TRANSACTIONS

OF THE

AMERICAN PHILOSOPHICAL SOCIETY

HELD AT PHILADELPHIA
FOR PROMOTING USEFUL KNOWLEDGE

NEW SERIES—VOLUME 55, PART 9
1965

BENJAMIN FRANKLIN
AND EIGHTEENTH-CENTURY AMERICAN LIBRARIES

MARGARET BARTON KORTY

THE AMERICAN PHILOSOPHICAL SOCIETY
INDEPENDENCE SQUARE
PHILADELPHIA

DECEMBER, 1965

Copyright © 1965 by The American Philosophical Society

Library of Congress Catalog
Card Number 65-27428

ACKNOWLEDGMENTS

This article is a shortened and revised version of a dissertation submitted to the Catholic University of America, in partial fulfillment of the degree, Master of Science in Library Science. I wish to acknowledge especially the aid and encouragement of Father Bernard Theall, my adviser, and Elizabeth Stone, reader, both of the Library Science Department of Catholic University. Thanks are also due to Gertrude D. Hess, assistant librarian of the American Philosophical Society, Charles D. Custer, reference librarian of Washington and Jefferson College, and Herbert Lawrence Ganter, archivist at the College of William and Mary, for making available materials from those institutions.

For permission to quote from manuscript and copyrighted materials, I am grateful to the following: American Philosophical Society (Franklin manuscripts, *The Papers of Benjamin Franklin* edited by Leonard W. Labaree and others, *Letters of Benjamin Rush* edited by L. H. Butterfield, *Benjamin Franklin and Catharine Ray Greene; Their Correspondence, 1755-1790* edited by William Greene Roelker, and *The Letters of Benjamin Franklin & Jane Mecom* edited by Carl Van Doren); Columbia University Libraries (two letters from Franklin to John Witherspoon, April 5, 1784, and to Clinton and Duane, August 9, 1784); Harvard College Library (letter from Franklin to Thomas Hancock, September 11, 1755); Historical Society of Pennsylvania (articles published in *The Pennsylvania Magazine of History and Biography);* Library Company of Philadelphia (Minutes, *A Short History of the Library Company of Philadelphia* . . . by George M. Abbot, and *Benjamin Franklin's Library* by Austin K. Gray); Library of Congress (Franklin manuscripts); Pennsylvania Hospital *(Some Account of the Pennsylvania Hospital from its first Rise to the Beginning of the Year 1938* by Francis R. Packard); University of Pennsylvania Press *(History of the University of Pennsylvania, 1740-1940* by Edward P. Cheyney and *Benjamin Franklin in Scotland and Ireland, 1759 and 1771* by J. Bennett Nolan); University of Pittsburgh Press *(Banners in the Wilderness; Early Years of Washington and Jefferson College* by Helen T. W. Coleman); Viking Press *(Benjamin Franklin's Autobiographical Writings* edited by Carl Van Doren); and Yale University Press *(The Papers of Benjamin Franklin* and *The Autobiography of Benjamin Franklin* edited by Leonard W. Labaree and others).

Direct quotations are verbally exact; capitalization and punctuation are conformed to current editorial practice.

Illustrations and facsimile reproductions have been provided by the American Philosophical Society, Historical Society of Pennsylvania, Independence National Historical Park Collection, Library Company of Philadelphia, the Library of Congress, and the University of Pennsylvania.

This list of acknowledgments would not be complete without some word of thanks to the regular staff members of the libraries consulted; to my husband, Vernon M. Korty, for his general assistance and over-all support; to the editor, George W. Corner, for his patience in guiding an inexperienced author through the maze of publication procedures; and to Whitfield J. Bell, Jr., for specific suggestions on Chapter IV.

M. B. K.

BENJAMIN FRANKLIN AND EIGHTEENTH-CENTURY AMERICAN LIBRARIES

MARGARET BARTON KORTY

CONTENTS

	PAGE
I. The Library Company of Philadelphia	5
Beginnings in the Junto	5
Formation and early years	7
Laboratory and museum	11
Agents	13
The Library Company, 1757-1790	15
Donations	18
The influence of the Library Company	20
Pennsylvania libraries	21
The Trenton Library Company	23
The Library Company of Burlington, N. J.	23
Charleston Library Society	24
Redwood Library, Newport, R. I.	24
New York Society Library	25
General influence in Philadelphia	25
II. The Loganian Library	26
III. Academic libraries	30
The Philadelphia Academy (University of Pennsylvania)	30
Harvard	36
Yale	39
The College of William and Mary	41
Rhode Island College (Brown University)	41
Dartmouth	42
College of New Jersey (Princeton)	42
The University of the State of New York	43
Dickinson College	44
Franklin (and Marshall) College	45
Washington (and Jefferson) College	46
IV. American learned societies	47
The American Philosophical Society	47
Origins and early years	47
The great exchange—American	51
The great exchange—European	52
Donations from friends in Europe	54
Donations from Franklin	55
Collection of Frankliniana	56
The American Academy of Arts and Sciences, Boston	56
The Connecticut Academy of Arts and Sciences, New Haven	57
V. Medical libraries	57
The Pennsylvania Hospital	57
Medical Society of New Fairfield, Connecticut	61
VI. Governmental libraries	61
New York Corporation Library	61
Pennsylvania Assembly Library	62
General Assembly of Rhode Island	64
United States Congress	65
VII. Religious and charitable organizations	67
Franklin, Massachusetts	67
The associates of the late Dr. Bray	69
German charity schools	70
Conclusion	72
Appendix	73
A. The long arm	73
B. Franklin's "Short Account of the Library" (Library Company of Philadelphia)	74
C. Catalogue of the Franklin, Massachusetts, Library—1786	75
Bibliography	76
Index	79

I. THE LIBRARY COMPANY OF PHILADELPHIA

BEGINNINGS IN THE JUNTO

When Benjamin Franklin arrived in Philadelphia for the first time, he noted that

there was not a good Bookseller's Shop in any of the Colonies to the Southward of Boston. In New-York and Philadelphia the Printers were indeed Stationers, they sold only Paper, &c., Almanacks, Ballads, and a few common School Books. Those who lov'd Reading were oblig'd to send for their Books from England.[1]

[1] *The Autobiography of Benjamin Franklin*, 1964: p. 141.

It is no wonder then, that this young man sought out friends who enjoyed books and enjoyed talking about them; he began to gather around him young men with similar interests. In the fall of 1727, he tells us,

I had form'd most of my ingenious Acquaintance into a Club for mutual Improvement, which we call'd the Junto. We met on Friday Evenings. The Rules I drew up requir'd that every Member in his Turn should produce one or more Queries on any Point of Morals, Politics or Natural Philosophy, to be discuss'd by the Company, and once in three Months produce and read an Essay of his own Writing on any Subject he pleased. Our Debates were to be under the Direction of a President, and to be conducted in the sincere Spirit of Enquiry after Truth, without Fondness for Dispute, or Desire of Victory; and to prevent Warmth all Expressions of Positiveness in Opinion, or of direct Contradiction, were after some time made contraband and prohibited under small pecuniary Penalties.[2]

Three of the members of this Junto were fellow workers at Keimer's printing shop: Hugh Meredith, later Franklin's partner; Stephen Potts, later Franklin's bookbinder; and George Webb. Others were Joseph Breintnall, "a Copyer of Deeds for the Scriveners"; Thomas Godfrey, a glazier and "self-taught Mathematician"; Nicholas Scull, a surveyor; William Parsons, a shoemaker; William Maugridge, a joiner; William Coleman, a merchant's clerk; and Robert Grace, the only member with some wealth. For the most part, these were men with more interest than principal. The Junto met at first in a tavern, but later moved to a room in a house owned by Robert Grace,[3] in Pewter-Platter Alley (or Jones's Alley).

On Franklin's first trip to England, he became familiar with the literary discussions that went on in the coffee-houses and taverns, and even became a participant as author of *A Dissertation on Liberty and Necessity, Pleasure and Pain.*

My Pamphlet by some means falling into the Hands of one Lyons, a Surgeon, Author of a Book intituled *The Infallibility of Human Judgment,* it occasioned an Acquaintance between us; he took great Notice of me, call'd on me often, to converse on those Subjects, carried me to the Horns a pale Ale-House in [blank] Lane, Cheapside, and introduc'd me to Dr. Mandevile, Author of the Fable of the Bees who had a Club there, of which he was the Soul, being a most facetious entertaining Companion. Lyons too introduc'd me, to Dr. Pemberton, at Batson's Coffee House, who promis'd to give me an Opportunity some time or other of seeing Sir Isaac Newton, of which I was extreamly desirous; but this never happened.[4]

Between this experience and his boyhood memory of Cotton Mather's neighborhood benefit societies in Boston, he worked out a plan for the Junto,[5] borrowing additional ideas from John Locke's plan for a mutual improvement society.[6]

Franklin was interested in reading, in discussion, and in self-improvement. These were the three functions which the Junto fulfilled for all of its members. Each member had to qualify himself by promising to love mankind, to respect one another, to believe in freedom of speech and of worship, and to love truth for truth's sake. The "Rules for a Club Established for Mutual Improvement" were drawn up in 1728 as regulations for the Junto. They were refined in later years, but remained essentially the same in that there were twenty-four "queries" which formed the basis of discussions of the group. Among these queries were:

1. Have you met with any thing in the author you last read, remarkable, or suitable to be communicated to the Junto? particularly in history, morality, poetry, physic, travels, mechanic arts, or other parts of knowledge.

2. What new story have you lately heard agreeable for telling in conversation?

Other questions dealt with morality, business, and hospitality.[7] Among the proposals which Franklin brought before the Junto in 1732 were these:

That these queries, copied at the beginning of a book, be read distinctly at each meeting; a pause between each, while one might fill and drink a glass of wine.

That, if they cannot be gone through in one night, we begin the next where we left off; ...

. . . .

When any thing from reading an author is mentioned, if it exceed a line, and the Junto require it, the person shall bring the passage or an abstract of it the next night, if he has it not with him.

When the books of the library come, every member shall undertake some author, that he may not be without observations to communicate.

In that year the queries were enlarged to include one on literary criticism: "How shall we judge of the goodness of a writing?" Franklin's own proposed answer was, in part: "To be good, it ought to have a tendency to benefit the reader, by improving his virtue or his knowledge.... it should be *smooth, clear,* and *short."*[8] Thus, the Junto was beginning to depend more upon books to stimulate discussion.

Not long after the club meetings had moved into a separate room in the house of Robert Grace, Benjamin Franklin proposed:

that since our Books were often referr'd to in our Disquisitions upon the Queries, it might be convenient to us to have them all together where we met, that upon Occasion they might be consulted; and by thus clubbing our Books to a common Library, we should, while we lik'd to keep them together, have each of us the Advantage of using the Books of all the other Members, which would be nearly as beneficial as if each owned the whole. It was lik'd and agreed to, and we fill'd one End of the Room with such Books as we could best spare. The Number was not so great as we expected; and tho' they had been of great Use, yet some Inconveniencies occurring for want of due Care of them, the Collection after about a Year was separated, and each took his Books home again.[9]

Franklin took advantage of this opportunity while the books still remained in the Junto meeting room. He set down on paper a few "Observations on my Reading History in Library, May 9. 1731." Noting the destruc-

---

[2] *Ibid.,* pp. 116-117.
[3] *Ibid.,* pp. 117-118, 130.
[4] *Ibid.,* p. 97.
[5] Van Doren, 1938: p. 75.
[6] Grimm, 1956: pp. 441-446. See also Franklin's donation to the Library Company of Philadelphia, 1741 *Catalogue,* pp. 28-29.

[7] Sparks, 1836-1840: 2: pp. 9, 12.
[8] *Ibid.* 2: pp. 551-553.
[9] *Autobiography,* 1964: p. 130.

tive effect of private and party interests, he came to the conclusion that:

> There seems to me at present to be great Occasion for raising an united Party for Virtue, by forming the Virtuous and good Men of all Nations into a regular Body, to be govern'd by suitable good and wise Rules, which good and wise Men may probably be more unanimous in their Obedience to, than common People are to common Laws.

Franklin never carried out his plan for a dream world, though he from time to time kept making notes for starting on the *"great and extensive Project"* by establishing a "Society of the *Free and Easy,"* a society free from vice and easy from debt.[10]

Though the books were dispersed, the discussions continued, and this first abortive attempt at a library was not in vain. "Finding the Advantage of this little Collection, I propos'd to render the Benefit from Books more common by commencing a Public Subscription Library." Thus was born the first subscription library in America, the Library Company of Philadelphia. The Junto continued in existence for many years and became influential not only in furnishing intellectual and moral stimulation for its members, but also in "preparing the Minds of People"[11] for other public improvements to come.

FORMATION AND EARLY YEARS

It was only a matter of a few months between the dispersal of the Junto library and the establishment of the Library Company of Philadelphia. Franklin had recorded using the Junto library on May 9, 1731, and the Instrument of Association of the Library Company was drawn up on July 1, 1731.[12] Franklin's *Autobiography* reveals his genius for organization:

> I drew a Sketch of the Plan and Rules that would be necessary, and got a skilful Conveyancer, Mr. Charles Brockden to put the whole in Form of Articles of Agreement to be subscribed; by which each Subscriber engag'd to pay a certain Sum down for the first Purchase of Books and an annual Contribution for encreasing them. So few were the Readers at that time in Philadelphia, and the Majority of us so poor, that I was not able with great Industry to find more than Fifty Persons, mostly young Tradesmen, willing to pay down for this purpose Forty shillings each, and Ten Shillings per Annum. On this little Fund we began. . . . .
> . . . .
> The Objections, and Reluctances I met with in Soliciting the Subscriptions, made me soon feel the Impropriety of presenting one's self as the Proposer of any useful Project that might be suppos'd to raise one's Reputation in the smallest degree above that of one's Neighbours, when one has need of their Assistance to accomplish that Project. I therefore put my self as much as I could out of sight, and stated it as a Scheme of a *Number of Friends,* who had requested me to go about and propose it to such as they thought Lovers of Reading. In this way my Affair went on more smoothly, and I ever after practis'd it on such Occasions; and from my frequent Successes, can heartily recommend it. The present little Sacrifice of your Vanity will afterwards be amply repaid.[13]

Franklin's method of recruiting subscribers was a success, but it took several months to accomplish the purpose. The Junto members, too, were busily engaged in recruiting. All of the original members of the Junto became subscribers except Hugh Meredith, who one year before had sold out his printing partnership to Franklin to pay off his drinking debts and departed for North Carolina.[14] At length, the Instrument of Association had been completed by the signature of fifty subscribers. Benjamin Franklin wrote out a summons to the directors of the Library Company, and Joseph Breintnall, the secretary, signed it.

> To Benjamin Franklin, William Parsons, Thomas Godfrey, Thomas Cadwalader, Robert Grace and Thomas Hopkinson, Philip Syng Junr., Anthony Nicholas, John Jones Junr., [and] Isaac Penington.
>
> Gentlemen,
> The Subscription to the Library being compleated You the Directors appointed in the Instrument are desired to meet this Evening at 5 o'Clock, at the House of Nicholas Scull to take Bond of the Treasurer for the faithfull Performance of his Trust, and to consider of, and appoint a proper Time for the Payment of the Money subscribed, and other Matters relating to the said Library.
> Philada. 8 Novr. 1731 JOSEPH BREINTNALL, Secy.[15]

The treasurer was William Coleman. In this first official group, the treasurer, the secretary, and four directors (Franklin, Parsons, Godfrey, and Grace) were all members of the original Junto. Thomas Cadwalader was a physician; Thomas Hopkinson, a lawyer; Philip Syng, a silversmith; Anthony Nicholas, a blacksmith; John Jones, a cordwainer or leatherworker; and Isaac Penington, a landowner.

At the meeting of November 8, 1731, Franklin urged that the "monies" be collected from the first twenty-five subscribers. Members who lived in town could pay at Nicholas Scull's on November 10; members who lived out of town paid at Owen Owen's on November 22 and 29. By December 14, the twenty-fifth subscriber had paid his money. After New Year's Day, the subscription was thrown open again, and twenty-five more subscribers purchased their shares. Two directors, William Parsons and Isaac Penington, were tardy with their payments, but responded to a polite mandate from Franklin.[16] Franklin printed and distributed a final notice to the Library Company subscribers, dated March 25, 1732:

---

[10]*Ibid.,* pp. 161-163.
[11]*Ibid.,* pp. 142, 173.
[12]Abbot, 1913: p. 3.
[13]*Autobiography,* 1964: pp. 142-143.
[14]Van Doren, 1938: pp. 100-101.
[15]Labaree, 1959—: 1: pp. 209-210.
[16]Gray, 1937: pp. 7-8.

Sir. Next Saturday Evening Attendance will be given at N. Scull's, to receive the Money subscribed to the Library, of those who have not yet paid; when you are desired to appear without Fail, either to pay or relinquish; that it may then be known who are, and who are not concerned.[17]

With a capital of one hundred English pounds and an annual income of twenty-five pounds in dues, the Library Company was now ready for its first book order.[18] According to the Minutes of March 29, 1732,

Thomas Godfrey at this meeting informed us that Mr. Logan had let him know he would willingly give his advice of the choice of the books . . . and the Committee esteeming Mr. Logan to be a Gentleman of universal learning, and the best judge of books in these parts, ordered that Mr. Godfrey should wait on him and request him to favour them with a catalogue of suitable books.[19]

James Logan was a man of wealth and position in Pennsylvania. He had a large private library, devoted not only to classics, but also to mathematics, botany, astronomy, history, and literature. Franklin accompanied Godfrey out to Stenton, James Logan's home,[20] and the list was completed by March 31, for the first book order:

Puffendorf's Introduc'n 8vo.
Dr. Howell's History of ye World 3 vols. Fo.
Rapin's History of England 12 vols. 8vo.
Salmon's Modern History
Vertot's Revolutions
Plutarch's Lives in small vol.
Stanley's Lives of ye Philosophers
Annals of Tacitus by Gordon
Collection of Voyages 6 vols.
Atlas Geogra. 5 vols. 4to.
Gordon's Grammar
Brightland's English Grammar
Greenwood's   "   "
Johnson's History of Animals
Architect: by And^w Palladio
Evelyn's Parallels of the ancient and modern Architecture
Bradley's Improvmt. of Husbandry and his other books of Gardening
Perkinson's Herball
Helvicius's Chronology
Wood's Institutes
Dechall's Euclid
L'Hospital's Conic Sections
Ozanam's Course of Mathem. 5 vols.
Hayes upon Fluxions
Keil's Astronomical Lectures
Drake's Anatomy

Sidney on Government
Cato's Letters
Sieur Du Port Royal moral essays
Crousay's Art of Thinking
Spectator
Guardian
Tatler
Puffendorf's Laws of Nature etc.
Addison's Works in 12 mo.
Memorable Things of Socrates
Turkish Spy
Abrdgmt. of Phil. Trans. 5 vols. 4to.
Gravesend's Nat. Philos. 2 vols. 8vo.
Boerhaave's Chemistry
The Compleat Tradesman
Bailey's Dictionary — the best
Homer's Iliad and Odyssey
Bayle's Critical Dictionary
Dryden's Virgil
Catalogues[21]

Franklin's influence is shown in some of the books that he wrote about in his *Autobiography* — the *Spectator*, Socrates, Plutarch, *Moral Essays* of Du Port Royal, Addison, etc. This was a practical library; there was not one work of theology on order. Filled instead with dictionaries, grammars, an atlas, histories, and books on science and agriculture, it was suited to the tastes and purses of young tradesmen.

Thomas Hopkinson carried the order and the bill of exchange for forty-five pounds made out to Peter Collinson, mercer, in London. Collinson responded not only with aid in supplying the books, but also with the first donation to the Library — "Sr. Isaac Newton's Philosophy and Philip Miller's Gardening Dictionary."[22] Later he added Barclay's *Apology*.[23] Benjamin Franklin dictated the return letter of thanks on November 7, and it was "copied fair" and sent under the signature of the secretary. In it, Franklin pointed out that:

An Undertaking like ours, was as necessary here, as we hope it will be useful; there being no Manner of Provision made by the Government for publick Education, either in this or the neighbouring Provinces, nor so much as a good Booksellers Shop nearer than Boston.[24]

This was the first of many years of correspondence between Peter Collinson, agent in England, and the Library Company, much of it going through the hands of Benjamin Franklin.

The books arrived in October, 1732, and were unpacked and placed on shelves in the library room of the house owned by Robert Grace in Jones's Alley. A labeling committee was appointed, and the books were catalogued according to a system used in Queens'

---

[17] Labaree, 1959—: 1: pp. 229-230.
[18] Gray, 1937: p. 8.
[19] Abbot, 1913: p. 5.
[20] Library Company of Philadelphia, Minutes, 1: p. 6 (March 30, 1732). Tolles, 1957: p. 213.
[21] Gray, 1937: pp. 9-10.
[22] *Ibid.*, pp. 10-11.
[23] Library Company of Philadelphia, 1807: p. 16.
[24] Labaree, 1959—: 1: pp. 248-249.

College, Cambridge, England. This system lists size first (folio, quarto, octavo, and duodecimo), before any consideration is given to author or subject.[25] To protect the binding, the books were covered with sheathing paper.[26] Franklin printed the catalogue of the books; at the meeting of December 11, 1732,

B. Franklin was asked what his charge was for printing a catalogue . . . for each subscriber; and his answer was that he designed them for presents, and should make no charge for them.[27]

In all the time between July 1, 1731, when the Library was first formed, to November 14, 1732, there had been no librarian. The first librarian, Louis Timothée, was selected on November 14, 1732, and served to December 10, 1733.[28] Timothée, a language teacher, was a native of Holland, who had come to Philadelphia in 1731, and was employed by Benjamin Franklin as journeyman and editor of the *Philadelphische Zeitung*, first German-American newspaper.[29] He was at this time living in the house of Robert Grace, where the books were kept. The agreement between Timothée and the directors of the Library Company, written in Franklin's hand,[30] provided for a salary and room rental together of three pounds for the first three months, with future salary to be arranged. The librarian was to be in attendance on Wednesdays from two to three o'clock, and on Saturdays from ten to four; he was to lend to any subscriber one book or set of books at a time upon receipt of a promissory note to pay the value of the book set down in the catalogue; he "shall not lend to, or suffer to be taken out of the Library by, any Person who is not a subscribing Member any of the said Books, Mr. James Logan only excepted." Franklin printed the promissory notes according to the following form:

I promise to pay Lewis Timothee or his Order, the Sum of   for Value received. Nevertheless if within   from the Date hereof, I return undefaced to the said Lewis Timothee a Book belonging to the Library Company of Philadelphia entituled   which I have now borrowed of him this Bill is to be void. Witness my Hand the   Day of   .[31]

After Timothée (now Lewis Timothy) left for Charleston, South Carolina, to print the *South Carolina Gazette* in partnership with Franklin, Franklin served as substitute librarian from December 10, 1733, to March 11, 1734, a period of three months and one day. William Parsons was then selected as librarian and served until 1746.[32]

On April 26, 1733, Franklin inserted an advertisement in his *Pennsylvania Gazette* to give notice to the subscribers that May 7 would be the time for electing officers and for paying their first annual installment of ten shillings apiece, with a reminder that a penalty was exacted for late payment. Penalties were not only for the subscribers in general, but also for directors. Attendance at monthly meetings was disappointing, so Franklin conceived a novel cure for the situation and presented his proposal to the directors on May 28, 1733. Only five directors were present to sign the agreement that

upon every Failure of attending at any of the aforemention'd Meetings We will at our next Appearance in a Meeting of the said Directors . . . forfeit and pay for Each of us One pint of Wine. . . . No Reasons shall be pleaded for Absence.

The other directors endorsed the agreement later, and it became an annual ritual, with variations.[33] The agreement signed by the directors on May 22, 1738, required the payment of one shilling for absence. In that year, Franklin was tardy once and absent once (March 12, 1738/9); absentees ranged from two to six per meeting. The agreement of May 11, 1741, changed the penalty to sending a proxy in the shape of "two bottles of good wine."[34]

The directors now felt it time to court the favor of the proprietors, and on May 14, 1733, a committee composed of Franklin, Thomas Hopkinson, William Coleman, and Joseph Breintnall was appointed to draft an address to Thomas Penn, who had recently arrived in Pennsylvania. The language was rather flowery for a Quaker community, for example: "May your Philadelphia be the future Athens of America." Thomas Penn was pleased with the petition for his "Countenance and Protection," asked questions about the new venture, and gave a short oral reply. On May 31, Franklin and Hopkinson returned to receive the reply in writing because the directors wished to print his response:

I take this Address very kindly; and assure you, I shall always be ready to promote any Undertaking so useful to the Country, as that of erecting a *common Library* in this City.[35]

The business of the library went on as usual, but two major changes were made during the short term that Franklin served as librarian (December 10, 1733, to March 11, 1734). First, the library was opened to nonsubscribers upon a deposit equal to the value of the book and a rental fee.[36] Second, it was proposed in the Minutes of February 11, 1734, "that the time of the

---

[25] Gray, 1937: pp. 10-11.
[26] Library Company of Philadelphia, Minutes, 1: p. 19 (Jan. 8, 1732/3).
[27] Abbot, 1913: p. 7.
[28] Library Company of Philadelphia, 1807: p. xxxix.
[29] Labaree, 1959—: 1: p. 230 n. 2. Van Doren, 1938: p. 103.
[30] Wolf, 1956a: p. 15.
[31] Labaree, 1959—: 1: pp. 251-252.
[32] Library Company of Philadelphia, 1807: p. xxxix.

[33] Labaree, 1959—: 1: pp. 321-322.
[34] *Ibid.* 2: pp. 205-206.
[35] *Ibid.* 1: pp. 320-321. *Pennsylvania Gazette*, May 31, 1733.
[36] Library Company of Philadelphia, Minutes, 1: pp. 37-38 (Jan. 14, 1734, new style).

Librarian's attendance should be only one day in the week (it having been found by experience that the borrowers of books did not commonly come to the Library on Wednesdays)."[37] The hours were set for Saturday from four to eight o'clock. The care of the library was turned over to William Parsons on March 14; the books were removed to his house, and an inventory was taken. There were 239 volumes plus sixteen "Notes of Hand" for books checked out, plus twenty-five periodicals, and a few other pamphlets and papers. The directors agreed that they would continue the "Printing the Notes to be given by all Borrowers of Books out of the said Library."[38]

Book selection was done in various ways, but most of the selection was done by the directors themselves with some help from the subscribers. Suggestions were taken from John Clarke's *An Essay upon Study* and John Locke's *Some Thoughts Concerning Education,* and the library eventually acquired *A General History of Printing,* by Samuel Palmer, the London printer who had hired Franklin back in 1725.[39]

New members were admitted from time to time. An example of the form used was one written by Franklin on August 27, 1734, for the admission of John Mifflin, a Quaker merchant.

> Such of the Directors of the Library Company as approve of John Mifflin's being admitted a Member are desired to shew their Consent by subscribing their Names hereto.[40]

In the fall of 1734, John Penn arrived from England, but it was the next May before the Library Company presented an address to him which had been written by Franklin, Coleman, Hopkinson, and Breintnall. The language of this address was also flowery, but it gives some hint that there was already some dissatisfaction with the Penn government, though it showed nothing of the future conflict between Franklin himself and the Proprietors. It, too, speaks of the Library Company as being a "Publick Library" erected to promote "Knowledge and Virtue." The address was printed in the *Pennsylvania Gazette,* June 5, 1735. In his reply to the Library Company, John Penn promised that:

> I shall always be ready with Pleasure to promote so good and necessary an Undertaking, as the erecting a Publick Library in this City.[41]

Both John and Thomas Penn had the welfare of the Library Company at heart. John donated an air pump, and Thomas donated a lot in 1738, located on the south side of Chestnut Street between Eighth and Ninth. The lot was never used for the intended purpose of building, but was used instead as rental property.[42]

The directors of the Library Company did not feel ready to build, but they did feel cramped for space. Franklin at this time was serving as clerk to the Pennsylvania Assembly, and it occurred to him to petition for use of a room in one of the vacant offices of the State House. Permission was granted in the fall of 1739, and the books were actually removed from the house of William Parsons, then librarian, to the "upper room of the westernmost office of the State House" on April 7, 1740.[43] This office was located in the west wing of the building, with an outside stairway, for the same wing also housed the doorkeeper of the Assembly and his family. The two wings of the State House had been constructed in 1736 to provide a safe place for the keeping of state papers. They were, however, not Indian-proof, and during the early years were subjected to indoor teepee fires when Indian delegations were lodged in the upper story of the eastern wing. Not until a separate building was constructed for the use of Indian guests, were the state papers and the books of the Library Company out of danger.[44]

After the books were moved to the State House, now known as Independence Hall, a committee, which included Franklin, was appointed to make a catalogue, and on April 13, 1741, reported "that they have done so; whereupon it is agreed that two hundred of them shall be printed by B. Franklin."[45] In 1733 and 1735, Franklin had printed broadsheet lists of the works available to members of the Library Company, but no copies of either list have survived. The 1741 *Catalogue* recorded 375 titles listed according to size of book. History (114 titles), literature (69 titles), and science (65 titles) were the most popular subjects. Most of the books were in English. Only thirteen were in foreign languages; ten of them were gifts, and in each case of a foreign title order the Library Company also owned an English translation.[46] So far, the language policy followed Franklin's original scheme for an English library.[47] To fill up a blank page at the end of this 1741 catalogue, Franklin wrote "A short Account of the Library." It was approved by the directors and included in the printed catalogue.[48]

Obviously at this time, Franklin was doing all the printing work of the Library Company; besides forms and catalogues, he inserted advertisements of its meetings in the *Pennsylvania Gazette,* did bookbinding and repair work, furnished account books and paper, and even took care of "ye mending Library stairs."[49] He had been excused from two years of annual payments

---

[37] Abbot, 1913: p. 8.
[38] Labaree, 1959— : 1: pp. 360-361.
[39] Wolf, 1956b: pp. 14, 34.
[40] Labaree, 1959— : 1: p. 373.
[41] *Ibid.* 2: pp. 33-35.
[42] *Ibid.* 2: pp. 207-210.
[43] Abbot, 1913: p. 9.
[44] U.S. National Park Service, 1956: p. 3.
[45] Abbot, 1913: p. 9.
[46] Wolf, 1956b: pp. 13-15.
[47] Smyth, 1905-1907: 10: p. 9.
[48] See Appendix for copy. A facsimile edition of the 1741 *Catalogue* with an introduction by Edwin Wolf, 2nd, was published by the Library Company of Philadelphia in 1956 to mark the 250th anniversary of the birth of Franklin.
[49] Eddy, 1929: p. 79.

(April 24, 1732) for his printing services.[50] Although he was in the business of selling books, he did not sell books to the Library Company; rather, he probably waited for the Library Company to order new books from London, and then, judging by how well they were received, ordered his own multiple copies for sale.[51] He also used materials owned by the Library Company in his publications. The 1741 *Catalogue* lists in the manuscript collection three documents of Pennsylvania history — Charles II's Charter to Penn, Penn's Charter of Liberties for Pennsylvania, and Penn's Charter of the City of Philadelphia. The year before, these three were gathered together and published by Franklin. Robert Grace donated Gauger's *Fires Improved* to the Library Company; since Grace was the manufacturer of Franklin's improved stove, it is likely that Franklin consulted that book in the design of it.[52] He printed his description of the stove, *An Account of the New-Invented Pennsylvanian Fire-Places,* in 1744.[53]

As early as 1739, the directors began to discuss the possibility of seeking a charter from the Proprietors. After some difficulty in getting approval on its exact wording and terms, the charter was finally signed by Governor Thomas on March 25 and approved by the subscribers on May 3, 1742; by-laws were also adopted at this time. Benjamin Franklin's name stood first in the charter list of subscribers. Franklin, Hopkinson, and Coleman prepared an address of thanks to the Proprietors, John, Thomas, and Richard Penn. In 1746 Franklin printed the text of the charter, the by-laws, and a list of "Books Added to the Library Since the Year 1741."[54]

Franklin took over the secretaryship of the Library Company after the death of Joseph Breintnall in 1746, and held this position until 1757, when he left for England. He was succeeded by Francis Allison, who served for a period of two years, and then by Francis Hopkinson.[55] Hopkinson decided to collect all the old minutes into one volume, but found that some had been lost because Franklin had written some of his minutes on scraps of paper and on backs of correspondence.[56] No wonder Hopkinson was confused — Franklin wrote the December, 1748, minutes on the bottom of Peter Collinson's bill for books sent to the Library between June 16, 1742, and October 15, 1745.[57] Franklin, himself, admitted "I found myself incorrigible with respect to *Order.*"[58]

Franklin played host to the visiting Swedish naturalist, Peter Kalm, sent over by the Swedish Academy of Sciences in 1748, and introduced him to Philadelphia's men of learning, including James Logan. Kalm was interested in every detail of life in the colonies, as is evidenced in the detailed diary he kept of his *Travels in North America.* He was particularly impressed by the size of the Library Company's book collection, kept in the State House, which he mistakenly called the "Town Hall."

On one side of this building stands the *Library* which was first begun in the year 1742 on a public spirited plan formed and put into execution by the learned Mr. Franklin. . . . There is already a fine collection of excellent works, most of them English; many French and Latin, but few in any other language The subscribers were kind enough to order the librarian, during my stay here, to lend me every book which I should want without any payment. The library is open every Saturday from four to eight o'clock in the afternoon. Besides the books, several mathematical and physical instruments and a large collection of natural curiosities are to be seen in it. Several little libraries were founded in the town on the same principle or nearly so.[59]

In the eyes of a European, the Library Company could hold its own.

LABORATORY AND MUSEUM

The Library Company soon expanded beyond the realm of books and became a center of scientific experiment. On May 1, 1738, a letter was delivered to the directors from John Penn, Proprietor:

Gentlemen—

It always gives me a pleasure when I think of the Library Company of Philadelphia, as they were the first that encouraged knowledge and learning in the Province of Pennsylvania. I have herewith sent you by Mr. Samuel Jenkins, the bearer hereof, an air-pump with some other things to shew the nature and power of the air; which will be both useful and pleasant; and Mr. Jenkins being a gentleman well acquainted with natural knowledge, and the mathematics, has been so kind as to offer his assistance in explaining the many experiments to be made thereon. I am with much regard, your sincere friend,

John Penn.
London, 31, Jan'y 1738.

The directors were so delighted with the present of the air pump, that it was

Ordered that B. Franklin, P. Syng and H. Roberts get a frame and case made, with glass lights in the door to receive and preserve the air-pump with its appendages, and to look ornamental in the Library room.

They also invited Samuel Jenkins, Proprietor Thomas Penn (who could not attend), and several other interested gentlemen to dinner at the house of Thomas Mullen, where it was reported that they enjoyed "a

---

[50] Library Company of Philadelphia, Minutes, 1: p. 10 (April 24, 1732).
[51] Wolf, 1956a: p. 16.
[52] Wolf, 1956b: pp. 33-34.
[53] Van Doren, 1938: p. 117.
[54] Labaree, 1959—: 2: pp. 345-349, 359.
[55] Abbot, 1913: p. 29 (not numbered).
[56] Wolf, 1956a: p. 15.
[57] Labaree, 1959—: 3: p. 351.
[58] *Autobiography,* 1964: p.156.

[59] The 1742 date refers to the date of charter. Kalm, 1937: 1: p. 25.

facetious agreeable conversation."[60] The air pump was taken to the law office of James Hamilton and assembled for experiments.[61] The directors appointed Franlin, William Coleman, and Richard Peters to draft a letter of thanks, finally sent on its way in August.[62]

After the Library Company had moved to the State House in 1740, Franklin requested and gained permission from the directors to use the air pump and the room adjoining the Library for demonstrations of lectures to be given by Isaac Greenwood, a former Harvard professor. An advertisement was inserted in the *Pennsylvania Gazette* on June 5, 1740, for a "Course of Philosophical Lectures and Experiments," to be performed "on Tuesday next, about 9 a Clock in the Morning," with later lectures to be presented at such times as would be agreeable to those interested.[63] The air pump became known as far away as Boston; James Bowdoin suggested to Franklin in 1751 that he try out certain electrical experiments with the Library Company's air pump.[64]

In 1741 John Penn added another magnificent gift, "a curious Microscope and Camera Obscura." Once again, Franklin, along with William Coleman and Thomas Hopkinson, was appointed to write a letter of thanks; this letter was entered in the minutes on August 10.[65]

In the spring of 1744, Dr. A. Spencer of Edinburgh arrived in Philadelphia, where he began a series of lectures which were to spark Franklin's famous Philadelphia experiments in electricity.[66] Franklin had met Spencer in Boston, probably in 1743, though he reports it in his *Autobiography* as 1746, and refers to him as

a Dr. Spence, who was lately arrived from Scotland, and show'd me some electric Experiments. They were imperfectly perform'd, as he was not very expert; but being on a subject quite new to me, they equally surpriz'd and pleas'd me.[67]

Dr. Spencer's Philadelphia lectures in the Library room at the State House lasted through July, 1744, when an advertisement in the *Pennsylvania Gazette* informed the public that this would be the last of the series, and that those who had followed earlier courses might attend this one at half-price, as well as some additional lectures on the "Globes."[68]

In 1746 Peter Collinson, the Library Company's agent in England, gave his greatest contribution, an electric tube, along with directions for using it. Franklin immediately seized upon the new instrument, making experiments whenever he could, and showing them to the "crouds" who came to see them. This was followed by a "compleat Electrical Apparatus" given to the Library Company by Thomas Penn in 1747. Thomas Penn's donation arrived in the hot moist weather of July, and "little has been done with it yet," although it had "come to Hand in good Order, and is put up in the Library." Once again, Franklin was on the committee to draft a letter of thanks to the Proprietor.[69]

These two donations set Philadelphia buzzing with interest in electricity. Philip Syng, in 1747, constructed a simple labor-saving portable machine for producing electricity by friction.[70] Professor Kinnersley called upon Franklin to get together a series of lectures and equipment which enabled him to travel extensively throughout the colonies and help spread the latest news of electrical experiments.[71] Glass-blowers of the Philadelphia area were put to work blowing glass tubes for export to other colonies.

Franklin began to make regular reports of his progress to Peter Collinson:

As you first put us on Electrical Experiments by sending our Library-Company a Tube with Directions how to use it; and as our honourable Proprietor enabled us to carry those Experiments to a greater Height, by his generous Present of a compleat Electrical Apparatus; 'Tis fit that both should know from Time to Time what Progress we make. It was in this View I wrote and sent you my former Papers on this Subject, desiring, that, as I had not the Honour of a direct Correspondence with that bountiful Benefactor to our Library, they might be communicated to him thro' your Hands. In the same View I write and send you this additional Paper. If it happens to bring you Nothing new . . . at least it will shew, that the Instruments put into our Hands are not neglected, and that if no valuable Discoveries are made by us, whatever may be the Cause, it is not a Want of Industry and Application.[72]

Through Collinson's interest, some of these letters were published anonymously in the *Gentleman's Magazine*. Submitted to the Royal Society, they were read at its meetings and were quoted but not published completely in the *Philosophical Transactions*. When publisher Cave brought them out as a pamphlet (seen through the press by Dr. John Fothergill), they at last gained fame, not only for Franklin, but also for the Library Company and the colonies.

Thomas Penn continued to show favor to the Library Company by a donation of a large reflecting telescope, along with "five Volumes of Voyages." The letter of thanks dated March 14, 1748/9, was sent under Franklin's signature since he was secretary at that time.[73] Other donations by Thomas Penn included a large pair of globes, a copy of George Adams' *Micrographia Illustrata; or, The Knowledge of the Microscope ex-*

---

[60] Abbot, 1913: p. 8.
[61] Grimm, 1956: p. 452.
[62] Labaree, 1959—: 2: p. 207.
[63] *Ibid.* 2: pp. 286-287.
[64] *Ibid.* 4: p. 219.
[65] *Ibid.* 2: p. 312.
[66] Cohen, 1941: pp. 49-54.
[67] *Autobiography*, 1964: p. 240.
[68] *Pennsylvania Gazette*, July 26, 1744.

[69] Labaree, 1959—: 3: pp. 115-119, 141, 156, 164.
[70] Grimm, 1956: p. 449.
[71] *Autobiography*, 1964: pp. 241-242.
[72] Labaree, 1959—: 4: p. 9.
[73] *Ibid.*, 3: pp. 351-352.

plained (London, 1746),[74] and (or?) *Observations in natural history by the microscope; with a variety of experiments explaining its use* (London, 1746).[75]

When the scientific world wanted to observe the transit of Mercury on May 6, 1753, it was Franklin who proposed to use the telescope belonging to the Library Company at one of the observation posts. Unfortunately, it was cloudy that day along the eastern coast, and Antigua was the only New World post with good visibility.[76] Far more favorable results were gained when the telescope was used for observing the transit of Venus in 1769, but Franklin was in England at this time and could only advise at a distance.

Besides the scientific instruments already mentioned, the library owned a twelve-inch concave reflecting mirror, given by Franklin, and a hydrostatical balance.[77] When the telescope needed repair in 1762, it was Franklin who made the arrangements in London, and saw that it was returned safely to Philadelphia.[78] Thus the Library Company filled a unique need in the growing colony, for though books could be purchased elsewhere, scientific equipment would have been out of the range of personal ownership for many citizens.

Besides the regular book collection and the scientific instruments, the Library Company also began to collect natural and historical specimens which gave it the air of a museum. Franklin would sometimes experiment, along with his friend, Joseph Breintnall, in making impressions of leaves of plants around Philadelphia. Joseph Breintnall became quite expert and gathered a large collection of these; after his death in 1746, they were given to the Library Company.[79]

Franklin also took pride in the fossil collection brought in by John Bartram in 1743, and several years later Franklin mentioned the collection in a letter to Jared Eliot, trustee of Yale:

the great Apalachian Mountains, which run from York River back of these Colonies to the Bay of Mexico, show in many Places near the highest Parts of them, Strata of Sea Shells, in some Places the Marks of them are in the solid Rocks. 'Tis certainly the *Wreck* of a World we live on! We have Specimens of those Sea shell Rocks broken off near the Tops of those Mountains, brought and deposited in our Library as Curiosities.[80]

A collection of "Instruments and Utensils of the Eskimaux" from Labrador was presented to the Library Company on November 9, 1754, by Captain Charles Swaine of the Northwest Company. Franklin had been instrumental in organizing and financing the expedition in search of a Northwest Passage, but at the time when Captain Swaine returned from his trip, Franklin was in Boston on a postoffice inspection tour.[81]

Ship captains docking in Philadelphia were encouraged to bring in mementos from their voyages to the far corners of the earth, and once a life membership was given in exchange for a fossil collection.[82] One morning a week was set aside for the local citizens to view the curiosities in the library museum. Besides the items already mentioned, the *Catalogue* of the Library Company (1770) lists the following: two manuscripts in rolls in the Russian language, given by Lewis Timothy (first librarian); a very beautiful concha, given by R. G. (Robert Grace, charter member); the hand and arm of an Egyptian mummy, presented by Benjamin West; fossils, snakes, scorpions, a piece of marble from the ruins of Herculaneum, an antique pewter dish, a Malabar manuscript on leaves, a sea feather, and ancient medals.[83]

AGENTS

PETER COLLINSON

Ever since the first book order of March 31, 1732, Peter Collinson had acted as the Library Company's book agent in England. A Quaker merchant busy with his own affairs, he yet found time to encourage the infant library through years of patient service, donations, and correspondence. Franklin developed a personal affection for this man, since much of the Library Company's business went directly through Franklin's hands, and he was so moved by the death of Peter Collinson in 1768 that he wrote a testimonial letter:

in the Year 1730,[84] a Subscription Library being set on foot in Philadelphia, he encouraged the [design] by making several very valuable Presents to it, and procuring others from his Friends; and, as the Library Company had a considerable Sum arising annually to be laid out in Books, and needed a judicious Friend in London to transact the Business for them, he voluntarily and chearfully undertook that Service, and executed it for more than 30 years successively, assisting in the Choice of the Books, and taking the whole Care of Collecting and Shipping them, without ever charging or accepting any Consideration for his Trouble. The Success of this Library (greatly owing to his kind Countenance and good Advice) encouraged the erecting others in different Places on the same Plan; ...

During the same time he transmitted to the Directors the earliest accounts of every new European Improvement in Agriculture and the Arts, and every philosophical Discovery; ...[85]

Shipments of books were disturbed in these years by numerous irritations — the capture of a ship by the

---

[74]*Ibid.*, 4: p. 3 n. 3. The microscope and camera obscura credited to Thomas Penn were given by John Penn; see the Library Company's letter in Labaree, 1959—: 2: p. 312.
[75]Library Company of Philadelphia, 1807: p. 2.
[76]Labaree, 1959—: 4: p. 416.
[77]Grimm, 1956: pp. 460-461.
[78]Wolf, 1956a: p. 15.
[79]Grimm, 1956: p. 457.
[80]Labaree, 1959—: 3: p. 149.

[81]*Ibid.* 5: p. 439. *Pennsylvania Gazette*, Nov. 14, 1754.
[82]Grimm, 1956: p. 451.
[83]Library Company of Philadelphia, 1770: pp. 4-5.
[84]Actually the Instrument of Association of the Library Company was dated July 1, 1731.
[85]Smyth, 1905-1907: 5: pp. 185-186.

French;[86] the special packaging needed for maps ("a Long Deal Case Marked L†C");[87] the loss of individual issues of magazines ("We are about to bind them up, and should have our Sets compleat");[88] the termination of periodical subscriptions ("It may be well enough to forbear sending the Universal Magazine for the future: it contains little of Value");[89] and even the long wait between order and receipt. But the orders were filled faithfully each year, and sometimes even a little extra was added. Peter Collinson sent to the Library Company pamphlets that had not been ordered, but which he thought would be valuable to a colonial library; they dealt with the early settlement of the colonies. Franklin returned a letter of thanks in June, 1755: "The old Accounts of the first Settlement of the Colonies, are very Curious, and very acceptable to the Library Company."[90] Evidently these pamphlets on Americana were appreciated by Franklin far more than by the other directors, for in later years the librarian was reluctant to announce the arrival of unordered pamphlets. Austin Gray, who has written a full account of *Benjamin Franklin's Library*, seems to think that these pamphlets were a matter of conspiracy between Collinson and Franklin.[91]

Peter Collinson had one vexatious fault. He was a practical packager, and insisted upon filling up the empty spaces of the Library Company's trunk. "For the sake of package I was Obliged to Mix the Books," he wrote to Franklin in 1750, "but they will be Easily found by the bills of Parcells."[92] This fault grew and grew; the parcels of books were now expanded to include seeds, dried daffodils, a microscope for James Logan, leathern breeches for John Bartram, etc., thereby turning the Library Company into a veritable parcel post office, for Collinson would write to his friends in Pennsylvania and ask them to pick up their parcels at the Library Company. After nearly thirty years, the directors rebelled, and, at a time when Franklin was not there to reason with them, a letter was sent to Collinson protesting his way of packaging. Collinson immediately resigned as agent, complaining of the ill treatment he had received from the directors. Franklin at this time (1759) was in London as colonial agent, and even he could not pacify his old friend.[93]

Despite Collinson's refusal to purchase books after 1759, he still was interested in the Library Company's welfare and continued sending items, but directed them only through Franklin. On December 7, 1762, Franklin wrote: "I have delivered ... to the Library Company what you sent by me."[94] On June 8, 1763, Collinson sent to Franklin "Books & Catalogues" for the Library Company, noting that, "As I have no Acct with the Lib: Com I make you Debtor for their Books So please to be reimbursed by them." He also advised: "Lett not the Lib: Com bind up the Colour'd Prints of Insects for I Expect 2 or 3 more Plates."[95] Shortly afterward, Collinson wrote again: "Mr Edwards has Left off publishing if the Lib: Com have a Mind to Compleat their Sett, if any is wanting Lett them Send in Time. He has published *Seven Volumes of 'Birds & Animals'* &c."[96] At this time, Franklin was briefly back in Philadelphia. After Franklin returned to London, Collinson probably approached him directly when he had any items which he felt would interest the Library Company. Thus, despite the misunderstanding with the directors, Collinson continued to serve the Library Company through his good friend, Benjamin Franklin.

WILLIAM STRAHAN

Somewhat overlapping with the agency of Peter Collinson, was the service rendered by William Strahan, printer and bookseller of London. Benjamin Franklin used Strahan in his private bookselling business. Strahan must have applied in 1744 for the business of the Library Company, for Franklin answered on July 4:

> We have already in our Library Bolton's and Shaw's Abridgements of Boyle's Works. I shall, however, mention to the Directors the Edition of his Works at large; possibly they may think fit to send for it.[97]

The following year, Franklin himself suggested that Strahan might deal with Peter Collinson:

> Our Library Company send yearly for about £20 worth of Books. Mr. P. Collinson does us the Favour to buy them for us. Perhaps on your speaking to that Gentleman he would take them of you.

And then, in order to help his friend obtain the business, less than two weeks later, December 22, Franklin wrote:

> Enclos'd is also a Letter to Mr. Collinson, containing an Order for Books for the Library, which when you deliver will have an Opportunity of proposing to furnish them.[98]

By 1746 Franklin was much more direct in his approach. He told William Strahan:

> I am sorry it so happen'd that Mr. Collinson had bespoke the Books. The next Catalogue sent to him will be accompanied with a Request that he should purchase them of you only.[99]

---

[86] Labaree, 1959—: 3: p. 284.
[87] *Ibid.* 5: p. 191.
[88] *Ibid.* 6: p. 171.
[89] Smyth, 1905-1907: 3: p. 366.
[90] Labaree, 1959—: 6: p. 84.
[91] Gray, 1937: pp. 24-26.
[92] Labaree, 1959—: 4: p. 4.
[93] Library Company of Philadelphia, Minutes, 1: p. 178 (Aug. 13, 1759). Gray, 1937: pp. 22-23.
[94] Smyth, 1905-1907: 4: p. 182.
[95] American Philosophical Society, Franklin MSS, 1: 75.
[96] *Ibid.* 1: 76 (June 28, 1763).
[97] Labaree, 1959—: 2: p. 412.
[98] *Ibid.* 3: pp. 49-50.
[99] *Ibid.* 3: p. 83.

In 1749 Franklin made another attempt to help Strahan obtain the commission of the books:

> The Library Company send to Mr. Collinson by this ship for a parcel of books. I have recommended you to him on the occasion, and hope you will have the selling of them. If you should, and the Company judge your charges reasonable, I doubt not but you will keep their custom.[100]

Was 1752 the first year that Franklin was successful in getting Strahan the book commission directly? In his letter of June 20 to Strahan, he said:

> Enclos'd is a Bill of £50 Sterling, . . . with a List of Books for the Library Company. As this is the first Time of their Dealing with you, they will inspect the Invoice pretty curiously, therefore I hope you will be careful to procure the Books as cheap as possible. The Company are unacquainted with some of the Books, so that if the whole should come to more than £50 with Charges of Insurance, &c. they desire you would omit so many as to bring it within that Sum; for their Money comes in but once a Year, and they do not chuse to lie so long in Debt.[101]

Strahan completed the order in August. Altogether, ninety-nine titles were sent; another thirteen which he could not supply were too expensive, out of print, or had not been published yet. Strahan wrote:

> I am very much obliged to you for your kind Recommendation, and hope the Prices are such as will give Satisfaction. I am sure they are as low as can be afforded. If there are any Mistakes, they shall be rectified next Occasion.[102]

There were, indeed, books mistakenly substituted for those ordered,[103] but considering that book orders of those days gave very scanty bibliographical information, Strahan had done well enough. With the help of Franklin, Strahan took over the book orders completely after Peter Collinson resigned as agent.

THE LIBRARY COMPANY, 1757-1790

Beginning in 1757, the relationship of Benjamin Franklin to the Library Company of Philadelphia changed radically, for on June 5 of that year, he left for England as a representative of the Pennsylvania Assembly. He had been a director of the Library Company from its founding in 1731; then starting in 1746, he served as both secretary and director until he left for England.[104] He immediately started making purchases in England in the name of the Library Company. His account books of 1757-1758 list a subscription of magazines from Henry and Cave, a subscription to "Mr. Stuart's Antiquities of Athens," and purchase of a "History of Arabians" (gift).[105] In addition, there may have been other purchases which were not specifically labeled "for the Library Company."

Franklin, too, was guilty of packaging personal items in the Library Company's trunk — "Writing Paper for Letters, and best Quills and Wax, all for Mrs. Moore, . . . having receiv'd such Civilities here from her Sister and Brother Scot, as are not in my Power to return," he explained in a letter to his wife.[106] Therefore, he was in full sympathy with Peter Collinson when the directors of the Library Company complained about such a practice.

With the help of Strahan, Franklin acted as agent for the Library Company most of the time he was in England. He returned to Philadelphia in November, 1762, and again for two years, served as director of the Library Company.[107] During this period, Franklin presided over a meeting called by outraged shareholders, who protested the action of the librarian, then Francis Hopkinson, in instituting a system of closed stacks. The by-laws made the librarian financially responsible for the loss of books, and since the shareholders and even the general public had been allowed to take what books they wanted from the shelves, this resulted in some loss charged against the librarian. Francis Hopkinson decided that all persons who wanted books must obtain them from the charging desk. A special meeting was held on August 27, 1764. Besides Franklin, there were three other directors, two shareholders and two sons of shareholders acting as proxies, with Francis Hopkinson, librarian, on trial. One of the proposals considered was "that any member wishing the freedom of the shelves should tender a bond whereby he made himself responsible for his proportionable part of any loss that might occur in books at the end of the year." But the shareholders themselves did not like this financial responsibility. Some sort of compromise was worked out to retain the charging desk and retain also a measure of freedom of the shelves. To mollify the librarian, his salary was raised, and he was promised assistance from members on Saturdays.[108]

Franklin left again for England in the fall of 1764, and once again began to make purchases for the Library Company. Among these were a "compleat set" (one hundred and twenty) of Hogarth engravings, purchased directly from Hogarth's widow. These were loaned out to members to hang on their walls for two weeks at a time, and were duplicated in 1770 when the original set became shop-worn. Franklin, the bookman, was not content to restrict purchases to those books ordered, but instead added, as his fancy saw fit, pamphlets on the early history of the colonies, the adventures of Captain John Smith, etc., all unappreciated by the directors with more mundane tastes. The directors instructed Mr. Peters to draw up a letter of protest to Franklin,

---

[100] *Ibid.* 3: p. 381.
[101] *Ibid.* 4: p. 323.
[102] *Ibid.* 4: pp. 350-353.
[103] *Ibid.* 4: pp. 379-380.
[104] Abbot, 1913: pp. 27, 29 (not numbered).
[105] Eddy, 1931: pp. 103, 110, 112.
[106] Smyth, 1905-1907: 3: p. 438.
[107] Abbot, 1913: p. 27 (not numbered).
[108] Gray, 1937: p. 22.

but they protested in vain;[109] the pamphlets on colonial history kept coming.

For many years, the Library Company had subscribed to the *Philosophical Transactions* of the Royal Society of London. Franklin felt that the time had come to subscribe to the transactions of other European philosophical societies. He suggested this to the directors in 1769, and they in turn asked him to inquire about the price of each set and also the price of the forthcoming French Encyclopaedia. Finding that the various transactions would cost £300, Franklin realized that that was beyond the budget of the Library Company. The directors agreed, but they did order the new edition of the French Encyclopaedia.[110]

In 1772 the Library Company petitioned the Pennsylvania Assembly for the right to build on State House Square, but the petition was denied. The next year, Franklin was informed:

since our last letter the Library has been removed to a new building called the Carpenter's Hall, in the centre of the square in which Friends' School stands, the books (enclosed within wire lattices) are kept in one large room and in another handsome apartment the apparatus is deposited and the Directors meet. [111]

Carpenters' Hall was then only three years old, and Franklin was glad to hear that the Library Company was satisfactorily situated in its new quarters.[112]

In the spring of 1775, with the "present unhappy" state of public affairs, the secretary informed him that their book order must be postponed.[113] This year marked the end of Franklin's pleasurable trips to the London book stores. He returned to Philadelphia on May 5, 1775, and the very next day he was elected a delegate to the Second Continental Congress, soon to meet in the Pennsylvania State House (Independence Hall). The Library Company opened its shelves to the Second Continental Congress, just as it had to the First, and the delegates made full use of the privilege. The proceedings of the Congress, whether in full session or in committee, were deposited in the Library. Members of the Library Company who served as delegates to the Congress were Franklin, Andrew Allen, John Dickinson, Thomas Mifflin, Robert Morris, John Morton, Samuel Rhoads, George Ross, Benjamin Rush, James Wilson, Thomas McKean, Francis Hopkinson, George Clymer, and James Smith.

The Library became a political institution. There was no time for anything else except the conflict with England. Book orders from abroad were stopped, but materials were still coming in from American presses, materials of a political nature. Directors were not attending meetings; shareholders were not attending special sessions. All attention was turned toward the Declaration of Independence, signed by ten members of the Library Company — Robert Morris, Dr. Benjamin Rush, John Morton, George Clymer, James Smith, James Wilson, George Ross, Francis Hopkinson, and Thomas McKean, with Benjamin Franklin taking a leading part.[114] Franklin served on the committee appointed to prepare the Declaration of Independence, but the committee wisely left the drafting of those memorable words to Thomas Jefferson, who declared that he "turned to neither book nor pamphlet" in preparing the famous document.[115] Despite the librarian's anxiety over the safety of the books, they remained in Carpenters' Hall throughout the Revolutionary War, surviving the British occupation of Philadelphia and the turbulence of the times.

Franklin was sent to France in October, 1776, and remained there for nine years. As long as the war was in progress, Franklin's attention was devoted to getting money and supplies from the French government; but after peace was declared, he heard once again from the Library Company. When in 1783 the directors received notice from Carpenters' Hall that their rent would be doubled, the Library Company considered the erection of a permanent building. They petitioned the Pennsylvania Assembly, in a joint request with the American Philosophical Society, for the erection of two buildings (one for the Library and one for the Society), facing one another on the State House Square. There was opposition to this request, and Samuel Vaughan, thinking that Franklin would have great influence, urged Franklin to write a letter to the Assembly quickly before the motion was made.[116] Denied the choice east side of the square, the Library Company withdrew from the petition.[117]

Franklin returned home to Philadelphia for the last time in 1785. Within two years, he was involved in daily attendance at the Constitutional Convention despite his increasing age and disabilities. The Convention was granted full freedom to borrow the books of the Library Company. On September 17, 1787, six members of the Library Company signed their names to the Constitution of the United States—Benjamin Franklin, Thomas Mifflin, Robert Morris, George Clymer, James Wilson, and John Dickinson.[118]

The library was in very good order in 1787, according to Manasseh Cutler:

This is a large and excellent collection, and is now become the public library of the University and the city.

---

[109] *Ibid.,* pp. 24, 26.
[110] American Philosophical Society, Franklin MSS, **3**: 42 and 94 (Library Co. to Franklin, Jan. 25, 1771, and April 27, 1772).
[111] Abbot, 1913: p. 11.
[112] American Philosophical Society, Franklin MSS, **45**: 78 (Franklin to R. Strettel Jones and Josiah Hewes, Feb. 18, 1774).
[113] *Ibid.* **4**: 45 (March 4, 1775).
[114] Gray, 1937: pp. 27-29.
[115] Morris, 1953: p. 91.
[116] American Philosophical Society, Franklin MSS, **28**: 75 (Vaughan to Franklin, May 3, 1783 [1784?]. The petition is dated March 12, 1784).
[117] Peterson, 1953: p. 130.
[118] Gray, 1937: p. 33.

Every modern author of any note, I am told, is to be met with here, and large additions are annually made. The books appeared to be well arranged and in good order. . . I was pleased with a kind of net-work doors to the book-shelves, which is made of a large wire sufficiently open to read the labels, but no book can be taken out unless the librarian unlocks the door. . . .

From the Library we were conducted into the Cabinet, which is a large room on the opposite side of the entry, and over the room where the Mechanical models are deposited. Here we had the pleasure of viewing a most excellent collection of natural curiosities from all parts of the globe. They are well arranged, and are contained principally on shelves which are inclosed, having glass casements in front, the panes of which are very large. . . There are several botanical volumes in this Museum, lately published. They are folios, and every plant is represented in large copper-plate cuts, colored from nature, very large and finely executed. The author's name I can not recollect. They were presents, and no person is to be permitted to take them out, but may examine them here as much as they please. For this reason they are in the Museum, and not in the Library.[119]

With such an excellent location, perhaps the Library Company might have tolerated a higher rent had it not been concerned about the danger of fire from combustible materials stored in the basement of Carpenters' Hall. Franklin, himself, held back a donation of books because he did not consider the building safe.[120]

The Library Company now realized that the time was ripe for a new building. In June, 1789, a meeting of the members was called, and it was decided to purchase two lots on Fifth Street, across from the State House Square. This was to be done as soon as one hundred new members had been added to the list. Recruiting must have gone very swiftly, for by August 31 the cornerstone was laid, and the Building Committee reported:

that upon the suggestion of Dr. Benjamin Franklin a large stone was prepared and laid at the southwest corner of the building with the following inscription, composed by the Doctor, except so far as relates to himself, which the Committee have taken the liberty of adding to it:—

Be it remembered
In honor of the Philadelphian Youth,
(Then chiefly artificers)
That in MDCCXXXI,
They cheerfully,
at the instance of Benjamin Franklin
one of their number,
Instituted the Philadelphia Library;
which tho' small at first,
Is become highly valuable & extensively useful,
And which the Walls of this Edifice
are now destined to contain and preserve;
The first Stone of whose Foundation,
was here placed
The thirty first Day of August, Anno Domini
MDCCLXXXIX.[121]

[119]Cutler, 1888: 1: pp. 282-283.
[120]Peterson, 1953: pp. 130-131.
[121]Abbot, 1913: pp. 13-14.

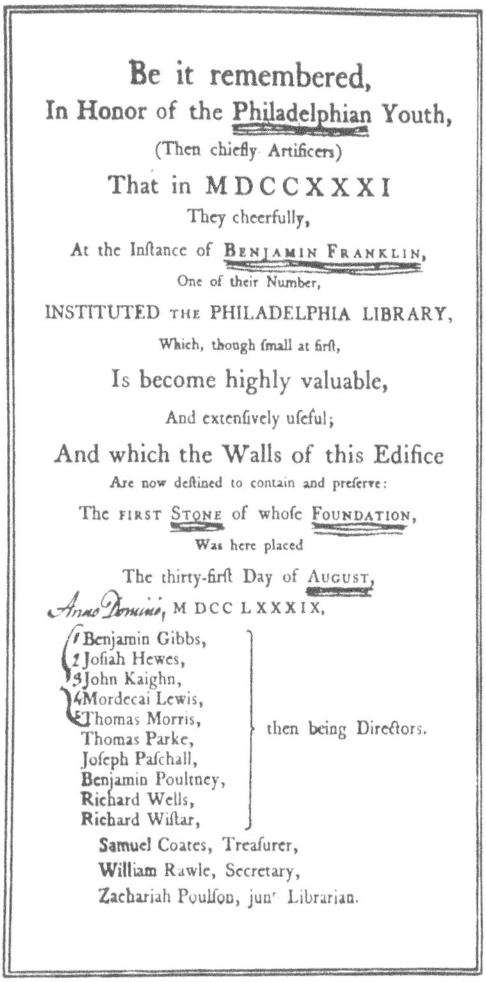
Be it remembered,
In Honor of the Philadelphian Youth,
(Then chiefly Artificers)
That in MDCCXXXI
They cheerfully,
At the Inſtance of BENJAMIN FRANKLIN,
One of their Number,
INSTITUTED THE PHILADELPHIA LIBRARY,
Which, though ſmall at firſt,
Is become highly valuable,
And extenſively uſeful;
And which the Walls of this Edifice
Are now deſtined to contain and preſerve:
The FIRST STONE of whoſe FOUNDATION,
Was here placed
The thirty-firſt Day of AUGUST,
Anno Domini, MDCC LXXXIX,
1 Benjamin Gibbs,
2 Joſiah Hewes,
3 John Kaighn,
4 Mordecai Lewis,
5 Thomas Morris,
Thomas Parke,
Joſeph Paſchall,
Benjamin Poultney,
Richard Wells,
Richard Wiſtar,
then being Directors.
Samuel Coates, Treaſurer,
William Rawle, Secretary,
Zachariah Poulſon, jun^r Librarian.

FIG. 1. Rare broadside of the Library Company's cornerstone inscription. Courtesy of the Library Company of Philadelphia.

Richard Wells had been appointed to confer with Franklin on this inscription, and had suggested that Franklin's name be placed on the stone. Franklin demurred in a formal note:

Dr. Franklin presents his Respects to Mr. Wells; he did not intend any Mention of himself in the propos'd Inscription, and even wrote it at first without the Words *'chearfully at the Instance of one of their Number,'* but in compliance with Mr. Wells's Idea, has added them tho' he still thinks it would be better without them. He cannot, however, but be pleased with every Mark of the Kind Regard of his Fellow-citizens towards him. It is his own being concern'd in promoting such

Testimonies that he thinks improper; and as that drawn by Mr. Wells may be understood as proceeding from him, he wishes it may be so considered.

Then followed the inscription as written by Franklin, giving 1732 as the date of founding,[122] although he had often quoted 1730 in the past. Franklin was overruled, and his name was recorded in stone along with the official date of 1731. He was the last survivor of that band of young men who had founded the Library Company. The new building was not yet completed when Franklin died in April, 1790, but his spirit lingered on in the form of a white marble statue donated by William Bingham and placed in a niche above the main door.[123] The present Library Hall of the American Philosophical Society, built in 1959, has on its façade (which reproduces that of the original Library Company building) a replica of the Franklin statue.

made the change is not clear; since Franklin was on his way to England in 1757, taking William along, he perhaps felt that his daughter would be less able to provide books for herself. It would have been very unusual for a woman to own a share in the Library Company at that time, although by 1774 women were accepted as subscribers.[125] In his will of 1788, Franklin changed the legacy once more: "My share in the Library Company of Philadelphia, I give to my grandson, *Benjamin Franklin Bache,* confiding that he will permit his brothers and sisters to share in the use of it."[126] Benjamin Franklin Bache would have had to share it with three brothers and three sisters, all living in Franklin's house. He had been taken to France by Franklin when he was only seven years old, had been trained as a printer, and would have been almost twenty-one years old when the share in the Library Company became his.

FIG. 2. First permanent building of the Library Company of Philadelphia. From an engraving by W. Birch, 1800.

Throughout his life, Franklin treasured his share in the Library Company. In his will of 1750, he designated it for his son, William, but in that of 1757, he bestowed it upon his daughter, Sarah (Sally).[124] Just why he

DONATIONS

The Library Company gladly accepted donations in addition to the regular purchases made possible by annual dues; yet it still maintained high standards for books of learning and reference. It contained a great

---
[122]Library of Congress, Franklin MSS. No. 2056-2057; printed in Smyth, 1905-1907: 10: pp. 159-160.
[123]Peterson, 1953: p. 136.
[124]Labaree, 1959—: 3: p. 480 and 7: p. 200.

[125]Historical Society of Pennsylvania. Norris MSS. No. 454, Receipt for Mary Norris, May 2, 1774.
[126]Van Doren, 1945: p. 692.

many books of a practical nature, on government and on agriculture and other applied sciences. Even as late as 1774, only one per cent could be classed as "Fiction, Wit and Humour."[127]

The following list of books donated to the Library Company was taken mainly from *A Catalogue of the Books Belonging to the Library Company of Philadelphia* (1807) unless otherwise noted. "D," "O," "Q," and "F" refer to size (duodecimo, octavo, quarto, and folio) and were part of the classification system used by the Library Company.

1. *Books Donated by Franklin* (starred items were contributions mentioned in Minutes, February 19, 1732/3)

Burgersdicius, 362, D. Monitio logica; or an abstract and translation of Burgersdicius's logic. By a person of quality. London, 1697. *Gift of Benjamin Franklin.*
Collins, 629, O. Johannis Collins,[128] et aliorum commercium epistolicum de analysi promota. Londini. 1722. *Gift of Dr. Benjamin Franklin.*
591, Q. Descriptions des arts et métiers. Pars messieurs de l'académie royale des sciences de Paris. Avec figures en taille-douce. 18 tomes. A Neuchatel, 1771. *The bequest of Dr. Franklin* .
Franklin, 217 and 322, Q. Experiments and observations on electricity; made at Philadelphia, by Dr. Benjamin Franklin. To which are added, letters and papers on philosophical subjects; with plates. London, 1769. 5th edit. London, 1774. No. *217, the gift of the author.*
Locke, 393, O. Treatises on government. By John Locke. 5th edit. London, 1728. *Gift of Doctor Benjamin Franklin.*
―――, O. A Collection of several Pieces of Mr. John Locke, never before printed, or not extant in his Works, . . . Lond. 1720. [*Given by B. F.*][129]
515, D. Magna charta et cætera antiqua statuta. Londini, 1556. *Gift of Doctor Benjamin Franklin.*
Marigny, 540, O. The history of the Arabians under the government of the Caliphs, from Mahomet, to the death of Mortazem; containing the space of six hundred and thirty-six years. By the Abbé Marigny. Translated from the French. 4 vols. London, 1758. *Gift of Dr. Benjamin Franklin.*
60, F. Votes and proceedings of the house of representatives of the province of Pennsylvania, from October 4, 1682, to September 26, 1776, inclusive. 18 vols. Philadelphia. *Gift of Dr. Benjamin Franklin and David Hall.*
O. Essays of Michael de Montaigne: With an Account of the Author's Life. 2 Vols. 1685. (*Given by B. F.*)[130]
D. Logic, or, The Art of Thinking; containing, besides the common Rules, many new Observations, that are of great Use in forming an Exactness of Judgment. By Messrs. Port Royal. Translated by Ozell. 1707. (*Given by B. F.*)[131]
O. A new Method of Studying History, Geography, and Chronology; with a Catalogue of the chief Historians of all Nations, the best Edition of their Works, and Characters of them. By M. *Languet du Fresnoy*, Librarian to Prince Eugene. 2 Vols. 1730. (*Given by B. F.*)[132]

2. *Works of Franklin Not Designated as Gifts*

Franklin, 194, Q. New experiments and observations on electricity; made at Philadelphia, by Dr. Benjamin Franklin, Communicated in several letters to Peter Collinson, of London. 3d edit. London, 1760.
―――, 321, Q. Political, miscellaneous and philosophical pieces. By Doctor Benjamin Franklin. London, 1779.
―――, 1103, D. The life of Dr. Benjamin Franklin; with his essays and letters. 2 vols. London, 1792.
―――, 1008, D. The general magazine, and historical chronicle, for the British plantations in America; for January, February, April, May, and June, 1741. By Benjamin Franklin. Philadelphia, 1741.
Keimer, 177, F. The universal instructor in all arts and sciences; and the Pennsylvania gazette; from December 24, 1728, to the present time. By Samuel Keimer, Franklin and Meredith, Benjamin Franklin, Franklin and Hall, and Hall and Sellers. 24 vols. Philadelphia. *The first five volumes the gift of Mr. Hopkinson.*

Pamphlet, Quarto, 500. 1 Pownal's hydraulic and nautical observations on the currents in the Atlantic ocean; with a corresponding chart of that ocean; with notes, by Dr. Benjamin Franklin. London, 1787.
Pamphlet, Quarto, 644. 7 Dr. Franklin's account of the inoculation for the small pox, in England and America, with plain instructions for performing the operation. London, 1759.
Pamphlet, Octavo, 1589. 1 An account of Dr. Franklin's new-invented open-stoves; with plates. Philadelphia, 1744.

3. *Books from Franklin's Private Library*

In 1801 Zachariah Poulson, then librarian, purchased volumes of English tracts from Dufief, who was selling Franklin's private library, and presented them to the Library Company. William Mackenzie, a Philadelphia merchant very fond of rare books, also purchased part of Franklin's library. The Library Company acquired part of Franklin's library by the will of Mackenzie, and part by purchase from executors of Mackenzie's estate.[133]

4. *Books Donated through Franklin's Influence and Friendship*

Besides Peter Collinson, Franklin had many friends and correspondents whose philanthropic impulses were aroused by his friendship. As a result, the Library

―――
[127] Bridenbaugh, 1962: p. 89.
[128] Coincidentally, Franklin had a boyhood friend named John Collins, but this book was the posthumous publication of the English mathematician of the same name (1625-1683).
[129] Contains "Rules of a Society which met once a Week for the Improvement of useful Knowledge, and the Promoting of Truth and Charity," thought to have influenced Franklin's ideas for his 1727 Junto. Library Company of Philadelphia, 1741 (1956): pp. 28-29.
[130] Library Company of Philadelphia, 1741 (1956): p. 33.
[131] *Ibid.*, p. 48.
[132] *Ibid.*, p. 32.
[133] Wolf, 1962: pp. 9-12.

Company received many gifts of books from Europe. Among these were:

Dr. John Fothergill, Franklin's personal physician in London,[134] and his co-worker in trying to mend the rift between the British Ministry and the colonies (*Publii Virgilii Maronis Bucolica, Georgica et Æneis.* Birminghamiae, 1754).[135]

Dr. Alexander Small, English correspondent on ventilation and weather (*Homer's Illiad; in Greek.* Glasgow, 1756).[136]

Dr. Richard Price, English theologian and political philosopher, close friend of Franklin, author of many books and pamphlets in the Library Company although none are designated as gifts in the 1807 catalogue (subjects include civil liberty, morals, annuities, national debt, war with America, love of country, importance of American Revolution, etc.).

Dr. Joseph Priestley, English theologian and scientist, close friend of Franklin, author of many books and pamphlets in the Library Company although none are designated as gifts in the 1807 catalogue (subjects include air, vision, light, color, perspective, electricity, education, grammar, slavery, government, civil and religious liberty, and theology). Priestley offered to will his books to the Library Company in 1784, and Franklin answered: "Your *Companions* would be very acceptable to the Library, but I hoped you would long live to enjoy their Company yourself."[137]

Dr. John Calder of London (offer in a letter to Franklin, March 13, 1783, to give his books to the Library Company in Philadelphia).[138]

Marquis de Ponçins, French soil analyst (his own book on agriculture, which Franklin promised to place in the "public Library" of Philadelphia).[139]

Charles W. F. Dumas, U. S. secret agent in Holland (three copies of his edition of Vattel's *Le Droit des Gens* in 1775, one of which Franklin deposited in the Library Company. That copy, along with the one that Franklin kept, "has been continually in the hands of the members of our Congress, now sitting.").[140]

Peter Kalm, Swedish scientist (*Olavi Celsii hierobotanicum.* Upsal, 1745).[141]

5. Books Donated by Societies

The Library Company received the first volume of the *Transactions of the American Philosophical Society, held at Philadelphia, for promoting useful knowledge,* as a gift from the Society.[142] Franklin was president at the time of publication, 1771, and even though he was in England at that time, he set many of the exchange policies for the Society.

In 1789 the Library Company received two gifts from the Pennsylvania Society for the Abolition of Slavery — Frossard's *La cause des esclaves negres, et des habitans de la Guinée* (2 vols.; Lyon, 1789), and *The substance of the evidence of sundry persons on the slave-trade, collected in the course of a tour made in the autumn of 1788* (London, 1789).[143] Franklin was president of the Society, reactivated in 1787.

6. Medals

On September 16, 1789, Franklin wrote a letter recorded by transcript in the Franklin manuscripts at the Library of Congress, which is usually said to have been sent to James Logan (II). It concerns his donations of two medals to the "Public Library." However, since the actual transcript copy does not carry the name of the recipient, there is a possibility that the letter was sent to Zachariah Poulson, librarian of the Library Company from 1785 to 1806.[144] Franklin often used the phrase "Public Library" to designate both the Library Company and the Loganian Library, and he was already aware of the possibility of joining the two libraries. Since the union took place soon after Franklin's death, it matters little to which library he donated the medals or to which man he sent the letter. As a last gesture of turning over a public historical heritage to the care of the "Public Library," the letter speaks for itself:

Sir,
I send you herewith two Medals which I think are fit to be preserved in our Public Library, as they relate to interresting Events in the History of our Country. — The silver one was struck by Order of Congress, in honour of M. Fleury, who was the first that entred the Fort at Stony Point when taken by Gen. Wayne, for whom another of the same Impression was struck in Gold. — The Copper one is a Copy of one struck by me, partly as a grateful Compliment to France for the Assistance afforded us; and partly to record the two great Events of the Taking Burgoyne & Cornwallis with their Armies. I presented one of these in Gold to the King & another to the Queen, which were extremely well taken. I distributed also a Number of Silver ones among the Ministry, and the Officers of the French Army that had served in America.—

I am
Your's respectfully[145]

THE INFLUENCE OF THE LIBRARY COMPANY

Benjamin Franklin was proud of the success of the Library Company, and mindful of the great influence it had among the colonists.

The Institution soon manifested its Utility, was imitated by other Towns and in other Provinces, the Librarys were augmented by Donations, Reading became fashionable, and our People having no publick Amusements to divert their Attention from Study became better acquainted with Books, and in a few Years were observ'd by Strangers to be better

---

[134] Sparks, 1836-1840: **7**: p. 150.
[135] Library Company of Philadelphia, 1807: p. 278.
[136] *Ibid.*, p. 133.
[137] Smyth, 1905-1907: **9**: p. 266.
[138] American Philosophical Society, Franklin MSS, **27**: 191.
[139] Hays, 1908: **3**: p. 244.
[140] Smyth, 1905-1907: **6**: p. 432.
[141] Library Company of Philadelphia, 1807: p. 51.
[142] *Ibid.*, p. 363. American Philosophical Society, 1885: *Proceedings* **22**, 3: p. 62.
[143] Library Company of Philadelphia, 1807: pp. 101, 335.
[144] *Ibid.*, p. xxxix.
[145] Library of Congress, Franklin MSS, No. 2070.

instructed and more intelligent than People of the same Rank generally are in other Countries.[146]

He had started the Library Company because "there was not a good Bookseller's Shop" in Philadelphia. "Those who lov'd Reading were oblig'd to send for their Books from England."[147] There was also a lack of a public educational system.

As the library grew and prospered, other towns followed suit, and so, like the ripples of a pond, the influence of the Library Company spread through Pennsylvania and spilled over into other colonies. Franklin called the Library Company

the Mother of all the N American Subscription Libraries now so numerous. It is become a great thing itself, and continually increasing. These Libraries have improv'd the general Conversation of the Americans, made the common Tradesmen and Farmers as intelligent as most Gentlemen from other Countries, and perhaps have contributed in some degree to the Stand so generally made throughout the Colonies in Defence of their Privileges.[148]

It is true that in Philadelphia library members were stimulated to an intellectual level far beyond their formal education. Because Philadelphia was especially blessed with a liberal intellectual atmosphere brought by the Quakers, the Library Company made a greater impact upon the community than it might have had if located elsewhere.

Franklin's term "mother" implies that it was first of a direct line. The Library Company of Philadelphia was certainly the first subscription library established in North America, but we cannot prove that it was the parent of "all" the North American subscription libraries. Only two years, for example, after the founding of the Library Company of Philadelphia, a second subscription library was established in Durham, Connecticut. The Book Company of Durham was organized on October 30, 1733, by eight men who subscribed twenty shillings each and opened the doors to other subscribers. One of the founders, Elihu Chauncey, was the son of the town minister, the Reverend Nathaniel Chauncey, a graduate and Fellow of Yale College. The Book Company of Durham was later patronized by other fellows and presidents of Yale.[149] Just two months before the founding of this library, Benjamin Franklin journeyed to Boston to visit his parents, and stopped off at Newport for a reconciliation with his brother James,[150] public printer and publisher of the *Rhode Island Gazette*. He announced his return to Philadelphia in the October 18 issue of the *Pennsylvania Gazette*. This brash young traveler, bolstered by his success as a publisher while still in his twenties, could surely be expected to brag a bit about Philadelphia in general

and the Library Company in particular. His total concern with the world of books had for years paved the way to many new friendships, and he had more recently proved his own interest in New England libraries by reporting Dean (later Bishop) George Berkeley's gift of books to Harvard and Yale in the July 12 and August 30 (1733) issues of the *Pennsylvania Gazette*. It would be difficult to trace the circulation of the *Pennsylvania Gazette* to know whether it traveled as far as Connecticut by 1733 with its news of the Library Company of Philadelphia. However, we do know from Franklin's *Autobiography* that he used the inter-colonial postal system to distribute copies of his newspaper by "Bribing the Riders who took them privately."[151] There is no record of any connection between the Library Company of Philadelphia and the Book Company of Durham, Connecticut, but the possibility of influence does exist even though it cannot be proved.

The establishment of other subscription libraries can definitely be traced to the example of the Library Company of Philadelphia. Like seeds of learning, these libraries sprang up in the towns of Pennsylvania, in Trenton and Burlington, New Jersey, in Charleston, South Carolina, in New York, and even in Newport, Rhode Island.

PENNSYLVANIA LIBRARIES

Philadelphia

In the city of Philadelphia, three subscription libraries were established that for a while were rivals of the Library Company, but later merged with it. One of the reasons that other libraries developed was the very high cost of a share in the Library Company. The share at first had a value of forty shillings, but each year the value was increased by ten shillings, the annual payment. No wonder the Library Company prospered; as the cost of a share rose steadily, one new member in time increased the book-buying fund by the huge sum of £21. The matter was rectified in the year 1768, when Francis Hopkinson, secretary, announced in the *Pennsylvania Gazette,* March 24:

THE LIBRARY COMPANY OF PHILADELPHIA, INCORPORATED by charter, and the first institution of that sort set on foot in this city, having hitherto computed the value of a share in the said company's books and effects, by adding the payment of Ten Shillings per annum, since their first establishment, to the original subscription money, by which computation the price of a share amounted to upwards of *Twenty One Pounds*, whereby many persons, desirous to become members, were discouraged on account of the expence; *Have* taken this matter into consideration, and lately enacted a law for reducing and fixing the purchase money of a share at *Ten Pounds*, Pennsylvania currency.

In 1747 the Union Library Company was founded with twenty-six members, and by the time they received

---

[146] *Autobiography*, 1964: p. 142.
[147] *Ibid.*, p. 141.
[148] *Ibid.*, pp. 130-131.
[149] Fowler, 1866: pp. 45-50, 103-106.
[150] *Autobiography*, 1964: p. 169.

[151] *Ibid.*, p. 127.

a charter in 1759, they had set the limit at one hundred members.[152] One of the charter members was James Chattin, printer, former apprentice to Benjamin Franklin.[153] Printing work was hired out to Franklin and Hall.[154] Their agent in England was none other than Benjamin Franklin, after his arrival there in 1757. His account books show that one of his first purchases for the library was "sundry optical instruments." The books were purchased from George Keith,[155] but William Strahan also served as book-seller.[156] In 1769 the Union Library joined with the Library Company, bringing to the joint library the use of its building at Third and Pear Streets. The members of the Library Company held a meeting on March 13 to consider the union, and with agreement on both sides, the members of the Union Library could pick up their certificates of admission by May 1, 1769.[157]

In 1757 the Association Library was founded by forty-six members, paying twenty shillings each. David Hall, printing partner of Franklin, and William Bradford, printer, were members of this library. Within ten years, the Association Library had gained two hundred members.[158] The library was housed in a room on Chestnut Street after 1766, and its catalogue of books was printed by William Bradford in 1765, not by Franklin and Hall. The Association joined with the Union Library on February 17, 1769, only a few months before the Union Library joined with the Library Company.[159]

The third library, called the Amicable Company and composed mostly of workingmen, maintained a room on Third Street. It expanded its activity to include lectures on electricity in 1765, just as the Library Company had done years before. In 1766 it united with the Union Library.[160] Thus, in this series of mergers, the Library Company became the foster-mother of the Union Library, the Association Library, and the Amicable Company.

Germantown

The Germantown Library Company was organized in 1745. It advertised yearly meetings in the *Pennsylvania Gazette,* and purchased books and printing services from Franklin and Hall,[161] including the printing of its Instrument of Partnership.[162]

Darby

A library was organized at Darby, Pennsylvania, on March 10, 1743. Darby was situated seven miles southwest of Philadelphia, and was the home town of John Bartram, pioneer botanist. Twenty-nine men subscribed twenty shillings each and five shillings a year. It was John Bartram who suggested Peter Collinson as book agent.[163] Bartram had been in close touch with Peter Collinson in connection with his botanical work, was a close friend of Benjamin Franklin, and at the time this library was established, was working on the founding of the American Philosophical Society. Bartram would have been very familiar with the Library Company and was given a free membership in it in 1743.[164] For lack of funds, the Darby Library later purchased more of its books in the colonies than in England.

Lancaster

The citizens of Lancaster, Pennsylvania, becoming aware of the "Attention to public Libraries, there not being less than four in Metropolis [Philadelphia], and in almost every Town of Note, one," took action in 1759 to establish the Juliana Library. Fifty-eight subscriptions raised a total of £200 sterling. A "few generous Gentlemen" paid ten pounds, and no subscription was under forty shillings. The library was favored by gifts from Thomas Penn and Governor James Hamilton, and received a charter in 1763. It began as the Lancaster Library Company, but was renamed in honor of Lady Juliana Penn,[165] who gave it an orrery, a pair of globes, a reflecting telescope, and five books. The first librarian was Samuel Magaw, a schoolteacher under the Society for the Education of Germans[166] (Society for the Relief and Instruction of Poor Germans), which Franklin helped establish. Edward Shippen, formerly of Philadelphia, but now of Lancaster, was very active in the founding of this library.[167] He became a trustee of the Juliana Library Company. While in Philadelphia, he had been the apprentice and later partner of James Logan and was familiar with the working plan of the Library Company.[168] He maintained a book account with David Hall in Philadelphia, and made the Juliana Library Company "virtually a branch chapter of the American Philosophical Society."[169] The 1766 catalogue of the Juliana Library promised that "An Electrical Apparatus, on the model of the ingenious Messieurs Franklin and Kinnersley, will be added as soon as possible."[170] The Juliana Library advertised in the *Pennsylvania Gazette.*[171]

---

[152] Bridenbaugh, 1962: p. 87.
[153] Lamberton, 1918: pp. 195-196.
[154] Labaree, 1959— : 3: p. 271.
[155] Eddy, 1931: pp. 107-117.
[156] "Correspondence between William Strahan and David Hall 1763-1777," 1886-1888: *Pa. Mag. of Hist. & Biog.* 10: p. 462.
[157] Lamberton, 1918: pp. 206-207.
[158] Bridenbaugh, 1962: p. 87.
[159] Lamberton, 1918: pp. 202-206.
[160] Bridenbaugh, 1962: p. 88.
[161] Lamberton, 1918: pp. 222-225.
[162] Labaree, 1959— : 3: pp. 270-271.

[163] Lamberton, 1918: pp. 219-221.
[164] Gray, 1937: p. 17.
[165] Juliana Library Company, 1766: pp. ix, 12-13.
[166] Lamberton, 1918: pp. 227-230.
[167] Bridenbaugh, 1962: p. 93.
[168] Labaree, 1959— : 5: p. 195.
[169] Bridenbaugh, 1962: pp. 84, 340.
[170] Page 56.
[171] Lamberton, 1918: pp. 231-232.

Hatborough and Chester

The Union Library Company of Hatborough, Pennsylvania, was founded in 1755, and a library in Chester, Pennsylvania, in 1769. Both of these libraries advertised in the *Pennsylvania Gazette*. The first book order of the Hatborough library was entrusted to the Reverend Charles Beatty,[172] who served as chaplain to Franklin's forces in the defense of Pennsylvania (1755-1756) and who helped Franklin purchase books and scientific equipment for Princeton in 1769.[173]

THE TRENTON LIBRARY COMPANY

The Trenton Library Company was established by Dr. Thomas Cadwalader in 1750, when he gave to the citizens of Trenton, New Jersey, £500 as a foundation for a free library.[174] Dr. Cadwalader had been one of the original subscribers to the Library Company, serving as director from its founding to 1739 (except for one year), and then for another eighteen years after he returned from Trenton.[175] When he moved to Trenton around 1739, he became active in civic affairs and was made first burgess of the town (1746-1750). His magnanimous gift of £500 was given when he returned to Philadelphia in 1750. He was also the author of *An Essay on the West-India Dry-Gripes,* printed by Franklin in 1745.[176]

On July 19, 1751, Benjamin Franklin wrote to William Strahan:

This serves to cover the enclosed and recommend the affair to your care. I have assured the gentlemen concerned that you will serve them as well and cheap as any bookseller in London. They are men of ability, and will be constant customers.

Whatever was enclosed has not been found, but supposedly it was an order for books from the Trenton Library Company. The next March, Franklin informed Strahan:

The Books for the Trenton Library arrived safe, and I believe gave Satisfaction.[177]

On October 27, 1753, Franklin wrote once again to Strahan:

I have now received Bower's 2d Vol. and shall send to the Trenton Library to enquire after Crito and Delaresse.[178]

The Trenton Library Company was known as the first "public" library in New Jersey. It suffered very heavy damages by British soldiers in 1776, but was revived and lasted until 1855.[179]

Trenton was only thirty miles from Philadelphia, and Franklin had occasion to visit there in September, 1749, to meet a relative.[180] Moreover, as public printer of New Jersey, he would have known other residents besides Dr. Cadwalader. Two of the members of the American Philosophical Society lived in Trenton, John Coxe and David Martin.[181]

THE LIBRARY COMPANY OF BURLINGTON, NEW JERSEY

On the evening of November 22, 1731, when the Library Company was collecting "monies" from charter members at Owen Owen's, there appeared a lad of sixteen, Charles Read, Jr. (1715-1774).[182] Charles was related to Franklin's wife, Deborah, though the exact degree of cousinship has not been clearly established. He was also the nephew of James Logan, founder of the Loganian Library. His father, Charles Read, Sr. (1686-1737), was a well-to-do merchant and public official, with a love of owning and of sharing good books.[183] Franklin's ledger accounts record the sale, binding, and repair of books, and *Pennsylvania Gazette* subscription and advertisements charged to Charles Read, Sr., who no doubt sent his son on many errands to the printer's bookshop.[184] The familiarity with the print shop, the luxury of both Read's and Logan's private libraries, and the charter membership in the Library Company extended this young boy's appreciation of books beyond the accumulation of his own private library to the eventual establishment of a subscription library in Burlington, New Jersey, years later.

After the death of his father in 1737, Charles Read, Jr., attempted to recoup the family library by advertising in Franklin's *Pennsylvania Gazette* for the books that his father had lent to forgetful borrowers.[185] How many of the lost books were recovered in this manner is not known. Two years later, he established his home in Burlington, New Jersey, where he started his public career. His younger brother, James Read, remained a while longer in Philadelphia and maintained a closer relationship with Benjamin Franklin.[186]

Charles Read continued to purchase books and supplies from Franklin's shop in Philadelphia.[187] He maintained his membership in the Library Company of Philadelphia at least through the 1742 charter from the Pennsylvania proprietors, and he was listed in the 1741

---

[172] *Ibid.,* pp. 225-227, 233-234.
[173] See Chapter III, College of New Jersey (Princeton).
[174] New Jersey, 1894-1895: 11: p. 584 n. 1.
[175] Abbot, 1913: p. 27 (not numbered).
[176] Dulles, 1903: pp. 268-272.
[177] Labaree, 1959—: 4: pp. 147, 281.
[178] *Ibid.* 5: p. 81. These are probably books which Franklin thought might have been mixed up in shipment, for on May 9, 1753, he reported to Strahan that they were not in Mr. Hall's trunks (see Labaree, 1959—: 4: p. 487). He gave Bower's *History of the Popes* to Yale.

[179] Federal Writers' Project, WPA, for the State of New Jersey, 1939: p. 400.
[180] Van Doren, 1950*b*: p. 33.
[181] Labaree, 1959—: 2: p. 407.
[182] Gray, 1937: p. 8.
[183] Woodward, 1941: pp. 27-28.
[184] Eddy, 1928: pp. 38-40, 53-54.
[185] *Pennsylvania Gazette,* August 11, 1737, p. 4.
[186] Woodward, 1941: pp. 39, 43-44.
[187] American Philosophical Society, Franklin MSS, Ledger D, p. 97.

Catalogue of Books Belonging to the Library Company of Philadelphia as the donor of a four-volume set of *Cato's Letters* and another volume on the New Testament.[188] As secretary to the Provincial Council of New Jersey, he was instrumental in gaining a royal charter in 1758 on behalf of sixty citizens of New Jersey, who desired to establish a library company in Burlington. His name appeared first in the list of founders and first in the list of directors. He remained a director for four years and contributed books from his own private library. The Library Company of Burlington, like the Library Company of Philadelphia, was maintained by subscription, with an annual fee of ten shillings a year.[189]

Benjamin Franklin was in England when this library was founded, but for many years he had known the citizens of Burlington in his official position as public printer of New Jersey from 1734 on;[190] his *Autobiography* tells of the many influential friends he had gained in Burlington while working with Keimer on printing paper money for New Jersey.[191] When his son William was appointed Governor of New Jersey in 1763 and took up residence in the state capital, Franklin had even more opportunity to make friends with the citizens of Burlington.

CHARLESTON LIBRARY SOCIETY

In 1748 a library society was founded in Charleston, South Carolina, with the help of Peter Timothy. Peter was the son of Lewis Timothy (Louis Timothée), first librarian of the Library Company of Philadelphia, and former employee of Benjamin Franklin. In 1733 Lewis Timothy left Philadelphia to become the public printer of South Carolina and publisher of the *South Carolina Gazette*, in partnership with Franklin. He died in 1738, leaving his widow to carry on the partnership. She eventually bought the business for her son, Peter.[192]

The Charleston Library Society was first organized by a group of young men who pooled their funds "to collect such new pamphlets and magazines as should occasionally be published in Great Britain." The group had no name and worked together under a verbal agreement only. By December 28, 1748, enough interest was created to draw up a written agreement under the name of the Charleston Library Society, and books were added to the orders from England. By 1750 there were more than 160 members. Opposition from the Governor delayed a charter until 1755.[193] Once again William Strahan was chosen as agent in London, through the influence of Peter Timothy and Benjamin Franklin, for the Timothy-Franklin correspondence continued long after their partnership ended. Strahan retained the business until 1755, when the death of his "particular friend," John Sinclair (or St. Clair) shifted the favor of the Charleston Library Society to James Rivington, rival printer and bookseller. John Sinclair (or St. Clair) was a Charleston merchant who ordered paper from Franklin as late as 1754.[194] Strahan complained about the loss of business to David Hall, Franklin's partner in Philadelphia, and Franklin promised Strahan: "I shall not fail on every Occasion to recommend you to my Friends on the Book Account."[195] In later years (1767), Strahan had no sympathy for Rivington's financial difficulties:

J. Rivington, I find, is gone to pieces with you; an Event, which I wonder did not happen sooner. He owes a vast deal of Money here; but as those who gave him Credit knew whom they trusted, nobody pities them.[196]

REDWOOD LIBRARY, NEWPORT, RHODE ISLAND

The Redwood Library was established in 1747 by Abraham Redwood, who, according to the Charter, "generously engaged to bestow five hundred pounds sterling, to be laid out in a collection of useful books suitable for a Public Library proposed to be erected in Newport."[197] Redwood was a wealthy merchant, born in Antigua and educated in Philadelphia. He settled in Newport before the founding of the Library Company of Philadelphia, but must have made a return visit to Philadelphia on some of his voyages between Newport and Antigua, where he held large estates.[198] According to Peter Kalm, a "rich gentleman from Rhode Island" visited the Library Company of Philadelphia in the 1740's, "and when he had the opportunity of examining this institution he liked it so well that when he had returned home he persuaded some gentlemen in that state to build a house for a library, to which he made a gift of 500 pounds sterling for books."[199] Note the term "useful" that had been used in the Charter. Whatever else, the Library Company of Philadelphia had stressed "useful" books — not books for entertainment, not books on theolgy, but books on the practical matters of everyday living.

The Redwood Library was not the idea of Abraham Redwood alone. It was the outgrowth of the work of the Literary and Philosophical Society established in Newport by Bishop George Berkeley, and a gift of a tract of land from Henry Collins.[200] The final impetus, however, came from Abraham Redwood, inspired by his visit to the Library Company of Philadelphia.

---

[188] Pp. 30, 48.
[189] Woodward, 1941: pp. 46-47.
[190] Van Doren, 1938: p. 118.
[191] *Autobiography*, 1964: pp. 112-113.
[192] Van Doren, 1938: pp. 116-117. Van Doren gives 1743 as the founding date for the Charleston Library Society.
[193] Scudder, 1876: pp. 12-13.
[194] Eddy, 1929: pp. 112-113.
[195] Labaree, 1959— : **5**: p. 342; **7**: p. 115.
[196] "Correspondence between William Strahan and David Hall, 1763-1777," 1886-1888: *Pa. Mag. of Hist. & Biog.* **10**: p. 327.
[197] Redwood Library and Athenaeum, 1860: p. xxvii.
[198] *Dictionary of American Biography*, 1943: **15**: pp. 444-445.
[199] Kalm, 1937: **2**: p. 638.
[200] Redwood Library and Athenaeum, 1860: pp. iii-iv.

One of the secretaries of the Redwood Library (1753-1771) was Thomas Vernon,[201] whom Franklin commissioned as postmaster at Newport in 1754. Thomas was the son of Samuel Vernon,[202] who had trusted young Franklin to collect a debt in Pennsylvania for him, and waited patiently for Franklin to make good "one of the first great Errata of my Life,"[203] the misuse of Vernon's money.

Another contact between the Redwood Library and Franklin was through his friendship with Ezra Stiles, an honorary member (1755), who served as Redwood librarian from 1756 to 1764 and from 1768 to 1777.[204] Stiles claimed to have known Franklin since 1743 (when Stiles was only sixteen), and to have met Franklin personally in 1755.[205] The friendship was fostered by Franklin's gift of an electrical apparatus to Yale in 1749, when Stiles was a tutor there. Stiles used the apparatus to perform some of the first electrical experiments in New England.[206]

Another librarian of Redwood (1764-1766) was Henry Marchant,[207] who met Franklin in Edinburgh and in London in 1771.[208] The Edinburgh tour is described under the division on Yale.

During the 1730's, Franklin had three brothers living in Newport — James, John, and Peter. James had established his printing shop in Newport after leaving Boston and continued in the printing business there until his death in 1735. It is quite possible that the success of the Library Company of Philadelphia became known to Newport residents through Franklin's brothers.

The nineteenth century brought the likeness of Franklin to the Redwood Library through donations of a bust given by Andrew Robeson and a portrait given by Charles B. King.[209]

NEW YORK SOCIETY LIBRARY

The New York Society Library was first planned in March, 1754, by William Alexander (son of James Alexander), Philip Livingston, Robert R. Livingston, William Livingston, John Morin Scott, and William Smith, meeting in the Alexander home. Articles and the Subscription Roll of the New York Society Library were drawn up on April 2, requiring an initial payment of five pounds and an annual subscription of ten shillings by each member.[210] James Alexander was a correspondent of Franklin, a charter member of the American Philosophical Society of 1743, and was interested in Franklin's Albany plan of union for the colonies in 1754. The idea of a subscription library in New York is sometimes accredited to a suggestion by Mrs. James Alexander. She surely would have been familiar with the plan of the Library Company of Philadelphia, for it was she who traveled secretly to Philadelphia in 1735 to obtain the services of Andrew Hamilton to defend Peter Zenger after her own husband had been disbarred from the case.[211]

The real need for a subscription library was felt several years before with the failure of the New York Corporation Library to fulfill its function. James Parker, printing partner of Benjamin Franklin, gave up his attempts to keep the New York Corporation Library alive in 1747; his efforts along that line are discussed in more detail in the chapter on governmental libraries. The books of the New York Corporation Library were given over to the care of the New York Society Library; some were boxed for storage, but the rest remained in the City Hall. Subscribers looked forward to the day when they could erect their own building with space for a museum and observatory as well as a library.[212] Thus, the dream of New York was patterned after the Library Company of Philadelphia.

GENERAL INFLUENCE IN PHILADELPHIA

It would be hard to measure the influence of a library for the public good; too much depends upon subjective judgment. The influence of Franklin's Library Company must have been considerable. The public was allowed to use its books for reference purposes, and might borrow a book upon payment of a deposit and a fee for the use. Members of the Pennsylvania Assembly and the Continental Congress were freely given the use of the books. Later chapters will discuss the direct influence of the Library Company of Philadelphia upon the founding of the Philadelphia Academy (University of Pennsylvania) and the American Philosophical Society.

---

[201] *Ibid.*, p. xxxix.
[202] Labaree, 1959—: **5**: p. 451.
[203] *Autobiography*, 1964: p. 86.
[204] Redwood Library and Athenaeum, 1860: pp. xxxix, xlix.
[205] Stiles, 1901: **3**: pp. 390-391.
[206] *Dictionary of American Biography*, 1943: **18**: pp. 18-20.
[207] Redwood Library and Athenaeum, 1860: p. xxxix.
[208] Stiles, 1901: **1**: pp. 307-316.
[209] Redwood Library and Athenaeum, 1860: pp. lii-liii.

[210] Keep, 1909: pp. 130, 136.
[211] *Ibid.*, p. 135. Van Rensselaer, 1898: pp. 304-305, 382-384.
[212] Smith, 1830: **2**: p. 208.

II. THE LOGANIAN LIBRARY

Of all the scholars in Franklin's Philadelphia, James Logan was considered the dean. He had come to America as secretary to William Penn, and had served as provincial secretary, clerk and president of the Council, Chief Justice of the Supreme Court, and even as acting governor from 1736 to 1738.[1] He was suspicious of Benjamin Franklin's Junto when it was first formed, calling the members "the base and lying lackeys" of Sir William Keith. Governor Keith had favored issuing paper money; James Logan opposed it. Franklin, therefore, made an unfavorable first impression upon Logan when he printed his first American pamphlet, *A Modest Enquiry into the Nature and Necessity of a Paper Currency*.[2]

Though they disagreed about political affairs, James Logan soon came to respect the "ingenious" young man, Benjamin Franklin. A common bond of understanding between them was built upon their love of books. In March, 1732, when the members of the Library Company asked for advice on the choice of books, it was Benjamin Franklin, along with Thomas Godfrey, who went out to Stenton to see James Logan, "the best judge of books in these parts."

In his *Autobiography,* Franklin tells how he turned an enemy into a friend by capitalizing upon the man's love of books:

Having heard that he had in his Library a certain very scarce and curious Book, I wrote a Note to him expressing my Desire of perusing that Book, and requesting he would do me the Favour of lending it to me for a few Days. He sent it immediately; and I return'd it in about a Week, with another Note expressing strongly my Sense of the Favour. . . . And he ever afterwards manifested a Readiness to serve me on all Occasions, so that we became great Friends, and our Friendship continu'd to his Death. This is another Instance of the Truth of an old Maxim I had learnt, which says, *He that has once done you a Kindness will be more ready to do you another, than he whom you yourself have obliged.*[3]

This is precisely the technique that Franklin used in cultivating the friendship of James Logan, for Logan was a man of learning. He knew Greek, Hebrew, French, and could write Latin as easily as English. He owned a carefully selected library of over two thousand volumes, described in Franklin's *Proposals Relating to the Education of Youth in Pensilvania* (1749):

It contains many hundred Volumes of the best Authors in the best Editions, among which are the Polyglot Bible, and Castel's Lexicon on it, in 8 large Vols. Aldus's Septuagint, Apocrypha and New Testament, in Greek, and some other Editions of the same; most of the Fathers; almost all the Greek Authors from Homer himself, in divers Editions (and one of them in that of Rome, with Eustathius's Commentaries, in 4 Vols.) to near the End of the 4th Century, with divers later, as Photius, Suidas, divers of the Byzantine Historians; all the old Mathematicians, as Archimedes, Apollonius, Euclid, Ptolomy's Geography and Almagest, with Theon's Commentaries and Diophantus, in the whole above 100 Vols. in Greek Folio's. All the old Roman Classics without Exception, and some of them in several Editions (as all Tully's Works in four Editions). All Graevius, Gronovius, Salengre's and Poleni's Collections of Roman and Greek Antiquities, containing above Five Hundred distinct Discourses in 33 Tomes, with some Hundreds of late Authors in Latin, as Vossius, Lipsius, Grotius, &c. A good Collection of Mathematical Pieces, as Newton in all three Editions, Wallis, Huygens, Tacquet, Dechales, &c. in near 100 Vols. in all Sizes, with some Orientals, French and Italian Authors, and many more English, &c.[4]

More than just a scholar, James Logan was a man who generated learning. With his encouragement, Thomas Godfrey was transformed from a glazier to a mathematician and inventor; William Parsons, from a cobbler to a mapmaker and surveyor; John Bartram, from a farmer to an accomplished botanist. Franklin came a-borrowing; it was not long before he came a-lending. This was the start of many years of book exchanges between printer and scholar, until as the time passed on, the relationship changed into one between scholar and scholar.

James Logan was not only a reading scholar, but also a scholarly writer. He translated Cato's *Moral Distichs,* which Franklin begged for permission to print. It appeared in 1735, with Franklin's preface explaining:

It was done by a Gentleman amongst us (whose Name or Character I am strictly forbid to mention, tho' it might give some Advantage to my Edition) for the Use of his Children; But in my Opinion, it is no unfit or unprofitable Entertainment for those of riper Years. For certainly, such excellent Precepts of Morality, contain'd in such short and easily-remember'd Sentences, may to Youth particularly be very serviceable in the Conduct of Life, since there can scarce happen any Affair of Importance to us, in which we may need Advice, but one or more of these Distichs suited to the Occasion, will seasonably occur to the Memory, if the Book has been read and studied with a proper Care and Attention.[5]

This was the first literary work in a classical language to be translated and printed in the American colonies. Nine years later, Franklin published Cicero's *Cato Major* (translated by Logan), taking special care with large, clear type, fine paper, broad margins, and a handsome rubricated title page.[6] This publication was prized by Franklin as his printing masterpiece. Franklin also printed a missing title page for Logan's copy of Euclid's *Elements* (Paris, 1516).[7]

James Logan wrote two other books, both in Latin: *Experimenta et Meletemata de Plantarum Generatione* (Leyden, 1739), and *Demonstrationes de Radiorum Lucis . . .* (Leyden, 1741). The first, giving his experi-

---

[1] *Dictionary of American Biography,* 1943: 11: p. 361.
[2] Gray, 1937: p. 3.
[3] *Autobiography,* 1964: pp. 171-172.
[4] Labaree, 1959—: 3: pp. 401-402.
[5] Van Doren, 1945: p. 37.
[6] Tolles, 1957: p. 212.
[7] Labaree, 1959—: 3: p. 219.

ments on maize, was translated into English by Dr. John Fothergill,[8] who was later to become Franklin's personal physician in London. Logan probably gave a copy of the English translation to Franklin in 1748.[9]

In the house at Stenton, James Logan's library was kept on the second floor in a huge room which extended across the entire front of the house.[10] It was a magnificent room for a private library, and Franklin enjoyed riding out to chat with his friend whenever he could find time. Sometimes Logan would send a message, "to come up and See my Books." He never stopped collecting:

> Old as I am, now near 73, and much fail'd in all respects, I want to lay out about £200 Sterling more in Books which I shall do if I am so happy as to see a peace without farther disturbance and I have my Catalogue ready drawn. I should take it as a favour if I could see thee oftner here.[11]

The two men discussed Jared Eliot's *Essays upon Field-Husbandry in New England,* the language of the Picts, Captain John Smith's *True Travels, Adventures, and Observations . . . ,*[12] and Folard's *Polybius* (six volumes of military science in French), which Franklin had ordered for his son and had sold to Logan when his son lost interest in a military career.[13]

Their discussions began to reflect Franklin's public activities. Henry Ellis's *A Voyage to Hudson's Bay* and Charles Swaine's *An Account of a Voyage For the Discovery of a North-West Passage by Hudson's Streight*[14] were to stir Franklin into organizing and supporting another expedition to search for the Northwest Passage in 1753. There were also many discussions on books which Franklin used to gather ideas for founding his academy.

James Logan followed Franklin's public activities with interest, but probably he was even more excited by Franklin's scientific discoveries. On February 23, 1747, Logan wrote:

> Yesterday was the first time that I ever heard one syllable of thy Electrical Experiments, when John Bartram surpriz'd me with the account of a Ball turning many hours about an Electrified Body, with some other particulars that were sufficiently amazing. . . . I could therefore wish as soon as it can suit thee that thou wouldst step up hither bringing an Account with thee.

Logan owned books by Francis Hauksbee, Stephen Gray, Gowin Knight, and Georges-Louis Le Clerc, Comte de Buffon, but "your own Experiments in my judgment exceed them all."[15] When James Logan suffered from a stroke a couple of years later, Franklin tried to help with electrotherapy.

> I send you herewith a new French piece on electricity, in which you will find a journal of experiments on a paralytic person. I also send Neal on Electricity, and the last Philosophical Transactions, in which you will find some other pieces on the same subject. If you should desire to see any of the experiments mentioned in those pieces repeated, or if any new ones should occur to you to propose, which you cannot well try yourself, when I come to fetch the apparatus they may be tried. I shall be glad to hear that the shocks had some good effect on your disordered side.[16]

The method of treatment followed was written down by Franklin in a letter to John Pringle years after James Logan's death.[17]

Logan was also fascinated by Franklin's mathematical dexterity with magic squares, and dragged out his French folio by Frenicle, and a smaller "arithmetical book" by Stifelius for consultation and comparison. The magic squares were the result of "doodling" when Franklin became bored with the dull speeches of the Pennsylvania Assembly, while he was serving as clerk. He admitted to Logan that he was "rather ashamed to have it known I have spent any part of my time in an employment that cannot possibly be of any use to myself or others."[18]

James Logan was the only nonmember permitted to withdraw books from the Library Company. He followed its development with interest, asking to be supplied with a catalogue of its books in 1747, and registering surprise at the length of the list,

> which I did not the least apprehend would be sufficient to fill so much as one Quarter of a sheet of common paper, and indeed I am surpriz'd to hear the number is so considerable since the year 1742 as to require the Press. But for my justification thou may'st remember I had from thee about two years since (I think it was) a written List from thy own hand of the last Addition before.

The list which Logan had asked for was a twenty-eight page supplement, *Books added to the Library since the Year 1741,* printed by Franklin in 1746.[19]

About 1744 James Logan began to make plans to carry out his dream of founding a public library. From then until his death, he sought inspiration by reading about famous European libraries, and particularly accounts of Sir Thomas Bodley and Cardinal Mazarin. He built a small wooden building at Walnut and Sixth Streets, across from the State House Square, deposited his books there, and opened it for public use. Borrowers had to be properly introduced and must certify that the books would be treated with care. In 1745 he designed a more permanent building, a "handsome Building above 60 Feet in front";[20] his 1749 will bequeathed the library to the public of Philadelphia, "in order to prevail on them (having such assistance) to acquaint

---

[8] Gray, 1937: p. 74.
[9] Labaree, 1959—: 3: p. 323.
[10] Tolles, 1957: p. 187.
[11] Labaree, 1959—: 3: pp. 146-147, 380.
[12] *Ibid.* 3: pp. 285, 379, 389-390.
[13] Wolf, 1962: p. 8.
[14] Labaree, 1959—: 3: p. 325.
[15] *Ibid.* 3: pp. 110-111.

[16] *Ibid.* 3: p. 433.
[17] Van Doren, 1945: pp. 73-74.
[18] Sparks, 1836-1840: 6: pp. 100-102.
[19] Labaree, 1959—: 3: p. 113.
[20] *Ibid.* 3: pp. 350-351, 380, 402.

themselves with literature." The librarianship of the Loganian Library was to be hereditary, passing from eldest son to eldest son. In the event of no male heir, a female should carry on in the family tradition, and the trustees might appoint a librarian if none of the family qualified. The librarian must be a classical scholar, able to read both Latin and Greek.[21] He arranged an endowment by rental of lands to pay £35 Sterling per annum to buy books. He canceled the deed to the one-story brick building which now held the library in order to put the trust in different terms,[22] but he died on October 31, 1751, before completing it.

All Philadelphia mourned the passing of this learned man. The obituary which appeared in the *Pennsylvania Gazette* may have been written by Franklin himself.

FIG. 3. The Loganian Library. Courtesy of the Historical Society of Pennsylvania.

But the most noble Monument of his Wisdom, Publick Spirit, Benevolence, and affectionate Regard to the People of Pennsylvania, is his Library; which he has been collecting these 50 Years past, with the greatest Care and Judgment, intending it a Benefaction to the Publick for the Increase of Knowledge, and for the common Use and Benefit of all Lovers of Learning. It contains the best Editions of the best Books in various Languages, Arts and Sciences, and is without Doubt the largest, and by far the most valuable Collection of the Kind in this Part of the World, and will convey the Name of Logan thro' Ages, with Honour, to the latest Posterity.[23]

When Peter Collinson from across the sea wrote to ask, "Pray what becomes of James Logan Library,"[24] Franklin answered:

The Heirs of our Friend Logan have honourably settled the Library agreable to their Father's Intention. I am one of the Trustees. The Books are now plac'd in the Library House he built and gave for that purpose. They deserve Praise for this Conduct; for some Children would have taken Advantage of the Settlement not being perfected by the Father, and refus'd to comply with it.[25]

---

[21]Gray, 1937: pp. 78-79.
[22]Lamberton, 1918: p. 209.
[23]Nov. 7, 1751; printed in Labaree, 1959—: 4: p. 207.
[24]Labaree, 1959—: 4: p. 320.
[25]*Ibid*. 6: p. 89.

A deed of trust was drawn up on August 28, 1754. Although it was never officially recorded, it held until it was replaced in 1760 by one very similar. The rents from the lands in Bucks County were by 1761 valued at the amount of £35 sterling per annum. The librarian was to attend every Saturday from 3 to 7 P.M. in the summer and "so long as one may see to read" in the winter. The library was open to all "residents of Pennsylvania educated in reading and writing, especially in Latin, or who studied any of the mathematical sciences or medicine." A borrower might keep a folio volume for three weeks, a quarto for two, and an octavo for one week; each was to give his receipt, promise not to abuse the book or write therein, keep it under cover, return it on time, and not carry it out of Philadelphia. The Logan family might borrow twice as many books for twice as long. The librarian was to keep a genealogical record to determine the right of succession. Besides Benjamin Franklin, the trustees signing this document were Israel Pemberton, Jr., William Allen, and Richard Peters, serving as party of the second part, and for the Logan family, William and James Logan, sons of the deceased; Hannah Logan Smith, daughter; and John Smith, son-in-law, all of the first part.[26] In 1760 a catalogue of the books was printed.[27]

The trustees, unfortunately, were an incompatible group. Political factions caused divisions between them, and this led to the neglect of the library. Franklin's absence from the country so much of the time after 1757 was also a factor in this neglect. Because the building was situated close to a dusty street and its windows had to remain closed during the heat of the summer, the library lost its appeal except to the most devoted of scholars.

William Logan, first librarian, died in 1776, a time of turmoil when the library was used less than ever. In 1777 General Gates ordered the building used to store ammunition, and the books were not accessible to the public again until 1792.[28] After the British soldiers withdrew from Philadelphia, and the first fever of war was tempered by time, Dr. George Logan, the hereditary librarian, returned to Philadelphia in 1780. Shocked by the state of the library, he set about wiping off the dust of neglect.[29] Only two trustees were living — George's uncle, James Logan, and Benjamin Franklin. Franklin was still in France, still occupied with the more important business of maintaining the supply of money and materials to the colonies, but George Logan felt moved to write to Franklin for "some directions respecting the Loganian library. I wish it to answer the purpose of its institution, and should think no

---

[26]*Ibid*. 5: pp. 424-426.
[27]Gray, 1937: p. 79.
[28]Lamberton, 1918: pp. 211-212.
[29]Tolles, 1953: p. 47.

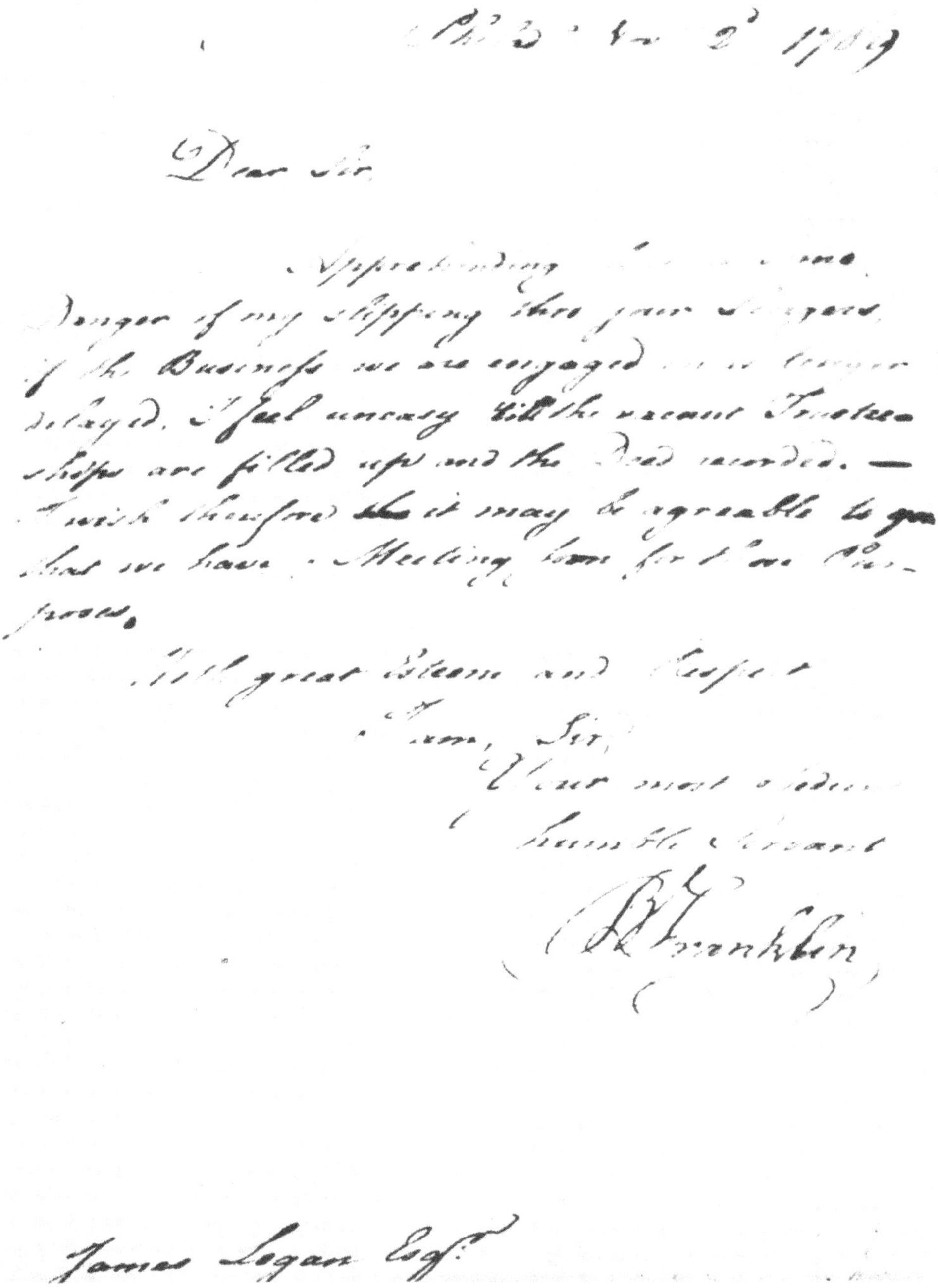

Phila. Nov. 2d 1789

Dear Sir,

Apprehending [some]
Danger of my slipping thro' your Fingers
if the Business we are engaged in is longer
delayed, I feel uneasy till the vacant Trusteeships are filled up and the Deed recorded. —
I wish therefore if it may be agreable to you
that we have a Meeting soon for those Purposes.

With great Esteem and Respect
I am, Sir,
Your most obedient
humble Servant
B Franklin

James Logan Esqr

Fig. 4. Letter concerning the trusteeships of the Loganian Library. Courtesy of the Library of Congress.

labour of mine too great to accomplish it."[30] Whether Franklin had any advice to give at that time is not known, but the next contact across the ocean came from Samuel Vaughan in Philadelphia. Vaughan inquired about a plan for uniting the Library Company and the Loganian Library, asking Franklin to send James Logan his answer.

> The present Idea is to have them under Trustees in the Same building but in different appartments, & with the former Same Names in order to perpetuate that of the Benefactor One librarian (if sufficient) to attend on both, at such distinct times as shall be judged most for public Utility.[31]

This James Logan was the son of the library's founder. He had recently served as a director of the Library Company (1778-1781),[32] and probably was convinced by this time of the wisdom of joining his father's older collection to a library of more current interest.

After Franklin returned to Philadelphia in 1785, he had more direct contact with the Logan family. George Logan would drop by on his way to and from the Assembly,[33] and Franklin, too, was busy with state affairs in his official position as President of the Supreme Executive Council of Pennsylvania. But even Franklin could not go on forever; as he was forced to restrict his activities more and more by the state of his health, he began to settle his earthly affairs. On November 2, 1789, he sent a poignant letter to James Logan concerning the trusteeship of the Loganian Library:

> Apprehending there is some Danger of my slipping thro your Fingers, if the Business we are engaged in is longer delayed, I feel uneasy 'till the vacant Trusteeships are filled up and the Deed recorded. — I wish therefore that it may be agreable to you that we have a Meeting soon for those Purposes.[34]

The Loganian Library was joined to the Library Company in 1792, after the Library Company had erected its first building and after the death of Franklin.

III. ACADEMIC LIBRARIES

THE PHILADELPHIA ACADEMY (UNIVERSITY OF PENNSYLVANIA)

Benjamin Franklin was a man with very little formal education, yet today he is remembered as the founder of the University of Pennsylvania. The University can trace its development through earlier stages of a Charity School, the Philadelphia Academy, and the College of Philadelphia, with Franklin most active in the affairs of the Academy.

---

[30] American Philosophical Society, Franklin MSS, Bache Collection (July 15, 1781).
[31] *Ibid.* 31: 106 (March 8, 1784).
[32] Abbot, 1913: p. 28 (not numbered).
[33] Tolles, 1953: pp. 68-69.
[34] Library of Congress, Franklin MSS, No. 2086.

In 1739 Franklin and other citizens of Philadelphia were so stirred by the powerful preaching of George Whitefield that a public subscription was collected to build an evangelical hall. This building, used for the first time in November, 1740, was devoted to nondenominational services; so that the building would be doubly useful, a charity school was opened to provide an education for poor children of the city.[1] The trusteeship of the building was carefully divided to avoid weighting in favor of any denomination, and Franklin was chosen because he was "merely an honest Man, and of no Sect at all."[2]

Franklin began to formulate plans for a formal system of education in 1743, and

> drew up a Proposal for establishing an Academy; and at that time thinking the Revd. Mr. Peters, who was out of Employ, a fit Person to superintend such an Institution, I communicated the Project to him. But he having more profitable Views in the Service of the Proprietors, which succeeded, declin'd the Undertaking. And not knowing another at that time suitable for such a Trust, I let the Scheme lie a while dormant.[3]

In 1749 Franklin resumed his plan for founding an academy. He had just retired, turning over the active part of his business to his partner, David Hall, and now had more time to prosecute the venture. As in all of his other public efforts, Franklin knew the value of advance suggestion and announced in the *Pennsylvania Gazette* of August 24 that a proposal "for establishing an Academy in this province" would soon be forthcoming.

> The first Step I took was to associate in the Design a Number of active Friends, of whom the Junto furnished a good Part: the next was to write and publish a Pamphlet intitled, *Proposals relating to the Education of Youth in Pennsylvania*. This I distributed among the principal Inhabitants gratis; and as soon as I could suppose their Minds a little prepared by the Perusal of it, I set on foot a Subscription for Opening and Supporting an Academy; it was to be paid in Quotas yearly for Five Years; by so dividing it I judg'd the Subscription might be larger, and I believe it was so, amounting to no less (if I remember right) than Five thousand Pounds. In the Introduction to these Proposals, I stated their Publication not as an Act of mine, but of some *publick-spirited Gentlemen;* avoiding as much as I could, according to my usual Rule, the presenting myself to the Publick as the Author of any Scheme for their Benefit.[4]

In his *Proposals,* he made plans for a library:

> That the House be furnished with a Library (if in the Country, if in the Town, the Town Libraries may serve) with Maps of all Countries, Globes, some mathematical Instruments, an Apparatus for Experiments in Natural

---

[1] Shores, 1935: p. 37.
[2] *Autobiography,* 1964: p. 194.
[3] *Ibid.,* p. 182.
[4] *Ibid.,* pp. 192-193.

Philosophy, and for Mechanics; Prints, of all Kinds, Prospects, Buildings, Machines, &c.[5]

The town libraries that Franklin had in mind were the Library Company and the Loganian Library. He had written to James Logan in September:

> Please to favour me with the short Account of your Library, contain'd in the Paper I read the other Day at your House, that I may insert it in a Note to the Proposals for an Academy.[6]

A description of the Loganian Library appeared in a long footnote in *Proposals Relating to the Education of Youth in Pensilvania*, printed in the fall of 1749.[7] Franklin drew heavily upon the books of both the Loganian Library and the Library Company for his ideas.

James Logan had at first refused to be active in supporting the Academy, probably because of his age and health; however, he finally gave in.

> I am willing my name Should be inserted amongst the Collegues of your Society, tho' very uncapable of being in any manner useful to it, yet I am very desirous to have it by all means promoted, tho' I expect to be excused from contributing any thing to it more than that £35 Sterl. per an. Settled on my Library for ever.

When the Constitutions of the Academy were copied, Franklin inserted Logan's name at the head of the trustees.[8] Written by Franklin and Tench Francis, the Constitutions contained a provision that donations would be "cheerfully and thankfully accepted" to furnish "Books of general Use, that may be too expensive for each Scholar; Maps, Draughts, and other Things generally necessary for the Improvement of the Youth."[9]

As President of the Board of Trustees,[10] Franklin negotiated the purchase of the hall built for Whitefield's evangelical meetings and superintended the necessary remodeling.[11] When all was ready, the school was moved from its temporary quarters where it had opened in January, 1751.[12] Books and supplies had been ordered the year before. On March 29, 1750, a committee including Franklin, Allen, Coleman, Peters, Hopkinson, and Francis were voted a sum not to exceed 100 pounds sterling to be disposed of in Latin and Greek authors, maps, drafts, and instruments for the use of the Academy. Orders were made out and forwarded to Peter Collinson, who in turn purchased the materials from various dealers. Among the books ordered were *Compendious System of Natural Philosophy* by John Bonning and *Way of Teaching Languages* by J. Thomas Philipps. These two titles along with "Map of the World" and "Rectifer" appeared in a marginal note in Franklin's handwriting.[13] The books were purchased from John Whiston, and Peter Collinson wrote: "I Acquainted him and showed Him the Constitutions. He has promised Mee to Encourage so Laudable a Work, He will contribute on his part in the price of his Books." Instruments purchased from Adams were "of such a Length I could not pack them in your Trunk," and so had to be sent with the goods of a merchant in Trenton, New Jersey; "so please to send for them."

> The whole Designe of the Academy is generally Approved by all my Ingenious knowing Friends and all Wish its prosperity but . . . They Think you Grasp at too much your Plans to Large for a Begining.

Collinson also furnished valuable contact with the Proprietor, Thomas Penn:

> Your proprietor in General approves your Academy Butt thinks it a Little too premature. Shall be glad if the Colony is come to such a Maturity as to support so Beneficial a Work.
> He Designs to Encourage It. I regret my not Showing Him your List of Instruments, for He Intended if I had not first bespoke them to have Sent them himself. Perhaps when I Show Him the Cost He may Yett Do It.[14]

About one-half of the money had been spent for "mathematical and philosophical" apparatus, probably under the influence of Franklin.[15]

As long as Franklin lived, a member of the faculty served as librarian.[16] The library was

> a small, though carefully selected body of books, established in locked cases in one of the central rooms of College Hall. It was under the administration of a committee of the Board of Trustees and of one of the professors, who acted as librarian in addition to his teaching duties, and was present to unlock cases and give out and receive books only at certain appointed hours in the week.[17]

Its purpose was supplemental only, because of the presence of other libraries in the city, the limited book-purchasing power of the students, and the textbook method of teaching. The library was enlarged at the expense of the trustees, who "Agreed unanimously that no Holliday [sic.] be granted to the Scholars at the request of any Person, unless at the same time he made a present to the Academy of a Book of Ten Shillings value." Absences from the meetings of the trustees brought a "Fine of One Shilling, . . . to be applied towards buying Books, Paper, &c for the Scholars in the Charity School."[18] This scheme of fining the trustees and appropriating the funds toward the purchase of books is strongly reminiscent of Franklin's system of fines imposed upon the Library Company directors for absence from meetings; there can be little doubt that it was Franklin who proposed the idea to the Academy trustees.

---

[5]Labaree, 1959—: 3: pp. 401-402.
[6]*Ibid.* 3: p. 389.
[7]*Ibid.* 3: pp. 401-402.
[8]*Ibid.* 3: p. 456.
[9]*Ibid.* 3: p. 426.
[10]Cheyney, 1940: p. 173.
[11]*Autobiography*, 1964: pp. 194-195.
[12]Bridenbaugh, 1962: p. 43.
[13]Montgomery, 1900: pp. 125-126.
[14]Labaree, 1959—: 4: pp. 3-6.
[15]Cheyney, 1940: p. 37.
[16]Shores, 1935: p. 271.
[17]Cheyney, 1940: pp. 322-323.
[18]Montgomery, 1900: pp. 154-155.

From the very start, Franklin's idea of the Academy was for the provision of education for business and agriculture, stressing more science and English than was commonly provided for in most schools. In order to gain support of the wealthier citizens, he had compromised in favor of those who would support only a Latin school. The Academy was to be half Latin, half English, with equal emphasis on both parts. First and foremost, Franklin felt that a basic knowledge of our native tongue was indispensable; he did, however, realize the value of other modern languages. He had acquired a reading knowledge of French, Italian, and Spanish by his own intensive program of study. He considered Latin a dead language, wasted on many students who did not continue on in higher education.[19] He was upheld in this by Cadwallader Colden, to whom he had sent his *Proposals Relating to Education* for comment. Colden suggested that all the sciences be taught in English, that there be no language other than English taught except the learned languages for students of "Divinity, Law and Physic," and French for future merchants.[20]

In 1750 Franklin wrote his "Idea of the English School, Sketch'd out for the Consideration of the Trustees of the Philadelphia Academy." The first and lowest class would stress grammar and orthography, using Croxall's *Fables*. The second class would emphasize oral reading, using the *Spectator*, stories, speeches, sermons, plays, and poetry. The third class would stress public speaking, using speeches, plays, Rollin's *"Antient and Roman Histories,"* and *Spectacle de la Nature* (natural and mechanic history). The fourth class would study composition of letters, using letters of Sir William Temple, Pope, etc., with the addition of history, geography, and ethics, especially Dr. Samuel Johnson's *Ethices Elementa, or first Principles of Morality*. The fifth class would study essays and poetry, history, and logic, using Dr. Johnson's *Noetica, or first Principles of human Knowledge*. The sixth class emphasized English literature, history, rhetoric, moral and natural philosophy, with such authors as Tillotson, Milton, Locke, Addison, Pope, Swift, "the higher Papers in the *Spectator* and *Guardian*," translations of Homer, Virgil, Horace, *Travels of Cyrus*, etc. Thus, the classics were not neglected but were appreciated in English, and instruction in composition followed Franklin's own method of learning by imitating examples in the *Spectator*. Franklin believed in encouraging personal libraries and urged that "fine gilt Books" be given as prizes in competitions. He would have the advanced class study also arithmetic, accounts, geography, use of globes, drawing, and mechanics. "Thus instructed,

[19] *Autobiography*, 1964: pp. 168-169.
[20] Labaree, 1959—: 3: p. 432.

FIG. 5. The College and the Academy of Philadelphia. Modern painting by Charles M. Lefferts from contemporary prints. Courtesy of the University of Pennsylvania. Original in the Edgar Fahs Smith Memorial Collection.

Youth will come out of this School fitted for learning any Business, Calling or Profession, except such wherein Languages are required."[21]

Franklin sent his "Idea of the English School" (for boys between eight and sixteen years of age) to Dr. Samuel Johnson of Stratford, Connecticut, author of several of the texts that he had recommended. He asked Johnson to amend this scheme, or to give them a complete one of his own, apologizing for being "indeed very unfit, having neither been educated myself (except as a Tradesman) nor ever concern'd in educating others."[22] Dr. Johnson was highly enthusiastic over the scheme.

Nobody would imagine that the draught you have made for an English education was done by a Tradesman. But so it sometimes is, a True Genius will not content itself without entering more or less into almost everything, and of mastering many things more in spite of Fate it self.[23]

The books which Dr. Johnson suggested and Franklin accepted in his published text were Blackwall's *An Introduction to the Classics,* Lamy's *The Art of Speaking,* Fénelon's *The Adventures of Telemachus,* and Ramsay's *The Travels of Cyrus.* In fact, Franklin accepted every one of Johnson's suggestions except Shakespeare![24] Most of the book titles which Franklin included were already owned by the Library Company and were mentioned in Clarke's *Essay upon Study.*[25]

The Academy now had a Latin School, an English School, and a Charity School, and was blessed with a charter and a gift of £500 from the Proprietors in July, 1753.[26] Franklin had tried to persuade Dr. Samuel Johnson to head the institution. Failing in that, he turned next to William Smith, who had just published his *General Idea of a College of Mirania.*[27] William Smith, at that time, was tutoring the sons of Colonel Josiah Martin of Long Island, while waiting for a more advantageous position. In making his appeal, Franklin described the advantages of settling in Philadelphia.

The English Library is a good one, and we have belonging to it a midling Apparatus for Experimental Philosophy, and purpose speedily to compleat it. The Loganian Library, one of the best Collections in America, will shortly be opened; so that neither Books nor Instruments will be wanting.[28]

Attracted by the cultural possibilities, William Smith visited Philadelphia and composed *A Poem on Visiting the Academy of Philadelphia,* which Franklin printed. Then he accompanied Franklin to Connecticut to pay a visit to Samuel Johnson at Stratford. William Smith proceeded on to England, where he stayed just long enough to be ordained as an Episcopal minister.[29] Upon his return, he accepted the position of head of the Philadelphia Academy. William Smith was an ambitious young man; under his administration, a college was added, with Smith as Provost, and Francis Alison, Vice-Provost. This meant the granting of an "Additional Charter" of the "College, Academy and Charitable School of Philadelphia in the Province of Pennsylvania." With power now to grant degrees, the College of Philadelphia became a real center of learning, and the trustees were empowered to set up branch schools in other parts of Pennsylvania and Delaware.[30]

Franklin continued in the financial affairs of the Academy and College. In 1754 he promoted a "Scheme Of a Lottery, for raising 3000 Pieces of Eight, for the Use of the Academy at Philadelphia."[31] He continued also with orders of books and equipment, Johnson's Dictionary, Blair's *Chronology of the World,* "Philosophical Implements to compleat our Apparatus for Natural Philosophy: . . . one of Mr. Smeaton's new Air Pumps, described in the late Transactions" — these all from Peter Collinson.[32] The Franklin and Hall printing firm showed accounts for the Academy and College between 1748 and 1766.[33] In 1756 Franklin attempted to get a grant from the Pennsylvania Assembly for the College, but by this time, political differences were arising between members of the Assembly and the administration of the College by William Smith, who was actively supporting the Proprietors, and so the grant was not furnished.[34]

Franklin complained about the decrease in enrollment because of Smith's party activities:

Smith continues still in the Academy; but I imagine will not much longer, unless he mends his Manners greatly; for the Schools decline on his Account: The Number of Scholars at present, that pay, not exceeding 118, tho' they formerly were 200."[35]

With the increase of power of William Smith in directing the affairs of the College, Franklin was replaced as President of the Board of Trustees by Richard Peters on May 11, 1756. He retained his position as trustee, but he and Smith ceased to be "on speaking Terms."[36] In January, 1757, a vacancy on the board of trustees was filled by the election of Benjamin Chew, "to the mortification of Mr. Franklin," according to a report by Richard Peters:

BF blames the Trustees that they did not beforehand consult him on his Election, saying it was a piece of Justice due to him as he was the Father and principal support of the Academy, and this is true, but for all that it was not

---

[21] *Ibid.* 4: pp. 101-108.
[22] *Ibid.* 4: p. 72.
[23] Smyth, 1905-1907: 3: p. 29 n. 1.
[24] Labaree, 1959—: 4: p. 75.
[25] Wolf, 1956b: p. 35.
[26] Labaree, 1959—: 5: p. 7.
[27] Bridenbaugh, 1962: p. 56.
[28] Labaree, 1959—: 4: p. 469.
[29] *Ibid.* 4: p. 511. Bridenbaugh, 1962: pp. 56-58.
[30] Labaree, 1959—: 6: pp. 28-37.
[31] *Pennsylvania Gazette,* Oct. 3, 1754, p. 1.
[32] Labaree, 1959—: 6: pp. 84-86, 171-172.
[33] *Ibid.* 3: p. 271.
[34] Cheyney, 1940: pp. 171-172.
[35] Labaree, 1959—: 7: p. 50.
[36] *Ibid.* 7: p. 12.

thought proper to gratify his Pride which now grows insufferable.

As the political differences could not be resolved, and Franklin was appointed by the Assembly to go to England to protest Proprietary action, he wrote to his friend, William Coleman, treasurer of the Academy, and gave instructions for applying a donation of £20 sterling left with him by Colonel Philip Ludwell, of Virginia.

As he was pleased to leave the particular Mode of applying it to me, I could wish it were put to Interest, and three Prizes purchas'd with the yearly Produce, to be distributed yearly for the three best Pieces of Writing (not exceeding 4 Lines each Piece) done by Boys under 14 Years of Age, who were taught at the Academy. One Prize of 18s. Value for the first. One Ditto of 13s. Value for the 2d. and one Ditto of 9s. Value for the 3d. Some useful Book neatly bound and gilt to be a Part of each Prize. But this I submit to the Trustees.[37]

Apparently, the trustees refused to accept the suggestion of granting books as prizes for compositions, and Franklin grew bitter over the policy decisions of the College and Academy. Two years later, he was still seething, when he wrote back to Professor Kinnersley, "Before I left Philadelphia, everything to be done at the Academy was privately preconcerted in a Cabal without my Knowledge or Participation."[38]

After Franklin left for England in 1757, William Smith was jailed by order of the Assembly and actually taught his classes in jail. Released by court order, Smith went to England to vindicate himself, but while there he hurt Franklin even more by slander and by undercutting the Franklin and Hall bookselling business in Philadelphia. Franklin wrote to David Hall, explaining how he dealt with the situation:

Parson Smith has been applying to Osborne for a large Cargo of Books, acquainting him that he could be of vast Service in selling great Quantities for him, as there was only one Hall at Philada. who demanded excessive Prices; and if another Shop was but open'd where People could be supply'd reasonably, all the Custom would run to it. I know not whether he was to sell them himself or employ some other. He gave Osborne a Catalogue. Osborne came to me and ask'd me if I knew him, and that he should be safe in trusting him. I told him I believ'd my Townsmen who were Smith's Creditors would be glad to see him come back with a Cargo of any Kind, as they might have some Chance of being paid out of it; And so I could not in Conscience dissuade him from trusting him. "Oh, says he, is that the Case; then he shall have no Books of me I assure you: He persuaded me to trust him 10 £'s worth of Books, and take his Note payable in Six Months. But I will have the Money immediately or the Books again."[39]

We can only wonder whether William Smith ever found out how his credit had been curtailed, but Franklin definitely considered Smith an enemy.

I made that Man my Enemy by doing him too much Kindness. 'Tis the honestest Way of acquiring an Enemy. And, since 'tis convenient to have at least one Enemy, who by his Readiness to revile one on all Occasions, may make one careful of one's Conduct, I shall keep him an Enemy for that purpose; . . .[40]

Despite the bitter feeling between the two men, they gradually resumed a cool correspondence, and Smith kept Franklin informed on the progress of donations for the college.[41]

Even though Franklin could no longer direct the policies of the Academy and the College, he still maintained interest in their welfare; many times some of the books that were given to the Academy were given through Franklin's friendship; such were the gifts from Peter Collinson. The Academy library received its basic start in 1749 by a gift from Richard Peters of books on theology and English literature; as time went on, so much of the Academy library was devoted to classical literature that Franklin felt it betrayed its original purpose.[42] In February, 1758, the trustees were notified that "many of the Students in the Philosophy School had been very deficient in their Exercises and otherways much retarded in their Studies for Want of a Library furnished with suitable Books in the different Branches of Science," so it was decided to devote some of the funds to the purchase of science books.[43] Franklin's account books of 1758 and 1759, while he was in England, show that he was the person to whom the Academy turned to purchase these books on science.[44] In 1762 Mr. William Dunlap, Franklin's printing partner and relative by marriage, presented the College with a substantial number of books.

Franklin returned to America in November, 1762, and remained for a couple of years. Since he was still a trustee during this period, he might have renewed his contacts with the Academy and College, but it was Richard Peters, Jacob Duché, and especially Professor Ewing, who actually were responsible for the inventory and the selection of the college library.[45] The library had been consigned to the "Apparatus Room" on the ground floor in January, 1762; there it sat surrounded by scientific instruments which Franklin had purchased in London, Kinnersley's electrical apparatus, and other science equipment donated by Thomas Penn.[46] Before sailing for France in October, 1776, Franklin gave to the college library a book by his friend, Joseph Priestley, *The History and Present State of Discoveries relating to Vision, Light and Colours* (London, 1772).[47]

---

[37] *Ibid.* 7: pp. 134-135.
[38] *Ibid.* 7: p. 12.
[39] Smyth, 1905-1907: 3: pp. 475-476.
[40] *Ibid.* 4: p. 195.
[41] American Philosophical Society, Franklin MSS, 3: 96 (Smith to Franklin, May 16, 1772).
[42] Bridenbaugh, 1962: p. 92.
[43] Montgomery, 1900: p. 336.
[44] Eddy, 1931: pp. 113, 116.
[45] Montgomery, 1900: pp. 336-337.
[46] Turner, 1953: p. 182.
[47] Pennsylvania, University of (Library), 1951: p. 47.

In 1779 the College was incorporated into the University of the State of Pennsylvania, later known as the University of Pennsylvania.

After peace had been restored in 1784, there arrived a gift of a hundred volumes of selected works contributed by King Louis XVI to the University of Pennsylvania. These were largely works by French writers on science and natural history, suggested by the known interests of Franklin, and for the most part printed by the royal press. There were thirty-six titles in all, including Buffon's *Histoire Naturelle* (30 volumes), Soulavie's *Histoire Naturelle de la France* (6 volumes), and Chastellux's *De la Félicité Publique (Public Happiness,* mentioned by Franklin to Joseph Reed). The entire catalogue of the gift collection is printed in C. Seymour Thompson's article, "The Gift of Louis XVI," *The University of Pennsylvania Library Chronicle,* 2, 4 (Dec. 1934): pp. 60-67. The idea of the gift originated with the Chevalier de Chastellux, a young French officer in Rochambeau's army, who had come over in 1780 with letters of introduction written by Benjamin Franklin to Joseph Reed, President of Pennsylvania (1778-1781), and a founder of the University of the State of Pennsylvania:

> I beg leave to introduce to your Excellency's acquaintance and civilities the Chevalier de Chastellux: major-general in the French troops, now about to embark for America, whom I have long known and esteemed highly in his several characters of a soldier, a gentleman, and a man of letters. His excellent book on *Public Happiness* shows him the friend to mankind, and as such entitles him, wherever he goes, to their respect and good offices. He is particularly a friend to our cause, and I am sure your Excellency will have great pleasure in his conversation.[48]

The university granted Chastellux an honorary degree of LL.D. (1782), and the American Philosophical Society, of which Franklin was president, elected him a member (1781).[49] Chastellux wrote Franklin that his letters of introduction had "procured him the kindest welcome in Philadelphia, from Mr. Reed and the Academical Society."[50] Upon his return to France, Chastellux urged Count Vergennes to recommend to the king to send a gift of books to the University of Pennsylvania and to the College of William and Mary.[51] Vergennes was the Foreign Minister of King Louis XVI and the man with whom Franklin dealt closely in his nine years of getting aid from France. The *Pennsylvania Gazette* announced the arrival of the gift on July 21, 1784:

> A well chosen collection of books is arrived at New-York in the French packet le Courier de l'Amerique: they are sent by order of the King of France to his Consul General, to be presented to the Universities of Philadelphia and Williamsburg. They have been given at the joint request of the Count de Vergennes, and of the Chevalier (and since his brother's death) Marquis de Chatellaux.

Just how much credit should be given to Franklin for this valuable donation is debatable. Franklin had spent so many years soliciting funds, ammunition, etc., for the very survival of his country, that he had formed a definite prejudice against soliciting foreign donations for colleges, feeling that it was time that these new American colleges gained their support from the people they served. However, it is not likely that he would have refused a donation suggested by a Frenchman, for he was well aware of the sensibilities of the French court, America's indebtedness to France, and diplomatic finesse requiring graciousness and tact. As for Chastellux, he continued to correspond with Franklin, sending his *Journal of Travels in America* (in French) several years later.[52]

Even after the donation from King Louis XVI, the library did not impress Manasseh Cutler on his Philadelphia visit in 1787:

> The Library is very small, consisting only of a few antiquated authors, and the apparatus not much better. Mr. Rittenhouse's orrery is the only instrument worthy of notice; the Cabinet is trifling. But the want of these in the University is pretty well supplied by the large and valuable collection of books, instruments, and natural curiosities in Carpenter's Hall.[53]

Franklin was literally adored by the French people, but he was also admired and respected as a scientific genius. When the time came for him to leave France, he was presented with many donations of books. One of these was a pamphlet designated for "the principal academy" in the United States.[54] Surely, to Franklin, the "principal academy" would have been his own "academy" in Philadelphia, now grown into a university. Upon his arrival in Philadelphia in 1785, Franklin was given a grand welcome, including an address by the University of Pennsylvania, delivered by the Reverend John Ewing, Provost.[55]

In the last year of his life, Franklin sat down to review his accomplishments. He was no longer President of Pennsylvania and had more time for other matters. He was chosen President of the Board of Trustees in the reorganization of 1789, in which the college was restored, operating separately but under the same charter as the University of Pennsylvania, and the Board held some of its meetings in his house because of his ill health.[56] He obtained the minutes of the trustees and went through them, raking over the years of disappointment and bitterness over the policies that had been followed. In June of 1789, he sat down and wrote

---

[48]Sparks, 1836-1840: **8**: p. 442.
[49]Thompson, 1934: p. 38.
[50]Hays, 1908: **2**: p. 348.
[51]Thompson, 1934: pp. 38-39.
[52]Bigelow, 1888: **3**: pp. 374-375. Franklin acknowledged receipt April 17, 1787.
[53]Cutler, 1888: **1**: p. 264.
[54]Hays, 1908: **3**: p. 255.
[55]Library of Congress, Franklin MSS, No. 1511 (Sept. 16, 1785).
[56]Cheyney, 1940: pp. 151, 171.

his *Observations Relative to the Intentions of the Original Founders of the Academy in Philadelphia.* The major factor of his discontent was the neglect and decline of the English School. In his original scheme, "my Ideas went no farther than to procure the Means of a good English Education." He had soon been pressed into facing reality in gaining support for the Academy, by providing for the establishment of two schools, the Latin and the English, with the promise that the two would always be equal. Even though he was the first President of the Board of Trustees, the partiality toward the Latin School was evident from the beginning. The title of Rector was given to the Latin master, and no title to the English master. The Latin master was given twice as much salary as the English master, and yet had only half as many students. It was Franklin who forced the raise of salary to the English master, because no one could be found at such a low salary. The second instance of partiality was the first book and supply order of March, 1750, "when 100 *l.* Sterling was voted to buy *Latin* and *Greek* Books, Maps, Drafts, and Instruments for the Use of the Academy, and nothing for *English Books.*"[57] Franklin probably forgot that he had not yet written or published his *Idea of the English School,* giving specific book titles, until several months after this order was made; also, half of the funds had been spent on science and mathematics, an idea strange to those educated in a Latin school. If this prejudice in favor of the Latin School existed when Franklin was still in Philadelphia serving as President of the Board of Trustees, it was intensified after he left the country. He noted in the minutes of July 23, 1769, that the trustees had decided to discontinue the English School, taking Professor Kinnersley off the salary roll on October 17, but permitting him to stay on the premises of the school on an individual fee basis. Despite the resolution to discontinue the English School, the trustees must have changed their minds, for on January 29, 1770, they voted to give a book of the value of one dollar as a prize to the boy best in English competition in July, while a book worth two dollars was to be given to the best Latin scholar. In oratorical competitions, English students and Latin students were on equal terms. Franklin pointed out that Latin and Greek schools developed because the only books available were in the classical languages, but after printing made books more available in the "Vulgar Tongues," learning "the ancient for the purpose of acquiring Knowledge is become absolutely unnecessary."[58] Latin and Greek, to Franklin, were the "quackery of literature."[59]

HARVARD

Had Benjamin Franklin followed his father's first ambition, he might have been a student at Harvard, headed toward the ministry, but life as a printer's apprentice made him see Harvard in a different light. When he was young and foolish, as he might have admitted himself later, he ridiculed the institution in his Silence Dogood papers, in an allegorical dream about the "Temple of Learning": "every Beetle-Scull seem'd well satisfy'd with his own Portion of Learning, tho' perhaps he was e'en just as ignorant as ever." He continued on to say that many of the graduates left to spend their lives "as poor as Church Mice, being unable to dig, and asham'd to beg, and to live by their Wits it was impossible."[60] The years softened Franklin's satire, sapping its strength till came the time in 1753 that he was willing to accept from Harvard his first honorary degree. Until such a time, Franklin paid scant attention to Harvard, except for a brief mention in the July 12 and August 30, 1733, issues of the *Pennsylvania Gazette,* concerning Dean Berkeley's gift of books to the Harvard library. This occurred on the eve of his first trip back to Boston as a successful business man.

As we have seen in the chapter on the Library Company of Philadelphia, Franklin's experiments in electricity caught the attention of the Royal Society in London, through the sponsorship of Peter Collinson, as early as 1747. In 1749 Franklin formulated his theories on the relationship between lightning and electricity. In April, 1751, his *Experiments and Observations on Electricity* were published in London. In February, 1752, they were translated and published in Paris. French scientists were thus stimulated to experiment with electricity; in May, Dalibard corroborated Franklin's theory about lightning. Franklin performed his own kite experiment in June and published the information in October. In March, 1753, the volume of *Supplemental Experiments and Observations* was published in London.[61] Harvard could hardly ignore this international recognition as a scientist, and granted Franklin an honorary master's degree on July 25, 1753.[62] This was conferred in person when Franklin was in New England attending to postal affairs. Harvard eventually acquired a copy of Franklin's *Experiments and Observations on Electricity . . .* with the 1753 *Supplemental Experiments and Observations,* presumably a gift from the author.[63]

From this time on, Franklin held Harvard in a higher regard than before. He corresponded with various officials of the college, but his chief contact for many years was through John Winthrop, professor of mathematics and natural philosophy from 1738 to 1779.[64]

[57] Smyth, 1905-1907: 10: pp. 10-11, 13.
[58] *Ibid.* 10: pp. 23-30.
[59] Rush, 1905: p. 27.
[60] Labaree, 1959—: 1: pp. 14-18.
[61] Cohen, 1941: pp. 78-103, 130, 141-147.
[62] Labaree, 1959—: 5: p. 17.
[63] Lane, 1907: p. 239.
[64] *Dictionary of American Biography,* 1943: 20: p. 415.

Although Franklin had been in Boston to receive his degree, he may not have met John Winthrop there, for Winthrop's wife was very ill at that time and died shortly thereafter. The following spring, John Winthrop traveled down to Philadelphia, bringing with him a letter of introduction from a mutual friend in New Jersey.[65]

In the fall of 1754, Franklin visited the Boston area again, this time with William Hunter, who served with him as joint deputy postmaster-general of North America. No doubt Franklin renewed his contact with Harvard at this time, for the next September (1755), he had a specific proposal for the development of the Harvard College Library. Franklin had learned through his experience with the Library Company of Philadelphia, the Philadelphia Academy, and various other public improvements which he supported, the value of the subscription plan by which contributors pledged a certain amount to be paid over a number of years. He wrote to Thomas Hancock, a wealthy Boston merchant and benefactor of Harvard College, outlining this subscription plan, enclosing an example of the scheme, together with his own pledge payable by an order on John Franklin, his brother, postmaster of Boston.

Five and twenty Subscribers at 4 Pistoles[66] Each per Annum would in five Years produce 500 Pistoles, which if all laid out in Books would make a handsome Addition to the Library, or if put to Interest, would produce a little Annual Income sufficient to procure the best new Books published in each Year. Some might perhaps subscribe more than four Pistoles per Annum and others less; and I think that a single Pistole or half a Pistole should not be refused; Tho' such small Sums might occasion a little more Trouble in Receiving or Collecting. I send withal an Order on my Brother, for my first Year's Payment. 'Tis but a Trifle compar'd with my hearty Good will and Respect to the College; but a small Seed properly Sown, sometimes produces a large and fruitful Tree; which I sincerely wish maybe the good Fortune of this.

Subscription Paper for Harvard College Library

We whose Names are hereunto subscribed, taking into Consideration, that in the Library of the College at Cambridge in New England, many Books useful to Students in the several Branches of Learning are yet wanting; and that as new Improvements are from time to time made in Science, new Books on many Subjects are continually coming forth, with which Seminarys of Learning especially should be early furnished, for the further Qualification of the Tutors, and Advantage of the Youth by them to be instructed. But inasmuch as there is not yet any Fund for such Purposes belonging to the said College, therefore to remedy that Deficiency in some degree for the Present, and farther to advance the Reputation of the College and the Public Good, We do each of us promise to pay Annually for Five Years to come, the Sums to our respective Names annexed, into the Hands of the Treasurer of the said College for the Time being, to be disposed of in the Purchase of such Books for the Library, as the President and Fellows shall from time to time order and direct.

Time of Subscribing	Names of Subscribers	Annual Subscription for Five Years.	Lawful Money £ s d
Septr.11.1755	Benja. Franklin of Philadelphia	Four Pistoles	4 8 0

Philada. Sept. 11. 1755

Pay to the Treasurer of Harvard College for the time being, Four Pistoles, or Four Pounds Eight Shillings Lawful Money, being my Subscription to the Library of the said College for one Year next ensuing the Date hereof, and charge the same to Account of Your Loving Brother

B FRANKLIN

£4 8s. 0d.

To Mr. John Franklin Postmaster Boston[67]

The order and the subscription plan remains in the Harvard College Library, but there is no record that the plan was ever used or that the order was ever paid.[68] The librarian of Harvard at that time was Mather Byles, great-grandson of Increase Mather.[69]

When Franklin was in England in 1758, he procured some electrical equipment for Harvard College. This had been specifically requested by Professor John Winthrop, who remembered Franklin's own electrical equipment seen in Philadelphia in 1754. Franklin informed Thomas Hubbard, treasurer of Harvard, that he had delivered to Mr. Joseph Mico, London agent for Harvard, a mahogany case lined with lead containing thirty-five square glass bottles, a glass globe mounted, and a large glass cylinder mounted.[70] In a postscript, Franklin added:

I beg the College will do me the favour to accept a Virgil, which I send in the case, thought to be the most curiously printed of any book hitherto done in the world.

Franklin had subscribed to six copies of this Baskerville edition, *Publii Virgilii Maronis Bucolica, Georgica, et Æneis.* The copy he sent to Harvard still can be seen proudly displaying the name of the donor on the handsome binding.[71]

The Harvard Library received a catastrophic blow when fire raged through Harvard Hall on January 24, 1764. Almost five thousand volumes went up in smoke, and only two or three hundred were saved. Gifts for the restoration of the library came pouring in from

---

[65] Labaree, 1959—: 5: p. 267.
[66] Spanish currency; see subscription pledge following for corresponding English currency value.
[67] By permission of the Harvard College Library. Labaree, 1959—: 6: pp. 180-181.
[68] Lane, 1907: p. 233.
[69] Potter and Bolton, 1897: p. 25.
[70] Eddy, 1931: pp. 109-110. Smyth, 1905-1907: 3: p. 436.
[71] Smyth, 1905-1907: 3: p. 437. Lane, 1907: p. 234.

near and far.[72] Franklin wrote to his friend, John Winthrop:

> I shall think of the affair of your unfortunate College, and try if I can be of any Service in procuring some Assistance towards restoring your Library.[73]

Faithfully, the college kept records of "Donations to the College, to Repair the Loss of Its Library and Philosophical Apparatus . . .," and under the name of Benjamin Franklin was listed "valuable instruments for the apparatus; also, a bust of Lord Chatham."[74] At the meeting of the president and fellows of Harvard College on January 4, 1769, they voted: "That the Thanks of this Board be given to D^r. Benj^a. Franklin for his very acceptable Present, of a fine Bust of that great Assertor of American Liberties, Lord Chatham." Lord Chatham (William Pitt, the Elder) worked with Franklin in an unsuccessful attempt to forestall the American Revolution; the bust, a plaster cast, was placed in the reading room of the college library.[75]

The making of scientific instruments was such a specialized craft that the death of craftsmen could cause long delays in concluding a purchase. In 1768 Franklin had ordered a telescope for Professor Winthrop from James Short; Short died before it was mounted, and Franklin had to claim it from the executors. At the same time, Franklin had ordered an equal altitudes and transit instrument from John Bird, who was "so singularly eminent in his way, that the commissioners of longitude have lately given him five hundred pounds merely to discover and make public his method of dividing instruments. I send it you herewith." These instruments were being prepared to observe the transit of Venus in 1769. In addition, Franklin sent along a pamphlet by Nevil Maskelyne, royal astronomer, and the latest volume of the Royal Society's *Philosophical Transactions,* with separately printed copies of Winthrop's article contained therein. Franklin also took charge of the "Glasses" of the long Galilean telescope which Mr. Ellicot presented to Harvard, put them into the hands of Edward Nairne, optician and electrician, to check, and forwarded them to Cambridge.[76] The president and fellows of Harvard voted their thanks on April 25, 1769, "to D^r. Franklin for his many very obliging acts of friendship; particularly for his care in procuring several valuable Instruments for the Apparatus, and that he be desired to continue his kind regards to the College."[77]

Soon after the publication of the 1769 edition of Franklin's *Experiments and Observations on Electricity . . . To which are added, Letters and Papers on Philosophical Subjects,* Franklin sent six copies to his sister, Jane Mecom, in Boston, with instructions to distribute them as directed.[78] One of these was directed to Harvard, one for Professor John Winthrop, and one for James Bowdoin. Franklin apologized to Winthrop "for inserting therein some part of our Correspondence without first obtaining your Permission; but, as Mr. Bowdoin had favoured me with his Consent for what related to him, I ventur'd to rely upon your Good-Nature, as to what related to you, and I hope you will forgive me."[79] The time and effort that Franklin put into these communications was not wasted, for Winthrop reported his observations on the transit of Venus in June, 1769, and on the transit of Mercury the next fall. Franklin submitted both letters to the Royal Society, and they were printed in the *Philosophical Transactions.*[80]

Franklin continued his ministrations, procuring an achromatic telescope in 1770,[81] and donating "many valuable books" to the college library in 1771.[82] The president and fellows voted:

> That the Thanks of this Board be given D^r. Franklin for his kind remembrance of Harvard College expressed in his many friendly Offices & valuable Donations to this Society, particularly in his late Present to our Library of two accurate Mathematical Treatises of Mr Maseres; and the learned & elaborate Work of Hoogeveen de Graecis Particulis. They also thank Dr Franklin for the Pleasure he has given them of placing his Effigies among those of their other Benefactors: and Voted that Professor Winthrop do transmit a Copy of this Vote to Dr Franklin.

The two mathematical treatises were *A Dissertation on the Use of the Negative Sign in Algebra* and *Elements of Plane Trigonometry, In which is introduced a Dissertation on the Nature and Use of Logarithms.* The Hoogeveen work was *Doctrina particularum linguae Graecae.* "Effigies" referred to a mezzotint engraving done by Fisher in 1771 from Chamberlin's portrait. It has hung for many years in the Librarian's office in the college library. The following year, Franklin presented to the college the work of Joseph Priestley, *The History & Present State of the Discoveries relating to Vision, Light & Colours.*[83] John Winthrop valued the gift as "a most noble collection of every thing relating to that science."[84]

In 1773, when Dubourg published *Œuvres de M. Franklin, Docteur ès Loix. Traduites de l'anglois sur la quatrième Édition . . . Avec des additions nouvelles. 2 tom.,* Franklin forwarded a copy to Samuel Cooper, then a fellow of Harvard: "There are in it several pieces

---

[72] Potter and Wells, 1911: p. 56.
[73] Smyth, 1905-1907: 4: p. 251.
[74] Quincy, 1840: 2: pp. 484, 491.
[75] Lane, 1907: p. 236.
[76] Smyth, 1905-1907: 5: pp. 136-138, 198-199.
[77] Lane, 1907: p. 237.
[78] Van Doren, 1950a: pp. 108-110.
[79] Smyth, 1905-1907: 5: p. 199.
[80] Quincy, 1840: 2: p. 222.
[81] Lane, 1907: p. 237.
[82] Potter and Wells, 1911: p. 41.
[83] Lane, 1907: pp. 237-238.
[84] Bigelow, 1887-1889: 5: p. 108.

not in the English. When you have looked them over, please to give them to Mr. Winthrop, for the college library." Harvard received it "with particular Pleasure, as it is a Testimony of the Sense *Foreigners* have of the Merit of these Writings, which must do honor to the Country that gave him Birth, as well as to every literary Society he is related to."[85]

After Franklin had returned to America, and in the midst of the troubled times of the Revolutionary War, Joseph Priestley sent to him "my second volume of Observations on air, . . . Not to burden my friend too much, I give him only one copy of my book, but I hope you will communicate it to Professor Winthrop, with my most respectful compliments."[86]

In 1775 Charles W. F. Dumas, who was later to become a secret agent of the United States, sent from The Hague, Netherlands, at least three copies of his edition of Vattel, designating that one be sent to the "College of Massachusetts Bay."[87] Franklin mailed it to James Bowdoin, who turned it over to the Harvard College Library as a present from Franklin. Harvard once again voted thanks to "the Hon^{le} Dr Franklin for a fresh Instance of his Regard to the College by the Present of Les Droits de Gens pars Monsr de Vattel to our Library."[88] Vattel's work was a world-renowned publication on international law; it was consulted time and time again by leaders of the American Revolution, searching for a solution of the conflict between England and the colonies. After the outbreak of the American Revolution, Franklin had little time to devote to college libraries, for he was sent to France to obtain aid for the colonies. Death claimed his friend, John Winthrop, in 1779, but another Winthrop (James, son of John Winthrop) carried on the family name at Harvard, serving as librarian from 1772 to 1787.[89] Franklin still maintained his correspondence with James Bowdoin, fellow of Harvard from 1779 to 1786,[90] and performed one last service requested by Thomas Pownall, colonial governor of Massachusetts, who had returned home to England:

I have taken the liberty to enclose to you two letters for my friends, Mr. Bowdoin and Dr. Cooper, with a power of attorney to them to make for me a deed of gift to Harvard College of five hundred acres of land which I have (and which was not confiscated) in Pownalborough, in the State of Massachusetts Bay. I have not directed the one for Mr. Bowdoin, as I should be sorry to be wrong in the mode of address. Will you be so good as to direct it, or tell the bearer of this how to do it?[91]

YALE

Yale College, established in 1700, used a senior tutor as librarian for its first century of existence.[92] Although overshadowed by the older Harvard College, it attracted the attention of Dean Berkeley and received a donation of books at the same time as his gift to Harvard; Franklin duly noted it in the August 30, 1733, issue of the *Pennsylvania Gazette*. Franklin's first personal contact with Yale was not through books, but through an electrical machine which he sent there in 1749. Ezra Stiles, a tutor at Yale, was one of the first in New England to do electrical experiments. Franklin also corresponded with the Reverend Jared Eliot, a trustee of Yale, and with President Thomas Clap.[93] Eager to promote scientific studies throughout the colonies, Franklin wrote to Thomas Clap on November 28, 1751, offering to contribute the electrical part of a collection of apparatus if the president of Yale would be able "to procure a Subscription to furnish your College with a compleat Apparatus for Natural Philosophy." It is doubtful that Franklin ever fulfilled this promise; the subscription was never promoted by President Clap. In his will of 1757, Franklin provided that his electrical apparatus should go to Yale College after his death, but this will was canceled by another in 1788.[94]

In November, 1751, Franklin also informed Thomas Clap of a donation to the college library, Archibald Bower's *The History of the Popes*, Volume I, which "has lain ever since in Mr. Parker's Hands at New York. He desires you would order one of your Boatmen to call for it." Franklin ordered the second volume "bound, dark sprinkled, filleted and letter'd,"[95] and again he asked that President Clap inquire of Mr. Parker in New York, for "he is at a loss how to end it, and desires you would order somebody to call for it."[96] Franklin also presented to the Yale College library a 1751 edition of his *Experiments and Observations on Electricity*, and at a later date Yale acquired Franklin's own volume of pamphlets including both the 1751 and the 1754 editions with marginal notes and corrections.[97]

In the year 1755, James Parker, Franklin's printing partner, set up a printing office in New Haven, Connecticut, started printing the *Connecticut Gazette*, and eventually became the printer for Yale College.[98]

Just seven weeks after Harvard had presented Franklin with his first honorary degree, Yale followed suit on September 12, 1753.[99] In his *Autobiography*, Franklin

---

[85] Lane, 1907: p. 238.
[86] "Some Letters of Franklin's Correspondents," 1903: *Pa. Mag. of Hist. & Biog.* 27: pp. 169-171.
[87] Smyth, 1905-1907: 6: p. 432.
[88] Lane, 1907: pp. 238-239.
[89] Potter and Bolton, 1897: p. 30.
[90] Quincy, 1840: 2: p. 409.
[91] Sparks, 1836-1840: 9: p. 492.

[92] Shores, 1935: p. 270.
[93] Montgomery, 1900: p. 208.
[94] Labaree, 1959—: 4: p. 213; 7: p. 201.
[95] *Ibid.* 4: pp. 213, 339.
[96] Sparks, 1836-1840: 6: p. 189.
[97] Labaree, 1959—: 3: p. 118.
[98] Van Doren, 1938: p. 120.
[99] Labaree, 1959—: 5: p. 58.

states that his Yale degree predates his Harvard degree,[100] but he may have been confused by the fact that he had a closer connection with Yale because of his gift of the electrical machine. A couple of months after receiving the degree, Franklin called President Clap's attention to a new kind of air pump described in the Royal Society's *Philosophical Transactions* by William Watson and John Smeaton, and suggested that Yale order one from England. The suggestion was accepted; Jared Eliot sent the order through Peter Collinson, but there was a great delay and it was May, 1756, before the instrument actually arrived.[101]

Through a mutual interest in science, Franklin came to know Ezra Stiles better. Stiles visited Philadelphia in 1754; when Franklin visited New Haven in 1755, it was Stiles who delivered the Latin oration in his honor.[102] From this time on, Franklin maintained a fairly regular correspondence with Stiles, lending him books from time to time.[103]

Stiles was a man of many talents. He was not only interested in science, but had studied law and theology also. In the fall of 1755, he answered the call of the Congregationalist Church in Newport, Rhode Island, drawn partly by the wealth of books to be found at the Redwood Library. He became librarian of Redwood in 1756 and held the position about twenty years.[104] The years passed; Franklin went off to England, and during his stay there traveled throughout Scotland and Ireland, visiting universities and libraries as he went. It was through recommendation from Franklin that the University of Edinburgh conferred a diploma of Doctor of Divinity on Ezra Stiles in 1765.[105] Franklin continued to cultivate the friendship of this talented scholar, sending him Reland's *Introduction to the Rabbinical Literature* and a book on Zoroaster, *Zend-Avesta, Ouvrage de Zoroastre, . . .* by Anquetil du Perron.[106]

Ezra Stiles in turn kept in touch with the activities of Benjamin Franklin at every opportunity. He pored through the travel diaries of Henry Marchant, who took a year's tour of England and Scotland, starting in July, 1771. Marchant was extremely interested in libraries and visited every one that he could, touring through Oxford and then going on to Edinburgh, where he met Franklin on October 28. Franklin had persuaded the University of Edinburgh to grant a degree of Doctor of Law to Professor John Winthrop of Harvard, and he offered to recommend Marchant also for a degree, but Marchant refused. At Edinburgh, Franklin introduced Marchant to the faculty of the university — David Hume, Principal William Robertson, Joseph Black, Adam Ferguson, James Russell — and visited the home of Lord Kames. Franklin returned separately to London, but after Marchant arrived there, Franklin introduced him to the Royal Society.[107] Ezra Stiles came to know Franklin better through membership in the American Philosophical Society,[108] by subscribing to Philadelphia newspapers,[109] and by interviewing Franklin's sister, Jane Mecom, at the home of Governor Greene of Rhode Island.[110]

In the year 1778 Stiles assumed the presidency of Yale. He probably changed the book-selection policy of the Yale library, for he had previously protested to President Clap about the removal of deistical books from the college library.[111] Even though Stiles himself was a minister, he felt that there should be a certain freedom of religion reflected in educational libraries. In January, 1790, less than three months before the death of Franklin, Ezra Stiles wrote to Franklin and asked for a picture for the college library:

We have lately received Governor Yale's portrait from his family in London, and deposited it in the College Library, where is also deposited one of Governor Saltonstall's. I have also long wished that we might be honored with that of Dr. Franklin. In the course of your long life, you may probably have become possessed of several portraits of yourself. Shall I take too great a liberty in humbly asking a donation of one of them to Yale College? You obliged me with a mezzotinto picture of yourself many years ago, which I often view with pleasure. But the canvass is more permanent. We wish to be possessed of the durable resemblance of the American Patriot and Philosopher.[112]

Franklin was glad enough to oblige, but by the time he answered the letter, on March 9, he was growing so weak that he feared that there might not be much time left.

I received your kind letter of January 28, and am glad you have at length received the portrait of Governor Yale from his family, and deposited it in the College Library. . . . The honour you propose doing me by placing mine in the same room with his is much too great for my deserts; but you always had a partiality for me, and to that it must be ascribed. I am, however, too much obliged to Yale College, the first learned society that took notice of me and adorned me with its honours, to refuse a request that comes from it through so esteemed a friend. But I do not think any one of the portraits you mention as in my possession, worthy of the situation and company you propose to place it in. You have an excellent artist lately arrived. If he will undertake to make one for you, I shall cheerfully pay the expense; but he must not delay setting about it, or I may slip through his fingers, for I am now in my eighty-fifth year, and very infirm.

---

[100]*Autobiography*, 1964: p. 209.
[101]Labaree, 1959—: 5: pp. 108-109.
[102]*Dictionary of American Biography*, 1943: 18: p. 18.
[103]Labaree, 1959—: 6: pp. 103, 192.
[104]*Dictionary of American Biography*, 1943: 18: p. 18.
[105]Stiles, 1901: 1: p. 17 n. 6.
[106]*Ibid.* 1: p. 70. Smyth, 1905-1907: 5: pp. 371-372.
[107]Stiles, 1901: 1: pp. 304-322.
[108]*Dictionary of American Biography*, 1943: 18: p. 18.
[109]Bridenbaugh, 1962: p. 76.
[110]Van Doren, 1950b: pp. 151-152.
[111]*Dictionary of American Biography*, 1943: 18: pp. 19-20.
[112]Sparks, 1836-1840: 10: p. 421.

In the same letter, Franklin also informed Stiles about his arrangements for his last donation to the Yale College library:

> I send with this a very learned work, as it seems to me, on the ancient Samaritan coins, lately printed in Spain, and at least curious for the beauty of the impression. Please to accept it for your college library. I have subscribed for the Encyclopædia now printing here, with the intention of presenting it to the College. I shall probably depart before the work is finished, but shall leave directions for its continuation to the end. With this you will receive some of the first numbers.
> ....
> P.S. Had not your College some present of books from the King of France? Please to let me know if you had an expectation given you of more, and the nature of that expectation. I have a reason for the enquiry.[113]

Dr. Stiles noted in his diary on March 27, "Rec^d a Box of Books from Dr Franklin . . . a Present to the College Library."

Then came the news of Franklin's death, and in his diary entry of April 27, Ezra Stiles made his final notes on the death, the funeral, and the life work of Benjamin Franklin.

> I have ordered a commemoratory Eulogium by one of the Orators next Commencement as he says he received his first academic Honors at Yal. College. . . . In 1755 I became acquainted with him personally, tho' I had known him from 1743. In 1753, . . . he received the honorary Degree of A.M. from Harv. Coll. Cambridge; & Sept. Commencem^t of the same year he received the Diploma of the same Degree from us at Yale College — which he calls his first academic Honors, because we from 1749 & onward adopted with Avidity & before all the rest of the learned World his Electrical & philosophical Discoveries. In 1755 I made a gratulatory Oration to him in the College Hall celebrat^g his philosophic Discoveries & congratulat^g his Honors from the Republic of Letters.[114]

THE COLLEGE OF WILLIAM AND MARY

Benjamin Franklin had very little contact with the College of William and Mary, one of the oldest in the country, although the College granted him a Master of Arts degree on April 2, 1756. Even though the diploma is dated April 2, it may not have been actually presented until April 20.[115] This was three years after Franklin had received like degrees from Harvard and from Yale, and at this time he was on an inspection trip through Virginia on post office business.

At the same time that the University of Pennsylvania was given a large donation of books by King Louis XVI of France, the College of William and Mary received a large donation also. This donation, too, originated from the suggestion of the French officer, Chastellux, who recommended it to the French government, after he returned from fighting in the American Revolutionary War. Chastellux had distinguished himself in the campaigns around Williamsburg, and had developed a friendship for Bishop James Madison, president of the College of William and Mary. The gift arrived in 1784 and consisted of "two hundred books in beautiful editions," among which was a splendid set of the *Encyclopédie Méthodique* in thirty-three folio volumes.[116] Only one book of this entire collection has been preserved — *Lettres sur l'Atlantide de Platon et sur l'Ancienne Histoire de l'Asie. Pour servir de suite aux Lettres sur l'origine des Sciences, adressées à M. de Voltaire par M. Bailly.* Prix, 3 livres 12 sols broché. A Londres, Chez M. Elmesly, et a Paris, Chez les Frères Debure, Quai des Augustins. M. DCC. LXXIX.[117] This gift, too, was a by-product of the love and esteem that the French people had for Benjamin Franklin, although he had no direct connection with it. It was part and parcel of the gift to the University of Pennsylvania, made possible by the good will generated by Franklin in France.

RHODE ISLAND COLLEGE (BROWN UNIVERSITY)

Benjamin Franklin's contacts with Rhode Island College (later renamed Brown University) began with his acquaintance with two of the founders, Ezra Stiles and Morgan Edwards. Ezra Stiles, whom Franklin had met at Yale, drew up the charter in 1763, trying to find a happy balance between the Congregationalists and Baptists, who were influential in establishing the college.[118] The Reverend Morgan Edwards represented the Philadelphia Baptist Association, dissatisfied with the sectarianism of the College of Philadelphia under the leadership of the Anglican Provost, the Reverend William Smith.[119]

Morgan Edwards traveled throughout America and England, soliciting funds for the new college in 1767. Franklin, then in England, received a letter from Joseph Galloway "recommending Mr. Morgan Edwards and his affair of the Rhode Island College." Franklin promised that he would endeavor to promote the college, "deeming the institution one of the most catholic and generous of the kind."[120]

During the colonial period, Franklin was willing enough to solicit funds from the mother country and even from Europe in order to help establish new colleges, but after the United States gained its indepen-

---

[113]Van Doren, 1945: pp. 783-785.
[114]Stiles, 1901: 3: pp. 386, 390-391.
[115]Labaree, 1959—: 6: p. 430.

[116]"Library of the College of William and Mary," 1910: *William and Mary Quarterly* 19, 1 (July): p. 49. Scudder, 1876: p. 28. The article in the *William and Mary Quarterly* contains several errors in the title, publisher, and date of Bailly's book, mentioned below.
[117]From a Xerox reproduction of the title page furnished by Herbert Lawrence Ganter, archivist at the College of William and Mary. Facing the title page is a notation: "Binder's error in recording book as volume 2. Separate title."
[118]*Dictionary of American Biography*, 1943: 18: p. 19.
[119]Bridenbaugh, 1962: p. 63.
[120]Smyth, 1905-1907: 5: p. 71.

dence, the story was quite different. We were no longer dependent, and he wanted the world to know it. While he was minister in France, he refused pointblank to solicit donations for American colleges, making his reasons very clear in letters to Princeton and the University of the State of New York. In his private journal of July 20, 1784, he noted that he had received "only one American letter by the packet, which is from the College of Rhode Island, desiring me to solicit benefactions of the King, which I cannot do, for reasons which I shall give them."[121] The letter, dated January 9, came from Stephen Hopkins, Chancellor, and James Manning, President. They were asking Franklin to solicit the patronage of the King by "establishing a Professor of the French Language and History" and by "presenting such Books in the French Language, or other Benefactions thereto as shall be most agreeable to that Munificent Monarch, . . ." They had been encouraged to make this request because they had heard that Yale had recently declined his Majesty's "generous Proffer of important literary Favours. . . ."[122]

The Rhode Island College library was very much in need of contributions. The college had been founded in Warren, Rhode Island, and had moved to Providence in 1770. For a time, the college depended upon the town library located in the new court house.[123]

DARTMOUTH

Dartmouth College was founded in 1769 by Eleazer Wheelock, known for his work in educating and Christianizing the Indian natives. He served as Dartmouth's first president, and was succeeded in that position by his son, John, in 1779.[124] John Wheelock set out for Europe in 1782 with his brother, James, to solicit contributions from France and Holland. He arrived in France armed with many letters of introduction, from George Washington,[125] Jonathan Trumbull, governor of Connecticut,[126] Jonathan Williams, Franklin's grandnephew at Nantes,[127] and Bezaleel Woodward, secretary of Dartmouth, who had served as librarian of the college from 1773 to 1777.[128]

Franklin discouraged the solicitation, but did give the Wheelock brothers a letter of introduction to Charles W. F. Dumas in Holland to try their luck there.[129] He wrote a rather full account of the incident to the next college representative who came a-begging, John Witherspoon from Princeton.

[121] Van Doren, 1945: p. 611.
[122] American Philosophical Society, Franklin MSS, 31: 13.
[123] Scudder, 1876: p. 19.
[124] *Columbia Encyclopedia*, 1950: pp. 509, 2137.
[125] Ford, 1905: p. 132.
[126] Smyth, 1905-1907: 9: p. 15 n. 2.
[127] American Philosophical Society, Franklin MSS, 38: 127 (Jan. 31, 1783).
[128] Hays, 1908: 4: p. 460. Shores, 1935: p. 271.
[129] Smyth, 1905-1907: 9: p. 15.

COLLEGE OF NEW JERSEY (PRINCETON)

One of Franklin's favorite means of soliciting funds was the lottery. About the time when Philadelphia was concerned with establishing its own academy and college according to Franklin's plan, the president and trustees of the College of New Jersey (Princeton) approached Franklin and got him to print eight thousand lottery tickets, which were distributed in Philadelphia, New York, Boston, and Charlestown. Boston tickets were sold by Franklin's brother, John;[130] the drawing was set for May 28, 1750. However, the competition from the Philadelphia Academy removed Philadelphia as a possible source of funds. There was also opposition from Presbyterian sponsors of the college, who brought suit against the managers for using the lottery.[131]

The College of New Jersey was founded as a Presbyterian college; while Franklin had been raised as a Presbyterian, he could not accept the doctrines of that denomination, and he was not especially prone to contribute to a purely sectarian college. However, he was pleased to watch the College of New Jersey join in the festivities when his son, William, was welcomed as Governor of New Jersey in 1763.[132] Evidently, Franklin discussed problems of education with the college president, Samuel Finley, for on March 7, Franklin sent back a "Plan of Education in the College of Glasgow." President Finley made a copy and returned the original to Franklin.[133]

From 1766 to 1769, the College of New Jersey was once again searching for a president and fixed its sights upon the Reverend John Witherspoon, who had been graduated from the University of Edinburgh and had created a popular following in his Presbyterian ministry at Paisley, Scotland.[134] Chiefly responsible for persuading Witherspoon to come to America were Dr. Benjamin Rush and the Reverend Charles Beatty. Both of these men were friends of Franklin, then stationed in London. Beatty had served as military chaplain when Franklin was concerned with the defense of Pennsylvania (1755-1756), and had taken Franklin's advice upon how to increase attendance at religious services:

"It is perhaps below the Dignity of your Profession to act as Steward of the Rum. But if you were to deal it out, and only just after Prayers, you would have them all about you." He lik'd the Thought, undertook the Office, and with the help of a few hands to measure out the Liquor executed it to Satisfaction; and never were Prayers more generally and more punctually attended.[135]

On his way to his new post, Dr. Witherspoon stopped in London to consult Franklin on the choice of

[130] New Jersey, 1894-1895: 12: pp. 611, 623, 630.
[131] Wertenbaker, 1946: p. 31.
[132] Van Doren, 1938: p. 304.
[133] Van Doren, 1947: p. 204.
[134] *Dictionary of American Biography*, 1943: 20: p. 436.
[135] *Autobiography*, 1964: p. 235.

books and scientific equipment for the College of New Jersey. "An orrery, a small telescope, [and] an electrical machine with a case of coated jars" were selected and ordered. Beatty lingered on in England for a few months and helped Franklin inspect the equipment on March 21, 1769, before its shipment to New Jersey.[136]

At the outbreak of the American Revolution, Witherspoon began to work for the independence of the colonies. He had long suspected Governor William Franklin of trying to woo the Presbyterian College of New Jersey into the arms of the Church of England. As a member of the Provincial Council of New Jersey, he voted to send William Franklin into exile and imprisonment in Connecticut in 1775, and taunted the governor on his illegitimate birth.[137]

Throughout the war, Franklin was stationed in France and sent money to London for the care and comfort of American prisoners of war. One of the men who worked most actively with these American prisoners was Thomas Wren, a Presbyterian minister. In 1783 Franklin wrote to Robert R. Livingston, Secretary of the Department of Foreign Affairs, to request that "some public notice should be taken of this good man. I wish the Congress would enable me to make him a present, and that some of our universities would confer upon him the degree of Doctor." Since Wren was a Presbyterian, Livingston turned the matter over to the College of New Jersey, which granted him a degree of Doctor of Divinity.[138] Franklin was delighted with this action, and he forwarded the diploma along with the thanks of the Congress.[139]

The war had been hard on the library of Princeton; "many of the books were taken out by the British troops, which they were not so complaisant as to return."[140] In 1784 Dr. Witherspoon wrote from London to say that he had been sent to Europe against his judgment by the trustees of the college to solicit contributions in England and in France. He had had little success in England, where both Americans and Presbyterians were unpopular, and was asking Franklin's advice about coming to France. Franklin answered in a letter which made his position very plain:

Passy April 5th 1784.
Reverend Sir,

I have received the Letter you did me the honour of writing me the 27th past. It would be a Pleasure to me to see you here, but I cannot give you any Expectations of Success in the Project of obtaining Benefactions for your College. Last Year Messrs Wheelock came hither with the same Views for their College at Dartmouth in New England, and they brought a Recommendation signed by a great Number of the principal People of our States. They apply'd to me for Advice and Assistance, and I consulted some knowing prudent Persons, well acquainted with this Country and Friends of ours. After well considering the Matter, they gave their Opinion that it was by no means adviseable to attempt a Collection here for such a Purpose; for tho' possibly we might get something, it would not be equal to the Expence and Trouble attending the Solicitation; and the very Request would be disgraceful to us, and hurt the Credit of Responsability we wish to maintain in Europe, by representing the United States as too poor to provide for the Education of their own Children. — For my own part, I am persuaded we are fully able to furnish our Colleges amply with every Means of Public Instruction, and I cannot but wonder that our Legislatures have generally paid so little Attention to a Business of so great Importance. One Circumstance in Messrs Wheelock's Application here made me somewhat ashamed for our Country. Being asked by a Gentleman, what Sums had been subscribed or Donations made by the many eminent Persons who had signed the Recommendation, they were not able to say that more than one had given any thing. — Meeting with no Encouragement from any other Quarter here, they went to Holland and England. What Success they had in those Countrys, I have not heard. With great Esteem & Respect, I have the honour to be,

Revd Sir,
Your most obedient
& most humble Servant
B Franklin[141]

THE UNIVERSITY OF THE STATE OF NEW YORK

The University of the State of New York was chartered in 1784 as the governmental department which supervises all the educational activities of the state. In this same year, Columbia College was reopened, having been closed because of war, and until 1787 title to Columbia College was vested in the regents of the University of the State of New York.[142] In 1784 Franklin was still in France, trying to wind up his affairs so that he could go home. He received a letter from George Clinton, Governor of the State of New York, and James Duane, Mayor of New York City, introducing Lieutenant Colonel Mathew Clarkson, who was coming to Europe to solicit donations for the University of the State of New York.[143] Franklin replied with his most forceful letter to date on this subject:

Passy Augt 9th 1784
Gentlemen,

I received the Letter you did me the honour of writing to me by Lieut. Col. Clarkson, respecting the purpose of his Mission, viz Soliciting Donations in Europe for the University of the State of New York. Yours is the fourth American Seminary that since the Peace has sent Persons hither, or empower'd Persons here to make such Solicitations, all of which I have declined being concern'd in; tho' I should certainly be exceedingly glad if I could by any proper Means be serviceable to the Interests of Learning in our Country. The Letter I wrote to Dr Wither-

---

[136]Nolan, 1938: pp. 116-117.
[137]Ibid., pp. 73-74, 216 n. 11.
[138]Sparks, 1836-1840: 9: p. 545.
[139]Smyth, 1905-1907: 9: p. 124.
[140]Cutler, 1888: 1: p. 247.

[141]By permission of Columbia University Libraries. Van Doren, 1945: p. 600.
[142]Columbia Encyclopedia, 1950: pp. 427, 1395.
[143]American Philosophical Society, Franklin MSS, 32: 15 (June 12, 1784).

spoon on the Subject, (of which I enclose a Copy) will show the Reasons I then had for not encouraging his Application here for Benefactions to the College of New Jersey. The Necessity we are still under for Credit in Europe where we have Loans opened, the Success of which may be hurt by Declarations of Poverty, (the only Excuse for Mendicity) make this Mode of procuring Money at this Time exceedingly improper: as do also the Orders just received by your Ministers to offer Treaties to twenty different European Powers, with whom it is fit we should stand in as respectable a Light as possible, and not appear a Nation that is either unable or unwilling to support among ourselves the common Expence of Education. I am making a large Collection of such French Books as I think may be serviceable in America, where I hope that Language, which contains abundance of useful Learning, will be more and more cultivated. I intend a part of these Books as a Present to your University, and shall be glad of any Opportunity of promoting its Interests & Prosperity; but in the Mode proposed I hope you will excuse my not acting with Mr Clarkson, to whom the only Advice I can give is; not to attempt here any such Solicitation. With great respect, I have the honour to be,
Gentlemen,
Your most obedient
& most humble Servant
B Franklin.[144]

DICKINSON COLLEGE

Dickinson College started as a school in Carlisle, Pennsylvania, and was chartered as a college in 1783 through the efforts of John Dickinson, Dr. Benjamin Rush, and others.[145] Franklin's influence was felt through his friendship for Rush, who had taken his medical degree at the University of Edinburgh in 1768. As a student, Rush had relied on Franklin's recommendations [146] to the university and introductions to important physicians in London, such as Dr. John Fothergill and Dr. John Coakley Lettsom.[147] Back again in Philadelphia, Dr. Benjamin Rush wrote to Franklin, thanking him for the "many advantages which I derived from your friendship whilst in London."[148]

Dr. Rush was the catalytic force behind the immediate development of a large library at Dickinson College. He gathered books from booksellers in Philadelphia — Robert Bell, Mr. Hall (son of Franklin's former printing partner), Jackson & Dunn — and from his friends in Europe — John Erskine of Edinburgh,[149] Granville Sharp, Dr. Richard Price, and Dr. Lettsom. Of these, the last three were correspondents of Benjamin Franklin. In his letter to Dr. Lettsom, Dr. Rush asked:

Will you give me leave to solicit your friendship to our College in begging a few books from your friends for our library? The sweepings of their studies will be very acceptable in our illiterate wooden country.[150]

When Franklin was returning home from France in 1785, he stopped at Southampton, England, receiving there letters and presents from his friends in London. In one of the letters, Dr. Lettsom informed Franklin of his donation to Carlisle College (Dickinson): "To promote this institution I have sent off a large Box, . . . filled with books. The cultivation of useful science, forms the best foundation for national happiness, . . ."[151] Franklin returned his thanks:

You have done a good deed in contributing to promote science among us, by your liberal donation of books to Carlisle College. Thanks for your good wishes in favour of our country, and of your friend and servant.
B. FRANKLIN.[152]

Dr. Rush was not as appreciative of receiving "the sweepings" as he had promised to be, for among the books sent by Dr. Lettsom were thirty volumes of the *Journals of the House of Commons*. Dr. Rush proposed to John Montgomery at Carlisle that the *Journals* be sold to the Pennsylvania Assembly, and that the money be used to purchase "more useful and necessary books for a college," placing Dr. Lettsom's name in the books purchased. Apparently, Montgomery did not approve of the suggestion, for Dr. Rush wrote again on February 20, 1786:

What! — not exchange the *Journals of the House of Commons* for modern history or books on mathematics! Why, my friend, they will not be worth to us their carriage to Carlisle. We had better sell them to a pastry cook and get a neat edition of them cut out in wood. I am sure my friend Dr. Lettsom will thank us for exchanging them, especially if we inscribe his name in the books we procure instead of our own.[153]

He appealed to the trustees of the college for permission to sell the thirty volumes of *Journals* in order to pay for the *"Encylopaeidia Britanica"* and books on mathematics:

They may be useful in the State house library, but it would distress me to hear that a student of Dickinson College had ever wasted half an hour in examining even their title pages. He would find nothing in them but such things as a scholar and a gentleman should strive to forget.

Dr. Rush had wasted more than half an hour in pleading, for the *Journals of the House of Commons* still remain in the Dickinson College Library as a gift from Dr. Lettsom.[154]

John Dickinson gave to the college the library of his late father-in-law, Isaac Norris, and by April, 1786, the

---

[144] By permission of Columbia University Libraries. Van Doren, 1945: p. 601.
[145] *Columbia Encyclopedia*, 1950: p. 539.
[146] Van Doren, 1945: p. 167.
[147] Rush, 1951: 1: pp. 27, 313 n. 1.
[148] *Ibid.* 1: p. 76.
[149] *Ibid.* 1: pp. 348-349, 374.
[150] *Ibid.* 1: p. 351 (April 8, 1785).
[151] American Philosophical Society, Franklin MSS. 33: 170 (July 24, 1785).
[152] Smyth, 1905-1907: 9: p. 371.
[153] Rush, 1951: 1: pp. 377-379.
[154] *Ibid.* 1: pp. 382-383.

library could boast of 2,700 volumes.[155] In the meantime, John Montgomery had applied for assistance for the college from the state legislature, asking for either a grant or a loan without interest. He begged Franklin to use his "intrest and influence" with the Assembly as President of the State of Pennsylvania, for "you know Sir that money is absolutly necessarry to make all the wheels of such a machine move with ease and harmony."[156]

FRANKLIN (AND MARSHALL) COLLEGE

In his last years, Franklin became a special patron of Pennsylvania colleges. He served as President of the State of Pennsylvania for a period of three years, from 1785 to 1788. Feeling that the public trust was satisfaction enough, he began to give away a large part of his salary to the frontier colleges which were just getting started. One of these, located in Lancaster, Pennsylvania, was to bear his name. From the "General Plan" of the college comes the statement: "From a profound respect for the character of His Excellency the President of the State, the institution shall be called Franklin College."[157]

Franklin College was a German foundation. Years before, Franklin had been alarmed at the overwhelming numbers of Germans who immigrated into Pennsylvania and clung to their native tongue without making any effort to learn English or to assimilate with English-speaking groups. Franklin had fought the language barrier by helping to establish German Charity Schools and through publications from his press in both German and English. However, there was considerable opposition from some of the German leaders to the German Charity Schools, which were eventually discontinued. A German department had been set up in the preparatory school connected with the University of Pennsylvania in 1780, but the Germans never really felt at home in these Anglican surroundings. The German department began to decline about the time that Franklin College was being established.[158]

Dr. Benjamin Rush, one of the founders of Franklin College, published a "Proposal of a German College" in "An Address to the Citizens of Pennsylvania of German birth and extraction," in the *Pennsylvania Gazette*, August 31, 1785.[159] A petition from the trustees of the prospective college was presented to the Pennsylvania General Assembly on December 11, 1786, accompanied by the "General Plan of the College." Of the forty trustees, fourteen were to be from the Lutheran Church and fourteen from the Reformed (or Calvinist) Church —this was to be a Christian, German college. The first Principal of the college was the Reverend Henry Muhlenberg, brother of Peter Muhlenberg, who was then Vice President of the Supreme Executive Council of Pennsylvania and therefore in constant communication with Franklin.

Although Franklin College was founded in the interest of the Germans, it was never intended to be an exclusively German college. English was taught and stressed there, and a knowledge of German was not required for admission. It stood forth as an institution where "German life and literature would be appreciated, and in which the sons of Germans might be educated without becoming alienated from the faith of their fathers."[160]

The charter of the college provided that one-sixth of the income derived would be used to support a charity school. Though the charity school was never established, the college did grant free tuition to a number of poor students.[161] This would have pleased Franklin, who throughout all his life had supported free education for the poorer classes.

Dr. Benjamin Rush, of Philadelphia, received "great pleasure in promoting the German College," and enthusiastically reported to John Montgomery: "Dr. Franklin has given us £200-0-0 in specie. The 10,000 acres of land to be granted to us will be situated next to the lands of our College at Carlisle."[162] The lands were a grant from the state of Pennsylvania, in accordance with Franklin's idea that the state legislatures ought to do more to develop their own colleges.

The dedication of the college took place on June 6, 1787. J. Hector St. John Crèvecœur wrote an account of this dedication, claiming that he had accompanied Franklin to Lancaster. This, however, has been disproved, and it is generally agreed now that Franklin did not attend the Lancaster dedication.[163] Franklin's name did not appear on the printed program of the dedication, nor in the *Pennsylvania Gazette* (June 13, 1787) account written by Dr. Benjamin Rush. In a letter to his mother-in-law, Annis Boudinot Stockton (June 19), Dr. Rush described the dedication service; he mentioned a toast to "The President and State of Pennsylvania," but made no other reference to Franklin.[164] Franklin wrote to the Abbé Morellet in France and described the affair as one of religious toleration, attended by Presbyterians, Episcopalians, Lutherans, Catholics, and Moravians,[165] but he could have obtained his information from Dr. Rush personally. At this time Franklin was extremely busy with the affairs of the Constitutional Convention being held at Philadelphia.

---

[155] *Ibid.* 1: pp. 300, 385.
[156] American Philosophical Society, Franklin MSS, 33: 255 (Montgomery to Franklin, Dec. 6, 1785).
[157] Dubbs, 1903: p. 19.
[158] *Ibid.*, pp. 9-14.
[159] Printed in Rush, 1951: 1: pp. 364-368.
[160] Dubbs, 1903: pp. 17-23, 46.
[161] *Ibid.*, p. 28.
[162] *Ibid.*, p. 21. Rush,, 1951: 1: p. 410.
[163] Adams, 1947: p. 27.
[164] Rush, 1951: 1: pp. 420-429.
[165] Sparks, 1836-1840: 10: p. 314.

He wrote to his sister, Jane Mecom, on September 20, 1787:

> The Convention finish'd the 17th Instant. I attended the Business of it 5 Hours in every Day from the Beginning, which is something more than four Months.[166]

Thus, while he was honored by the name of the college, and contributed about twice as much as other subscribers,[167] he was more deeply concerned at the moment in helping to form a new pattern of government for our country.

The nineteenth century brought Franklin College educational maturity. Its library was formally organized in 1819 when a room was "prepared for a library,"[168] and in 1853 it combined forces with Marshall College of Mercersburg, Pennsylvania.

WASHINGTON (AND JEFFERSON) COLLEGE

Washington Academy (later Washington and Jefferson College) at Washington, Pennsylvania, had its origin in classes taught in the homes of ministers. It was chartered in 1787, and on the first Board of Trustees were David Bradford, then Vice-President of the Supreme Council of Pennsylvania, and David Redick, surveyor and later Vice-President of the Council. Since Franklin was President of the Council at this time, both men knew him fairly well. The academy was granted lands by the state of Pennsylvania, but these lands were never used for building because they were too far away from Washington, and were sold years later.[169]

Franklin advised the founders and gave an early contribution of fifty pounds to start a library.[170] The money was held in reserve for several years. Thomas Scott, one of the trustees, wrote to David Redick on November 19, 1788:

> We have a high sense of our obligation to Dr. Franklin, not only for his generous donation to our accademy, but for his recommendation of a Tuter, in which we have the highest confidence: — but we feel particularly flatered, in that we have a view of the patronage of so Great and so good a man, Under which our Infant Institution may safely rest, and hope to prosper.[171]

Only six days later, on November 25, 1788, the trustees wrote again that they were refusing to appoint the tutor, Mr. Thomas, unless he met their academic standards. Although recommendations had been sent by both Redick and Franklin, "you have both been silent on one point, which we think ourselves bound to have well ascertained, that is his literary Accomplishments."[172] Even in the eighteenth century the cry of "Publish or Perish" rang through the academic world. But in spite of problems of obtaining a faculty, the Washington Academy officially opened on April 1, 1789, in the upper room of a log courthouse with Thaddeus Dod as the only teacher. On April 10, another English teacher, David Johnson, was hired. He was formerly a tutor at the University of Pennsylvania, and may have been recommended by Franklin.

The courthouse burned in 1790, and a year and a half later a committee was appointed to furnish David Redick with a list of books to be purchased with Franklin's donation. Finally, late in 1792, Redick turned over a list of books totaling £49.10.11½. Five books from Franklin's gift still remain in the Historical Collection of Washington and Jefferson College. They are:

Jeremy Bentham, *A Fragment of Government, being an Examination of What is delivered, on the Subject of Government in General, in the introduction to Sir William Blackstone's Commentaries* (1776)

Torbern Bergman, *Physical and Chemical Essays*, II (translated by Edmund Cullen from the Latin, 1784)

John Bonnycastle, *Elements of Geometry . . . of Euclid* (1789)

James Ferguson, *The Art of Drawing in Perspective Made Easy* (1778)

The Philosophical Dictionary: or, The Opinions of Modern Philosophers on Metaphysical, Moral, and Political Subjects, I (1786).

The library of Washington Academy was maintained in the home of David Redick, librarian, between the years 1792 and 1803. Many of the books were scattered and worn out.[173]

In a reprint of the April 29 - May 2, 1789, issue of the *Gazette of the United States,* there is an "Elogium" on Benjamin Franklin. A copy of this reprint ("Copyright by Back Number Budd, 1280 Broadway, N.Y.") is on file in the Historical Collection of Washington and Jefferson College, and the account runs as follows:

> Dr. Franklin has had the happiness of living to see science extended under his fostering hand, from one end of Pennsylvania to the other. What hath he not done in the cause of literature and freedom? Was he not a principal agent in the foundation of the first public school of any note in the State? Was he not the principal agent in the foundation of the first library in Philadelphia? What seminary hath not partook of his bounty? Hath he not after a constant exercise of his extraordinary abilities, at the very eye of life, exhibited a striking proof of the consequences of good habits, in taking by the hand an infant academy at Washington, the very extremity of the State? Did he not some time ago endow it with fifty pounds? Hath he not within a few days past directed Mr. Redick, one of the trustees of that school, to receive from the State the whole amount of his account for postages during the three years of his presidency, and which amounted to a very considerable sum? Yes, all these things he hath done. But to all these things and as much more as would fill a volume of such things, would be but the dust

---

[166] Van Doren, 1950a: p. 298.
[167] Van Doren, 1938: p. 741.
[168] Dubbs, 1903: p. 64.
[169] Coleman, 1956: pp. 2, 22-27.
[170] Moffat, 1919: p. 749.
[171] American Philosophical Society, Franklin MSS, **48**: 54.
[172] Coleman, 1956: p. 28.

[173] *Ibid.*, pp. 28-32, 248 n. 24.

of the balance to what this great, this good, this ornament to human nature, hath done for man.[174]

Franklin had served as President of the Supreme Executive Council of Pennsylvania from 1785 to 1788, and apparently he had paid his own postage charges for official business. He evidently submitted a claim after he left the office, for in the *Colonial Records* of Pennsylvania, there is an order drawn on the Treasurer on April 30, 1789, for £77 5 shillings and 6 pence to reimburse Franklin for the postage that he had paid for public letters.[175] Such a gift was in keeping with Franklin's ideas that public officials should not benefit by their public trust. Oddly enough, within a few days of this generous contribution, Franklin wrote an urgent letter to his partner, Francis Childs, in New York, stating that "my late heavy expense in building five houses (which cost much more than I was made to expect) has so exhausted my finances that I am now in *real and great* want of money."[176] This can have been no more than a temporary shortage of cash and may have been only a device to persuade Childs to pay some long overdue debts; yet it is strange that Franklin could have been so generous to Washington College when his own cash reserves were so low.

In 1791, about a year after the death of Franklin, an academy was founded in Canonsburg, Pennsylvania. Apparently while the academy was still in the process of organization, Franklin sent some books which he had selected in Paris; his portrait was presented to the academy in 1790 by one of his descendants.[177] This academy at Canonsburg developed into Jefferson College, which merged with Washington College in 1865.

IV. AMERICAN LEARNED SOCIETIES

THE AMERICAN PHILOSOPHICAL SOCIETY

ORIGINS AND EARLY YEARS

The American Philosophical Society was first established in 1743. In that year Benjamin Franklin printed "A Proposal for Promoting Useful Knowledge among the British Plantations in America." This was printed on a separate sheet, as a circular letter, and sent to his various correspondents. He proposed:

That One Society be formed of Virtuosi or ingenious Men residing in the several Colonies, to be called *The American Philosophical Society;* who are to maintain a constant Correspondence.

That Philadelphia being the City nearest the Centre of the Continent-Colonies, . . . and having the Advantage of a good growing Library, be the Centre of the Society.

That at Philadelphia there be always at least seven Members, viz. a Physician, a Botanist, a Mathematician. a Chemist, a Mechanician, a Geographer, and a general Natural Philosopher, besides a President, Treasurer and Secretary.

That these Members meet once a Month, or oftner, at their own Expence, to communicate to each other their Observations, Experiments, &c. to receive, read and consider such Letters, Communications, or Queries as shall be sent from distant Members; to direct the Dispersing of Copies of such Communications as are valuable, to other distant Members, in order to procure their Sentiments thereupon, &c.

. . . .

That every Member shall have Abstracts sent him Quarterly, of every Thing valuable communicated to the Society's Secretary at Philadelphia; free of all Charge except the Yearly Payment hereafter mentioned.

That by Permission of the Postmaster-General, such Communications pass between the Secretary of the Society and the Members, Postage-free.

. . . .

That at the End of every Year, Collections be made and printed, of such Experiments, Discoveries, Improvements. &c. as may be thought of publick Advantage: And that every Member have a Copy sent him.

. . . .

Benjamin Franklin. the Writer of this Proposal. offers himself to serve the Society as their Secretary, 'till they shall be provided with one more capable.[1]

The idea of a philosophical society had been suggested in 1739 by John Bartram, but it was not until 1743 when Franklin printed and circulated the proposal, that the society was actually formed with the aid of John Bartram and Dr. Thomas Bond. By April, 1744, several meetings had already been held, and Franklin wrote to Cadwallader Colden, in New York, informing him that the Philadelphia members were:

Dr. Thomas Bond, as Physician
Mr. John Bartram, as Botanist
Mr. Thomas Godfrey, as Mathematician
Mr. Samuel Rhoads, as Mechanician
Mr. William Parsons, as Geographer
Dr. Phineas Bond, as General Natural Philosopher
Mr. Thomas Hopkinson, President
Mr. William Coleman, Treasurer
Benjamin Franklin, Secretary

Of these, Godfrey. Parsons. Coleman, and Franklin were members of the original 1727 Junto, and all of them were members of the Library Company, with Bartram entering later. Members from other colonies were James Alexander from New York; Robert Hunter Morris, Chief Justice of New Jersey; Archibald Home, secretary of New Jersey; John Coxe and David Martin, of Trenton, New Jersey; with others expected to join

---

[174] By permission of Washington and Jefferson College Memorial Library. This "Elogium" does not appear in the original issue located in the Rare Book Room of the Library of Congress. "Back Number" Budd [Robert M. Budd] "& Sons, news," is a listing found in the 1894 (Vol. 108) and later issues of *Trow's New York City Directory* with various addresses including 1267 Broadway. Robert M. Budd is listed as early as 1883 with a 1216 Broadway address; the 1892 (Vol. 106) directory follows his name with "news, anything ever published, 1267 B'way, h L. I. City."
[175] Pennsylvania, 1853: **16**: p. 67.
[176] Van Doren, 1945: p. 770.
[177] Coleman, 1956: pp. 61, 250 n. 7.

[1] Labaree, 1959—: **2**: pp. 380-383.

from Virginia, Maryland, Carolina, New York, and New England.[2] After a brief flurry, the society languished, and by the end of 1745, Franklin proposed to stimulate interest by publishing an *American Philosophical Miscellany*, monthly or quarterly.[3] But this idea, too, was laid aside. However, Franklin had not given up the society altogether, for when he applied for the position of Deputy Postmaster-General of North America in 1751, he still had plans for granting franking privileges to the American Philosophical Society.[4]

About 1750 a group of younger Philadelphians organized another society named after Franklin's Junto of 1727 and in some respects patterned after it.[5] The original Junto was a self-improvement club; later its interests varied, and it aimed at public improvement, with the establishment of branch Juntos (the Vine, the Union, the Band, etc.) which Franklin describes in his *Autobiography*.[6] Still later, the Junto began to include more and more scientific questions in its debates. William Smith quoted some of these in a memorial eulogy before the American Philosophical Society in 1791. Included were such questions as:

Is sound an entity or body?
How may the phenomena of vapors be explained?
What is the reason that the tides rise higher in the Bay of Fundy than the Bay of Delaware?
How may smoky chimneys be best cured?
Why does the flame of a candle tend upwards in a spire?[7]

These questions were the result of Franklin's own scientific investigations.

The young men who established the 1750 Junto were also interested in science and "useful knowledge." Although the membership was entirely new, this Junto imitated Franklin's Junto in their rules and their adoption of Franklin's four qualifications of 1728.[8] Their existing minutes start with 1758.

The 1750 Junto underwent several changes of organization and name before finally becoming a part of the American Philosophical Society in 1769. The name changes include:

Sept. 22, 1758. The Junto, or Society for the Promotion of Useful Knowledge.
(Oct. 22, 1762 — April 25, 1766. Records missing.)
Dec. 13, 1766. The American Society for promoting and propagating useful knowledge, held at Philadelphia.
Sept. 23, 1768. The American Society held at Philadelphia for Promoting Useful Knowledge.

The Medical Society of Philadelphia was absorbed by the group on November 4, 1768.[9] The American Society was headed by Charles Thomson, published in the *Pennsylvania Chronicle* (an anti-Proprietary paper), held its later meetings in the rooms of the Union Library Company, and was on the side of Benjamin Franklin in his fight against Proprietary government. William Franklin had been a member since 1750;[10] Benjamin Franklin was elected a member on February 19, 1768, and elected president the same year on November 4.[11]

The success of the American Society led to revival of the dormant American Philosophical Society of 1743. The American Society had chosen not to elect to its membership a number of distinguished philosophers, physicians, and other eligible citizens who were active in the Proprietary Party or for other reasons were not acceptable to the younger society. In 1767, therefore, while Franklin was in England, the American Philosophical Society was resurrected. Eight of the original members of 1743 still survived, led once again by Dr. Thomas Bond.[12] However, it soon became the scientific weapon of the Proprietary Party, extending membership to Lieutenant Governor John Penn (patron), ex-Governor James Hamilton, Chief Justice William Allen, the Reverend Richard Peters, and the Reverend William Smith (Provost of the College of Philadelphia). It published in the *Pennsylvania Gazette*, now run by David Hall alone as a Proprietary paper. Its members were drawn chiefly from the Anglican and Presbyterian churches, and it met in the State House.[13] It enjoyed the patronage of the government; the Assembly granted £100 to purchase a reflecting telescope and micrometer to be lent to the American Philosophical Society to observe the transit of Venus across the sun, expected on June 3, 1769.[14]

The year 1768 was a year of rivalry between the Philosophical Society and the American Society. The two societies competed in publications and in memberships. Franklin, himself, had been in England for so many years that he was more concerned with the affairs of the Royal Society of London, which had awarded him the Copley Medal for his discoveries in electricity in 1753 and elected him a member in 1756. However, he was concerned that science should not suffer from political rivalry, and he was very glad to hear of plans for joining the two societies. The union was made possible by overlapping memberships of twenty-six men.[15] Among these were William Franklin,[16] Dr. Cadwallader Evans, Dr. Thomas Cadwalader, Francis Hopkinson, Ebenezer Kinnersley, Joseph Galloway, Jacob Duché,

---

[2] *Ibid.* 2: pp. 406-407.
[3] *Ibid.* 3: pp. 47-48.
[4] Van Doren, 1945: pp. 74-76.
[5] Conklin, 1963: p. 38.
[6] *Autobiography*, 1964: p. 171.
[7] Bigelow, 1888: 1: p. 189.
[8] Du Ponceau, 1914: p. 20.
[9] Sparks, 1836-1840: 1: pp. 577-578. Conklin, 1963: p. 39.

[10] Bridenbaugh, 1962: pp. 304, 334-337.
[11] Sparks, 1836-1840: 1: pp. 577-578.
[12] Conklin, 1963: pp. 39-40.
[13] Bridenbaugh, 1962: pp. 336-337.
[14] Du Ponceau, 1914: p. 41.
[15] Conklin, 1963: p. 40.
[16] Elected to American Philosophical Society on March 8, 1768. American Philosophical Society, 1885: *Proceedings* 22, 3: p. 12.

and David Rittenhouse. Agreements were worked out whereby both societies should receive equal treatment in the union, and the formal union took place on January 2, 1769. Benjamin Franklin was elected first president of the united society even though he was still in England, and the name of the society was henceforth to be The American Philosophical Society, Held at Philadelphia, for Promoting Useful Knowledge. Franklin was re-elected president each year until his death. Angry that his own candidate, James Hamilton, did not win the presidency, Lieutenant Governor John Penn refused patronage to the Society. In 1769 there were 251 members; ninety of these resided in other British colonies, and seventeen in Europe.[17]

Among the committee's recommendations for union were the following:

That the Books & all the Curiosities &c of the former Societies be deposited in the Cabinet or elsewhere as the United Society shall direct.

That in the joint Publication which it may be thought proper to make of the Transactions of the former Societies, no preference shall be given to the Papers of either, but they shall be arranged & digested according to their Subjects & Dates.

That there shall be a New Book of the future Transactions of the United Society; . . .

. . . .

This Book therefore is to contain only the Transactions of the United Society under the Name aforesaid. What further relates to the Terms of union, as, well as the former Transactions of each Society, being antecedent to the Commencement of this Book, may be found in the old Books deposited in the Cabinet.[18]

The Laws and Regulations, adopted in 1769, provided for three curators:

The Business of the Curators shall be to take charge of and preserve all specimens of natural productions whether of the animal, vegetable or fossil kingdom, all models of machines and Instruments and all other matters and things belonging to the society which shall be committed to them; to class and arrange them in their proper orders and keep an exact list of them with the names of the respective donors in a book provided for that purpose, which book shall be laid before the society as often as called for.

The curators were also placed under bond, and signed a receipt for all articles in their care.[19] In developing a plan for increasing the cabinet, the curators decided to request merchants, army officers, and ship captains to collect plants, animals, and fossils from all over the world, to insert the names of donors in the Books, to give public acknowledgment to worthy donations, to solicit from foreign members, and to request local members to return any items they had borrowed. It took time to gather together all the property of the former societies. Even in 1773 the minutes were still being recovered from I. and J. Paschall.[20] For a while the new society eyed the vacant building formerly owned by the Union Library as a "fit Place for the meetings of the Society, & for the Keeping the Cabinet." They applied to the current owner, the Library Company, but decided that the rent was too high.[21]

This was a bigger and better scientific society. Its success was due to support of other colonial scientists, first displayed by cooperative scholarship in the observation of the transit of Venus in June, 1769. The American Philosophical Society had decided to observe this rare event at three points in the Philadelphia area: one was in the State House yard, in which a platform was built to mount the telescope lent by the Pennsylvania Assembly; another was at the Norriton residence of David Rittenhouse, a gifted astronomer and instrument-maker; and the third was at Cape Henlopen, at which Owen Biddle used a telescope lent by the Library Company of Philadelphia.[22] Other observations were made at Cambridge, Massachusetts; Providence, Rhode Island; and New Jersey.[23] Dr. Thomas Bond wrote to tell Franklin that the "Telliscope" which Franklin had procured in London was used in the late observations of Venus, and now that the American Philosophical Society was again united, "with your Presence may make a Figure, . . ."[24] The Society reached out and stimulated activities in the Juliana Library Company at Lancaster, Pennsylvania, through the personalities of Edward Shippen and the Reverend Thomas Barton.[25]

So far, the Society had paid much more attention to its museum specimens than to its books. Many of the members belonged to the Library Company and had not felt the necessity of acquiring a large scientific library in the care of the Society. However, prospective borrowers made the books more desirable; in October, 1773, Captain Inglis requested the use of "the Book of Tables of Parallax & Refraction" which had been presented by the University of Cambridge, for his voyage to Jamaica. He was permitted to borrow the book, provided that he ordered a new book of the same kind to be imported by the first spring ship to replace it. "But this method of lending the Books of the Society to any but Members not to be drawn into precedent."[26] By 1773 the cabinet could no longer hold all the books; a new plain pine bookcase was promptly ordered on March 19 and billed for £6 in October[27] — the library

---

[17] Bridenbaugh, 1962: pp. 338-339.
[18] American Philosophical Society, 1885: *Proceedings* 22, 3: p. 22.
[19] *Ibid.*, pp. 27-28.
[20] *Ibid.*, pp. 53-54, 77-78, 85.
[21] *Ibid.*, pp. 49-50.
[22] *Ibid.*, pp. 30, 37.
[23] Bridenbaugh, 1962: p. 343.
[24] American Philosophical Society, Franklin MSS, 2: 179 (June 7, 1769).
[25] Bridenbaugh, 1962: p. 340.
[26] American Philosophical Society, 1885: *Proceedings* 22, 3: p. 84.
[27] *Ibid.*, pp. 79, 83. Another bookcase is mentioned in the printed minutes for March 19, 1775 (p. 97), but the minutes for this date duplicate those given for March 19, 1773.

was beginning to grow. With the approach of the American Revolution, the curators began to realize that they were in danger of losing books and specimens and made a concerted effort in February, 1774, to collect the books and other valuables belonging to the Society.[28] The first librarian, David Rittenhouse, was appointed in December, 1774, with power to lend the books to the members "under the same regulations as those of the city library";[29] before this, the curators had charge of the books. David Rittenhouse moved part of the library to his own house during the period of the Revolution.[30]

Not until 1780 did the Society receive a charter. Under the proprietary government, Lieutenant Governor John Penn had refused to grant a charter; it remained for the Declaration of Independence to pave the way. In the Act of Incorporation, March 15, 1780, the Society was empowered to receive "gifts and bequests of what nature so ever." They were also granted the right

at all times, whether in peace or war, to correspond with learned Societies, as well as individual learned men, of any nation or country, upon matters merely belonging to the business of the said Society, such as the mutual communication of their discoveries and proceedings in Philosophy and Science; the procuring books, apparatus, natural curiosities, and such other articles and intelligence as are usually exchanged between learned bodies, for furthering their common pursuits; Provided always, That such correspondence of the said Society be at all times open to the inspection of the Supreme Executive Council of this Commonwealth.[31]

This freedom of exchange, even during wartime, was very important to the members of the Society, for under the presidency of Benjamin Franklin the exchange program had become the Society's main source of scientific information.

In 1780 the American Philosophical Society obtained the use of the library room in Carpenters' Hall, and the curators "were requested to remove the Society's effects from the University."[32] Then from 1783 until the time that the American Philosophical Society built its permanent home, the library was shifted from place to place and separated partly at the discretion of the librarian. In March, 1783, David Rittenhouse proposed "that the Society's Library be made useful by removal to some member's house who should act as Librarian." In November of that year, it was reported that "Cases containing the Library and books of Natural History" were "put under the care of M^r. Rittenhouse untill a more convenient place could be procured." At the December meeting, Rittenhouse reported "that he had removed the Library (in part) and the Cabinet to his own house. He is requested to continue his endeavors to collect the remainder of the books." The curators were having difficulty in preserving the natural history specimens and were instructed to take immediate measures to protect them from further decay. They also continued to transfer books to the care of the librarian.[33]

Heretofore, meetings had been held mainly at the State House or at the University. Now, the Society felt that it was increasing sufficiently in membership and possessions to warrant its own building, and an order was given to begin to solicit donations. It was proposed to build jointly with the "City Library." Members of the Society were highly in favor of a joint petition with the Library Company of Philadelphia, to the Pennsylvania Assembly, for "two Lots of ground on the East and West sides of the State-House square" for their permanent buildings.[34] There was, however, some dissatisfaction on the part of the Library Company as to the lot assigned, and only the Philosophical Society actually built on the State House grounds. In the Act of March 28, 1785, the Pennsylvania Assembly granted the lot to the Society for "a public hall, library and other accommodations."[35] In the April meetings of 1785, the Society ordered a subscription drive for building funds.[36]

The year before Franklin returned from France to give personal direction to the American Philosophical Society, his way was prepared by a speech presented by Francis Hopkinson, who saw the danger of limiting scientific investigation to "men of profound learning and scholastic education." Hopkinson summarized the speech in a letter to Franklin:

I asserted, that the book of nature was the book of knowledge; that it was open to all; that it was not written in Latin, Greek, or Hebrew, but in a language intelligible to every one, who would take the pains to read and observe.[37]

A special meeting was held September 27, 1785, by the American Philosophical Society to welcome its president, Benjamin Franklin, home from France.[38] After being president in absentia for sixteen years, Franklin delighted in taking over the chair. He had four and a half busy years left, which he crammed with the affairs of the Society as well as affairs of government. His grandson, William Temple Franklin, who had served as his secretary throughout his French mission, was elected to membership on July 21, 1786.[39] In December, 1785, the artist Charles Willson Peale pre-

---

[28] *Ibid.*, p. 91.
[29] *Ibid.*, p. 89.
[30] Lingelbach, 1946: p. 51.
[31] American Philosophical Society, 1902: pp. 14, 19.
[32] American Philosophical Society, 1885: *Proceedings* 22, 3: pp. 107-109.
[33] *Ibid.*, pp. 116, 119-121.
[34] *Ibid.*, pp. 108, 124.
[35] Lingelbach, 1946: p. 53.
[36] American Philosophical Society, 1885: *Proceedings* 22: 3: p. 130.
[37] Sparks, 1836-1840: 10: pp. 90-91.
[38] American Philosophical Society, 1885: *Proceedings* 22, 3: pp. 132-133.
[39] *Ibid.*, pp. 143-144.

sented a portrait of Franklin, "copied from a much admired painting" by David Martin. Thanks were returned, and Mr. Peale was requested to keep the portrait "till the Society shall have a convenient place for its reception."[40]

Franklin built an extension to his house with a large meeting room on the first floor. In his later years, the Society held its meetings there because of his ill health.[41] He kept his private library on the floor above, and proudly displayed his books to any one who lingered after the meeting to talk. The building for the American Philosophical Society was under construction from 1785 to 1789. In November of 1787 Franklin came to the rescue with a second subscription of £100 to the building fund and offered a loan of £500, payable in one year.[42]

Since the Library Company still kept its books in Carpenters' Hall, the American Philosophical Society offered to rent a part of its new building to the Library Company, and Franklin wrote to the Directors. The Library Company appointed a committee "to wait on him and thank him for his friendly attentions," but they wished to inform the Society that it would not be convenient to remove their library from the building which they then occupied. The extra rooms in the new building were then rented to the University of Pennsylvania.[43] The American Philosophical Society itself continued to meet in Franklin's house until November 13, 1789.[44]

Franklin presided over a meeting on March 7, 1788, which ordered labels for the books belonging to the Society, and the meeting on February 6, 1789, which ordered that Poulson be paid 35 shillings for printing 1,000 labels and 500 blank notices. The librarian at that time was Mr. Patterson.[45] Then, finally in February, 1790, the curators were ordered to catalogue and arrange "the Library, the various specimens of natural history, & other articles of their Museum, & remove them from the place in which they are at present to one of the chambers in the Society's Building," the Treasurer to pay the necessary expenses.[46] The library was at last joined with the members in their new building.

THE GREAT EXCHANGE — AMERICAN

Ever since 1745, when Benjamin Franklin abandoned his idea to publish a periodical of *American Philosophical Miscellany*, he had promoted the publication of "useful knowledge" by other methods. He, himself, published some of the works of Cadwallader Colden, and from time to time forwarded the writings of American scientists to the Royal Society in London. It was with great joy, therefore, that he received the news in London that the united American Philosophical Society would be able to publish its first volume of *Transactions* in 1771. Here at last was concrete evidence of the caliber of scientific investigations being conducted in the colonies. The second volume of *Transactions* was delayed by a paper shortage due to war conditions,[47] and finally appeared in 1786.

On February 1, 1771, the Society ordered that a copy of the *Transactions* be

presented to the Proprietaries, the Governor, to each member of Assembly, the Assemblies Library [sic], the Library of Philadelphia, to the Library of every College, in America, to the Royal Society of London, each of the foreign Philosophical Societies and to the Pennsylvania Hospital; the Secretaries to have the care of presenting these Books.

The presentation was made to the members of the Pennsylvania Assembly and to the Assembly Library on February 22, 1771. A committee went out to wait upon the Philadelphia merchants for the remainder of their subscriptions for canal surveys and to present those who were not members with a volume of *Transactions*.[48]

Just how soon the libraries of "every College, in America" received their copies of the first volume of *Transactions* is difficult to trace, but after two years, President James Manning of Rhode Island College (Brown University) was just returning his thanks.[49]

Franklin was more thorough in keeping track of exchanges with American societies once he returned home. He promised the second volume of the *Transactions* to James Bowdoin of the Boston American Academy of Arts and Sciences in 1786,[50] and two years later offered to send another if it had miscarried, since he had not heard of its arrival.[51] The success of the American Philosophical Society, with the favorable reaction both in the colonies and abroad to its publications, was a prime factor in the establishment of the Boston and similar scientific societies in other colonies. These societies were not limited to general science; among them were medical societies, such as the Medical Society of New Haven County, which sent its "Cases and Observations" in 1789 and desired exchange.[52] American science was feeling the need of informational exchange.

---

[40] *Ibid.*, p. 136.
[41] *Ibid.*, pp. 153-154. Van Doren, 1945: p. 767.
[42] American Philosophical Society, 1885, *Proceedings* 22, 3: p. 156.
[43] *Ibid.*, pp. 168-169, 171.
[44] *Ibid.*, pp. 174-175.
[45] *Ibid.*, pp. 159, 169.
[46] *Ibid.*, p. 179.

[47] American Philosophical Society, Franklin MSS, 18: 49 (Thomas Bond to Franklin, April 27, 1780).
[48] American Philosophical Society, 1885: *Proceedings* 22, 3: pp. 61-63.
[49] *Ibid.*, p. 79.
[50] Van Doren, 1945: p. 664.
[51] Smyth, 1905-1907: 9: p. 652.
[52] American Philosophical Society, 1885: *Proceedings* 22, 3: p. 172.

THE GREAT EXCHANGE — EUROPEAN

When Franklin was first organizing the American Philosophical Society in 1743, he strongly recommended corresponding with other learned societies, notably the Royal Society of London and the Dublin Society.[53] One of Franklin's proposals for the Library Company was to purchase the transactions of all the learned societies in Europe, but unfortunately he was forced to give up the idea because of the prohibitive cost. He made the same proposal to the American Philosophical Society in 1770, and received a return letter from John Ewing:

> I mentioned to our Society your proposal to purchase the Transactions of the learned societies in Europe, and they have taken the matter under their consideration. They approved of your reasoning on the subject, when I read it to them; and nothing will prevent their coming into the resolution, if their poverty does not.[54]

An account of the Venus and Mercury observations had been drawn up by John Ewing by order of the American Philosophical Society to be transmitted through its president, Franklin, to the learned societies in Europe.[55] But with the publication of its own *Transactions* in 1771, Franklin's ideas changed. The American Philosophical Society arranged to send these *Transactions* to the learned societies in Europe, and in return, the European societies sent theirs. This started a magnificent example of international exchange of scientific information, much of it due to the personal effort of Franklin. He was serving as colonial agent in England at this time, and had made continental tours to France, Germany, Belgium, Holland, as well as tours up through Scotland and Ireland. Everywhere he went, he stopped and visited the universities and the learned societies. He was in contact with the London scientists through membership in the Royal Society, and through them was introduced to many foreign scientists. Franklin was indeed a center of exchange.

When the *Transactions* first came out, the American Philosophical Society held a special meeting and drew up a "List of most considerable Philosophical Societies." They also added the list of important foreign universities and important foreign scientists, to whom they intended to send a copy of their *Transactions*. The following were selected to be so honored:

Societies:
  London: Royal Society
           British Museum
           Society for Promoting Arts and Manufactures
           Royal College of Physicians
  Edinburgh: Philosophical Society
  Dublin: Society
  Paris: Royal Academy of Science
  Berlin: Royal Society
  Göttingen: Royal Society
  Uppsala: Royal Society
  Stockholm: Royal Society
  St. Petersburg: Imperial Society
  Bologna: Academy
  Turin: Academy of Science
  Florence: Academy
  Berne: Society
  Academia Naturae Curiosorum

Universities:
  Oxford
  Cambridge
  Dublin
  Edinburgh
  Glasgow
  St. Andrews
  Aberdeen

Individuals (all members of the Society):
  Georges L. Leclerc Buffon, Paris
  James Ferguson, London
  John Fothergill, London
  Karl von Linné, Uppsala
  Johann D. Hahn, Utrecht
  Nevil Maskelyne, Greenwich
  Richard Penn, England
  Sir George Saville, London
  Benjamin West, London[56]

These were not all sent the first year, but the Royal Astronomer of England, Maskelyne, requested and received his copy at once.[57] Those sent in 1772 to the philosophical societies were sent with the following address attached:

> The American Philosophical Society held at Phil[a]. humbly desirous to cooperate w[th] [the Society's name] in their laudable endeavors for the Advancement of useful Knowledge, request y[e] learned and respectable Body to accept this Vol. as the first Fruits of their Labors in this new World. — By order of the Society — William Smith, Robt. Strettell Jones, Secretaries.[58]

Some of the *Transactions* Franklin delivered himself, even to Ireland, for he visited Dublin in 1771 and presented a copy of the *Transactions* to the editor of the *Hibernian Magazine* which reviewed it in October, commending "the great progress the arts and sciences will one day make in the New World."[59] The copy for the University of Glasgow was turned over to Professor Patrick Wilson, who had been in London and was ready to return.[60]

The copy of the *Transactions* sent to the Academy of Sciences at St. Petersburg, was given over to Timothy, Baron de Klingstedt, who was Counsellor of State to the Empress of Russia. The Baron was so excited over

---

[53] Labaree, 1959—: 2: p. 382.
[54] Sparks, 1836-1840: 6: p. 331.
[55] *Ibid.* 6: p. 326.
[56] American Philosophical Society, 1885: *Proceedings* 22, 3: p. 63.
[57] American Philosophical Society, Franklin MSS, 3: 56 (William Smith to Franklin, May 3, 1771).
[58] American Philosophical Society, 1885: *Proceedings* 22, 3: p. 73.
[59] Nolan, 1938: p. 144.
[60] American Philosophical Society, Franklin MSS, 3: 114 (Patrick Wilson to Franklin, Aug. 3, 1772).

the *Transactions* that he immediately applied and was accepted for membership in the American Philosophical Society.[61] The copy for the Academy of Sciences at Paris was entrusted to Jean Hyacinthe de Magellan, who also became a member later.[62] The messenger who carried the *Transactions* to the academies at Turin, Bologna, and Florence, was Philip Mazzei, who later took up residence at Richmond, Virginia.[63]

The first volume of the *Transactions* was well received in Europe. Starting early in 1772, the harvest gathered by Franklin began to come in. First to be received were the *Philosophical Transactions* of the Royal Society in London, "who have directed them to be constantly sent you from the time you first sent them yours. Let me know if these are regular. . . . Methinks a Line or two of Thanks would be proper from the Society to each Benefactor." The Prussian Academy of Sciences sent its *Memoirs*.[64] From Göttingen came *Novi commentaree societates scientiarum gottingensis* tomi III — 4to and from Berlin, *Nouveaux memoires de l'academie Royale de sciences et belles lettres*, Annee 1770 — 4to.[65] The Batavian Philosophical Society sent six volumes of its transactions.[66] Four volumes from the Academy of Turin were brought by Philip Mazzei to Richmond, Virginia, in 1773;[67] because of the unsettled times of 1775-1776, Franklin wrote from Philadelphia:

If you have not yet sent the books, which the Academy of Turin have done us the honour to present us with, we must, I fear, wait for more quiet times before we can have the pleasure of receiving them, the communication being now very difficult.[68]

Still not received by 1779, the secretaries made arrangements to send for them from Richmond, Virginia.[69] Abbé Jacob Hemmer, of the Palatinate Academy of Sciences, sent suggestions for overcoming language barriers between various societies and a catalogue of books that would be helpful in establishing a German society in Philadelphia.[70]

Franklin's hopes that these *Transactions* would "procure us the Correspondence of those Societies" were coming true. They were also in demand for individual sale; when they were first published, he was often asked "by the Curious how it happens that none are to be bought here," so arrangements were made for the sale of the *Transactions* through Dilly, the bookseller, in London.[71]

Franklin also constantly watched for suitable printed materials, which he sent to the American Philosophical Society to be read at the meetings.[72] One such piece, a French treatise on recent balloon experiments, he sent to Dr. Benjamin Rush to translate for the Society in 1784; the Society, like Franklin, was so pleased with the piece that it decided to publish it in translation.[73] Franklin had followed the French balloon experiments with considerable interest, and could see their possibility of use long before the general public.

By the time the second volume of *Transactions* was published in 1786, Franklin had returned to America and taken over the chair. He served on a committee with Vaughan and Hopkinson "to forward the sales of the Volume . . . and send, in donations, any number not exceeding 20 copies, to such Societies and particular persons in Europe, as they shall think entitled to this respect." When it appeared that twenty would not be a sufficient number, thirty copies were allotted for distribution.[74]

New societies just formed were being added to the list for exchange. The Cercle des Philadelphes, located at Cap François, Haiti, sent its publications, and Franklin reciprocated with the second volume of the *Transactions*.[75] In 1788 Franklin presented to the American Philosophical Society books sent to him by the secretary of the Patriotic Society at Milan, books from the Royal Academy of History at Madrid, and the *Memoires* of the Societá Italiana of Verona. "Through some mistake, or derangement with respect to conveyance, the books and papers from Milan were not received 'till very lately, although sent above two years ago, from Italy." The secretaries were ordered "to take the earliest opportunity" to return thanks and explain the delayed acknowledgment, and a copy of the second volume of the *Transactions* was sent to the Patriotic Society of Milan through Dr. Rush.[76]

The Royal Irish Academy sent its *Transactions*, Volume I, in 1789; and the American Philosophical Society returned two volumes of its *Transactions* in exchange.[77] The President of the Imperial Academy of Sciences at St. Petersburg, Princess Catherine Dashkov, recognized Franklin as the center of this exchange program, and thanked him for the *Transactions* "in the

---

[61] American Philosophical Society, 1885: *Proceedings* 22, 3: p. 75.

[62] Smyth, 1905-1907: 6: p. 29.

[63] American Philosophical Society, 1885: *Proceedings* 22, 3: p. 86.

[64] Smyth, 1905-1907: 5: pp. 386-387; 6: p. 237.

[65] Lingelbach, 1946: p. 51.

[66] American Philosophical Society, 1885: *Proceedings* 22, 3: p. 120.

[67] *Ibid.*, p. 86.

[68] Smyth, 1905-1907: 6: p. 455.

[69] American Philosophical Society, 1885: *Proceedings* 22, 3: p. 102.

[70] Hays, 1908: 1: p. 510 (Oct. 8, 1778).

[71] Smyth, 1905-1907: 5: p. 387. American Philosophical Society, Franklin MSS, 3: 96 (William Smith to Franklin, May 16, 1772).

[72] Smyth, 1905-1907: 6: p. 20.

[73] American Philosophical Society, 1885: *Proceedings* 22, 3: p. 124.

[74] *Ibid.*, pp. 143-144.

[75] Smyth, 1905-1907: 9: p. 526. Hays, 1908: 3: pp. 300, 316, 356.

[76] American Philosophical Society, 1885: *Proceedings* 22, 3: pp. 162-163.

[77] *Ibid.*, p. 175.

most polite terms for this mark of his attention." She had become acquainted with Franklin in Paris, and was elected to membership in April, 1789.[78]

The great exchange with the European learned societies was intensified by Franklin's membership in so many of the European societies. He was invited to join the following:

London: Royal Society, 1756
    Society for Promoting Arts, Manufactures, and Commerce, 1755 (Royal Society of Arts)
    Medical Society, 1787
    Society of Antiquaries
    Literary Society
Manchester: Literary and Philosophical Society, 1785
Edinburgh: Royal Society of Edinburgh, 1783
    Philosophical Society, 1759
Paris: Académie Royale des Sciences, 1772
    Royal Medical Society, 1777
Orleans: Société Royale de Physique, d'Histoire Naturelle, et des Arts, 1785
Lyons: Academy of Sciences, Belles Lettres, and Arts, 1785
Madrid: Royal Academy of History, 1784
Milan: La Société Patriotique, 1786
Turin: Royal Academy of Arts and Sciences, 1783
Padua: Royal Academy of Arts and Sciences, 1782
Bologna: Academy of Sciences, Letters and Arts, 1782
St. Petersburg: Imperial Academy of Sciences, 1789
Göttingen: Königliche Gesellschaft der Wissenschaften, 1766
Rotterdam: Bataafsch Genootschap der Proefondervindelijke Wijsbegeerte, 1771

DONATIONS FROM FRIENDS IN EUROPE

Through his personal contacts while he was in England and France, Franklin was also responsible for gathering great numbers of donations from Europeans. According to a memorandum left by Mrs. Deborah Logan, one of the donations came from Louis XVI, but never reached the library of the American Philosophical Society. It was a thirty or forty volume set ("in 12 quarto") on "the Jesuits' Account of China, and their translations of Chinese literature published after their expulsion from China and return to France." The books had been kept temporarily by Franklin in his Philadelphia home, and were confiscated by Major André during the American Revolution.[79]

Donations from other Europeans were often given out of personal regard for Franklin. Some donors became members of the American Philosophical Society through recommendations from Franklin, as president of the Society. Throughout the long years spent abroad in the service of his country, Franklin came to know many European scientists personally.

[78]*Ibid.*, pp. 169, 172.
[79]"Books Taken from Dr. Franklin's Library by Major André," 1884: *Pa. Mag. of Hist. & Biog.* **8**: p. 430.

The following composite list of European donations forwarded by Franklin is taken from many sources.[80] Asterisks indicate donors who gained membership through the influence of Franklin; dates of membership appear in parentheses after names of donors.

Donors and Donations	Date Given
*Buffon, Georges—Louis LeClerc, Comte de (1769, Paris)	
"Directions for Preserving Subjects of Natural History"	1774
Histoire Naturelle des Oiseaux, 4 vols., folio,	1774
with colored plates and	1787
Histoire Naturelle de Mineraux	1787
*Campomanès, Conde de (1784, Madrid)	
Books	1787
*Carmichael, William (Madrid)	
Books	
*Court de Gebelin, Antoine (1783?, French philologist)	
First four volumes of *The Primitive World*	1783
Decquemare, Abbé	
"Essay on Sea Anemones"	1775
Defay (Paris and Orleans)	
Works by Gastellier of Gatinais	1782
Work on natural history	1782
Dennis	
Astronomy	1775
Dunn, Samuel	
A New Atlas of the Mundane System	1774
Flores, Don Joseph Miguel de (1789, Madrid)	
Books	1787
Forster, John Reinhold	
Kalm's *Travels through North America*	1772
Bosser's *Travels through Louisiana*	1772
Catalogue of North American Animals	1772
*Fothergill, John (1770, London physician)	
Miller's Botanical Collection	1779
Herschell, William (1785)	
Catalogue of 1000 New Nebulae and Clusters of Stars	1787
Hewson, Mrs. William	
William Hewson's *Experimental Enquiries into the Lymphatic System*	1774
*Ingenhousz, Jan (1786, physician, Vienna)	
Experiments upon Vegetables	1785
German edition of his writings	1786
Books	1787
Nouvelles Experiences, 2 vols.	1790
*Lavoisier, M. (1775, Paris)	
Opuscules Physiques et Chemiques	1774
L'Héritier, Charles Louis	
Work on botany	1785
*Le Roy, Jean Baptiste (1773) and Julien David (1786)	
Precis de Recherches en France depuis l'Anée 1730, pour la Determination des Longitudes	1774
Materials on boats for river navigation	1786
Books	1786
Ludlam, William	
Box of books	1772

[80]The sources used were Hays, *Calendar of the Papers of Benjamin Franklin in the Library of the American Philosophical Society;* Ford, *List of the Benjamin Franklin Papers in the Library of Congress;* Smyth, *The Writings of Benjamin Franklin;* American Philosophical Society, "Old Minutes of the Society, from 1743 to 1838," *Proceedings,* Volume 22, Part 3 (1885); and *List of the Members of the American Philosophical Society, Held at Philadelphia, for Promoting Useful Knowledge, from Its Establishment, 2d January, 1769, to the 20th of April, 1838.*

DONATIONS FROM FRANKLIN

Franklin's own donations to the American Philosophical Society were varied, reflecting his many interests. He was always searching for materials on new scientific discoveries in Europe, and these he would send back to Philadelphia to be read at the meetings. Occasionally he would suggest the need of translation from the French, usually done by Dr. Benjamin Rush.[83] The following list shows some of the materials that he sent to the Society:

	Date Given
Maskelyne, Nevil (1771, Royal Astronomer, Greenwich)	
Astronomical Observations Made at Royal Observatory at Greenwich, 1765-1769, annual	1774
Other issues up to 1786	1788
Nairne, Edward (1770, London)	
De Luc's Hygrometer	1788
*Priestley, Joseph (1785, Birmingham)	
His "latest philosophical work"	1779
Pringle, Sir John (President of the Royal Society, London)	
A Discourse on the Different Kinds of Air	1774
Work on "the Torpedo"	1775
Abstract of Captain Cooke's last voyage, not yet published in England	1775
Rolland (President of Collège de Louis le Grand)	
Book on education	1783
Rozier, L'Abbé (1775, Paris)	
Observations sur la Physique, sur l'Histoire Naturelle . . . &c., Vol. 1 and 2	1774
2 copies of Vol. 3 and 4	1775
*Small, Alexander (1773, physician, London & Edinburgh)	
Journals of Weather in Jamaica	1772
Circular Scheme for Noting the Variations of the Barometer	1772
Paper "On Ventilation"	1789
Viel de St. Maux	
Lettres sur l'Architecture	1785
Whitehurst, John (1786, London)	
"Inquiry"	1787
An Attempt to Obtain Invariable Measures from the Mensuration of Time	1787
Copies of the Standard Troy Weight	1787

In addition to the donors listed above, other donations probably came from friends and correspondents of Franklin in the following list of those admitted to membership in the American Philosophical Society:

1773: Torbern Bergmann (Professor of Mathematics, Stockholm)
    Timothy, Baron de Klingstedt (Russia)
1774: Lord Stanhope (England)
    Lord Mahon (son of Lord Stanhope)
1775: Marquis de Condorcet (listed again in 1786)
    Barbeu Dubourg, translator of Franklin's works
1781: Chevalier de Chastellux
1784: Count de Vergennes (French Foreign Minister)
    John Hyacinth de Magellan (London)
1785: Richard Price (London)
1786: Duc de La Rochefoucauld (Paris)
    Jean L. G. Soulavie (Abbé)
    René G. Gastelier (Doctor of Physics, Montargis)
    Pierre J. G. Cabanis
    Louis Le Veillard
    Aimé A. J. Feutry (Mechanician, France)
    Benjamin Vaughan (London)
    Dr. Thomas Percival (Manchester)
    Jacques A. C. Charles
    Guillaume Grivel
1787: Sir Edward Newenham (Baronet of Ireland)
    Dr. John Coakley Lettsom (London)
    Sir Joseph Banks (President of Royal Society, London)
1789: J. Hector St. John (Michel Guillaume Jean de) Crèvecœur
    Princess Catherine Dashkov (St. Petersburg)[81]
Other names recommended by Franklin:
    Humbert (or Thibert?) Gerbier
    Eli de Beaumont[82]
    Le Begle du Presle

---

[81] American Philosophical Society, 1838: pp. 5-12.
[82] Library of Congress, Franklin MSS, No. 2316.

1770: Letter on silk culture
1774: Von Stæhlin's *Account of the Northern Archipelago lately discovered*
    J. Walsh's letter to Franklin "of the electric property of the Torpedo," pamphlet[84]
1780: Some "valuable books which I intend to present to the Society, but shall not send them till safer times." [85]
1782: The "new Encyclopædia" (French)[86]
1783: L'Abbé Soulavie's *Natural History S. of France*, 6 Vols.[87]
1788: A "specimen of the ancient shorthand"
    An engraving of the Duke de Chaulnes' improvement of Franklin's Electrical Kite
    F. A. Eckhardt's description of his Canal Dredger
    Proposals of the Society for the Encouragement of Arts, &c., of a premium for an invariable standard of Weights and Measures
    A description of the Chinese method of making large sheets of Paper
    An account of Ingenhousz's experiments on the heat-conducting power of Metals, under Franklin's direction[88]
    Franklin's letter (from Passy, September 22, 1782) to the Abbé Soulavie, "containing a new & ingenious theory of the formation of the Earth" [89]
1790: Legacy arranged by his will of 1788, *History of the Royal Academy of Sciences* at Paris, 91 volumes noted received by the Society on August 20.[90]

Books written by Franklin and listed in the 1824 catalogue of the American Philosophical Society were:

Experiments and observations on electricity (London, 1774).
Political, miscellaneous, and philosophical pieces, with plates (London, 1779).
Historical Review of the Constitution and Government of Pennsylvania (London, 1759) — Ascribed to Franklin at the time; financed and published by Franklin, but written by Richard Jackson.
Examination of Doctor B. Franklin, before an august Assembly, relating the repeal of the Stamp Act, &c. (1766).
The Pennsylvania Gazette, from January 13, 1742-3, to February 11, 1745-6 by B. Franklin, Philadelphia.
Plain Truth, or serious considerations on the present state of the City of Philadelphia and Province of Pennsylvania (1747).
Remarks on a late protest against the appointment of B. Franklin an agent for this Province (Philadelphia, 1764).
The case of Great Britain and America, addressed to the King and both houses of Parliament (London, 1769).
Rules for reducing a great empire to a small one (London, 1793, Reprinted).

---

[83] Smyth, 1905-1907: 6: p. 236.
[84] American Philosophical Society, 1885: *Proceedings* 22, 3: pp. 47, 88.
[85] Van Doren, 1945: p. 480.
[86] Smyth, 1905-1907: 8: p. 647.
[87] American Philosophical Society, 1885: *Proceedings* 22, 3: p. 118.
[88] *Ibid.*, p. 161.
[89] *Ibid.*, p. 165.
[90] *Ibid.*, p. 183.

Lettre a Monsieur David Le Roy contenant différentes observations sur la marine en mer a bord du Paquebot le London, Capt. Truxtun, du mois d'Août, 1785 (Paris, 1787).

"Philadelphia almanacs from 1719 to 1744 inclusive, collected by Dr B Franklin, and bound together in one volume. Among these are several printed by himself under the name of Richard Saunders or Poor Richard. The year 1730 is wanting."

Poor Richard's (Franklin's) Almanac for 1758, in which the Doctor s celebrated moral piece, *"The Way to Wealth,"* is published for the first time.

Franklin s *Works* 3 vols Philadelphia, 1818.

Letters of Franklin on the conduct of the executive, and the treaty negotiated by the Chief Justice of the United States with the Court of Great Britain (Philadelphia, 1795).[91]

COLLECTION OF FRANKLINIANA

After Franklin's death on April 17, 1790, the collection of Frankliniana began. On February 3, 1792, Richard Bache, son-in-law of Franklin, presented the chair which Franklin used when meetings were held in his house.[92] This was the famous stepladder chair

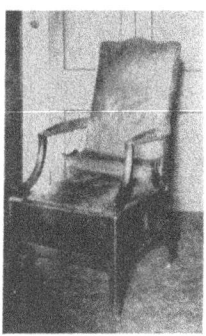

FIG. 6. Franklin s ladder-chair in the possession of the American Philosophical Society

which Franklin had invented for his own library to reach the higher levels of learning In order to acquire books which would be especially useful to the work of the Society, a committee was appointed to attend the sale of Franklin's library by Dufief in 1801. The minutes report an expenditure of $107.62 on October 2, $91 50 on October 16, and $20 on November 6. Then on March 18, 1803, the librarian, John Vaughan, reported that he had spent $89 15 at the Franklin library sale.[93]

Franklin s personal papers were longer in the process of collection. In 1840 the Fox collection was presented to the Society library, and gradually over the last century, the American Philosophical Society has become the chief depository of Franklin's papers. In 1936, over 1,100 items were purchased from the Bache family, in

[91] American Philosophical Society, 1824 *passim*.
[92] American Philosophical Society 1885 *Proceedings* 22, 3 p. 202
[93] *Ibid* pp 314-317 335.

1944 the Jane Mecom correspondence was acquired, and even more recently, the letters to Richard Jackson, colonial agent in England.[94] Other collections include Franklins correspondence with Catharine Ray Greene, Madame Brillon, and Francis Childs. Those papers that were in the possession of the American Philosophical Society in 1906 were gathered together by I. Minis Hays and listed chronologically in a five-volume work entitled *Calendar of the Papers of Benjamin Franklin in the Library of the American Philosophical Society* Currently, the Society is cooperating with the Yale University Press in the publication of all *The Papers of Benjamin Franklin*.

THE AMERICAN ACADEMY OF ARTS AND SCIENCES, BOSTON

The American Academy of Arts and Sciences was established at Boston in 1780, chiefly through the efforts of James Bowdoin. For thirty years Bowdoin had corresponded with Franklin on scientific matters, and with the successful example of the American Philosophical Society at Philadelphia, felt that it was time to organize a scientific society in the Boston area. Franklin was elected to membership in the American Academy on January 31, 1781 Notice of his nomination came from Bowdoin, its first president,[95] but a formal notice of election followed from Joseph Willard, with a catalogue of the officers, the act of incorporation and the President's oration. Franklin was still in France at this time, and Joseph Willard asked him to send information on recent French publications on "natural Philosophy, Mathematics and Astronomy," with a special request for observations of certain eclipses made at the Royal Observatory at Paris.[96] In a letter to Samuel Cooper, a fellow member, Franklin promised that he would gather whatever materials he could.

I am very sensible of the honour done me by the American Academy of Arts and Sciences, in choosing me one of their Members I wish I could be of some Utility in promoting the noble Design of their Institution. Perhaps I may, by sending them from time to time some of the best Publications that appear here. I shall begin to make a collection for them.[97]

Franklin made the necessary contact with the French Royal Observatory and continued to forward French materials to Boston as long as he stayed in France.[98]

Franklin also introduced individual French scientists and their writings to the Boston American Academy One of these was Antoine Court de Gebelin, a philol-

[94] Lingelbach, 1945 pp. 60, 65.
[95] American Philosophical Society. Franklin MSS, 21 18 (Jan. 11, 1781).
[96] *Ibid.* 21 · 55 and 86 (Feb 9 and March 1, 1781)
[97] Smyth, 1905-1907 8 p 257
[98] American Philosophical Society Franklin MSS, 32 173 (Jeaurat to Franklin, Nov 13, 1784)

ogist interested in the possibility of similarities between the Phoenician and the American Indian languages, an active member of the Académie des Inscriptions et Belles Lettres in Paris, and of the American Philosophical Society (1783). Franklin assured Court de Gebelin that "Our new American Society will be happy in the correspondence you mention, and when it is possible for me, I shall be glad to attend the meetings of your Society, which, I am sure, must be very instructive."[99]

Shortly before Franklin left France in 1785, he received his first piece of air mail, delivered by John Jeffries, who made a balloon flight from England to France on January 7. Jeffries wrote an account of his flight and sent a copy to Franklin. Franklin, in turn, sent a copy to James Bowdoin, as "it might afford some Amusement to you and to your Society;" the account was not for publication because it was under consideration by the Royal Society of London. Franklin also sent his *Maritime Observations* to Jonathan Williams to be read before the Boston society, but warned that the piece was being printed in the second volume of the American Philosophical Society *Transactions,* and it would not be "proper" for the Boston society to print it.[100] Jonathan Williams had requested the piece on behalf of James Bowdoin. Franklin continued to supply the American Academy of Arts and Sciences with philosophical papers, sending four more in January, 1786, to Jonathan Williams to be communicated to Bowdoin. Among these was a description of his own invention of the "long Arm, a new Instrument for taking down Books from high Shelves."[101] (See Appendix for copy.)

The exchange between the two American scientific societies was carried on by Franklin, but he had just missed his own first copy of the *Memoirs* of the Boston society, by passing it somewhere in mid-ocean between Passy, France, and Philadelphia.[102]. The second volume of the American Philosophical Society *Transactions* fared not much better; two years after publication in 1786, it had still not reached Boston and had to be sent again.[103]

In his will of 1788, Franklin provided that his folio edition of *Les Arts et les Métiers* be given to the American Academy ("*American Philosophical Society,* established in New England").[104] Franklin described it to James Bowdoin as "voluminous, well executed, and may be useful in our country. . . . but if they have it already, I will substitute something else."[105] Bowdoin replied:

The french work sur les Arts, & les Metiers, which you mention you have bequeathed by your Will to our philosophical Society, the Society is not possessed of; and it is my wish, and without doubt will be theirs, . . . that they may for a long time be kept out of possession of it.[106]

THE CONNECTICUT ACADEMY OF ARTS AND SCIENCES, NEW HAVEN

The Connecticut Academy of Arts and Sciences was founded in New Haven in 1786. Representing the literary arts more than science, the Society chose Ezra Stiles, president of Yale, as its corresponding secretary. He wrote to Franklin in July, 1787, asking for a list of scientific societies in Europe to which they might apply for publications, with the idea that the Connecticut Academy would reciprocate when it published its first literary collections.[107] Franklin advised Ezra Stiles to wait until the Connecticut Academy could "send forth a Volume" before asking other societies for theirs.[108] However, Franklin did send a list of the European scientific societies, along with a duplicate made with a letterpress copier, and the second volume of *Transactions* of the American Philosophical Society. These were carried back by the Reverend Manasseh Cutler, who had just visited Franklin at Philadelphia.[109]

V. MEDICAL LIBRARIES

THE PENNSYLVANIA HOSPITAL

The Pennsylvania Hospital, America's first permanent hospital and home of the first American medical library,[1] was born from the inspiration of Dr. Thomas Bond and the promotion of Benjamin Franklin. Convinced of the need of a hospital to care for "poor sick Persons," Dr. Bond attempted to secure subscriptions for it, but met with little success. Franklin relates in his *Autobiography* the secret of securing public support.

In 1751. Dr. Thomas Bond, a particular Friend of mine, conceiv'd the Idea of establishing a Hospital in Philadelphia, . . . At length he came to me, with the Compliment that he found there was no such thing as carrying a public Spirited Project through, without my being concern'd in it; "for, says he, I am often ask'd by those to whom I propose Subscribing, Have you consulted Franklin upon this Business? and what does he think of it? And when I tell them that I have not, (supposing it rather out of your Line) they do not subscribe, but say they will consider of it." I enquir'd into the Nature, and probable

---

[99] Van Doren, 1945: pp. 507-509.
[100] Smyth, 1905-1907: **9**: pp. 479-480.
[101] Library of Congress, Franklin MSS, No. 1553 (Franklin to Jonathan Williams, February 12, 1786). Sparks, 1836-1840: **6**: pp. 562-564.
[102] Van Doren, 1945: p. 664.
[103] American Philosophical Society, Franklin MSS, **36**: 64 (James Bowdoin to Franklin, June 28, 1788).
[104] Van Doren, 1945: p. 691.

[105] Smyth, 1905-1907: **9**: p. 652.
[106] American Philosophical Society, Franklin MSS, **36**: 64 (June 28, 1788).
[107] *Ibid.* **35**: 90 (July 3).
[108] *Ibid.* **35**: 97 (Stiles to Franklin, July 31, 1787).
[109] Stiles, 1901: **3**: p. 272.
[1] Packard, 1938: p. 63.

FIG. 7. Pennsylvania Hospital. Engraving by W. Birch & Son, 1799. Courtesy of Independence National Historical Park.

Utility of his Scheme, and receiving from him a very satisfactory Explanation, I not only subscrib'd to it myself, but engag'd heartily in the Design of Procuring Subscriptions from others. Previous however to the Solicitation, I endeavoured to prepare the Minds of the People by writing on the Subject in the Newspapers, which was my usual Custom in such Cases, but which he had omitted.

The Subscriptions afterwards were more free and generous, but beginning to flag, I saw they would be insufficient without some Assistance from the Assembly, and therefore propos'd to petition for it, which was done.[2]

Meeting with some resistance both from citizens of the town and from the rural representatives of the Assembly, Franklin proposed a scheme whereby he pitted one faction against the other. He inserted a conditional clause in the bill which provided that the Pennsylvania Assembly would grant two thousand pounds for the building of a hospital if the sum of two thousand pounds was secured by private donations.

This Condition carried the Bill through; for the Members who had oppos'd the Grant, and now conceiv'd they might have the Credit of being charitable without the Expence, agreed to its Passage; And then in soliciting Subscriptions among the People we urg'd the conditional Promise of the Law as an additional Motive to give, since every Man's Donation would be doubled. Thus the Clause work'd both ways. . . . And I do not remember any of my political Manoeuvres, the Success of which gave me at the time more Pleasure. Or that in after-thinking of it, I more easily excus'd my-self for having made some Use of Cunning.[3]

The hospital opened in temporary quarters in February, 1752, but a cornerstone with an inscription by Franklin was laid for a permanent building on May 28, 1755.[4] Sixty years later, Dr. Benjamin Rush recalled the day of the cornerstone laying:

On their way Dr. Bond lamented that the Hospital would allure strangers from all the then provinces in America. "Then," said Dr. Franklin "our institution will be more useful than we intended it to be."[5]

---

[2] *Autobiography*, 1964: pp. 199-200.
[3] *Ibid.*, p. 201.
[4] Labaree, 1959—: 4: pp. 110-111.
[5] Rush, 1951: 2: p. 1063.

Franklin's original contribution to the Pennsylvania Hospital was £25.[6] He served on the Board of Managers from 1751 to 1757, as its first secretary from 1751 to 1752, and as president of the Board of Managers from 1755 to 1757. He was given power of attorney while he was in England from 1757 to 1762 in order to solicit donations.[7] In 1754 he wrote *Some Account of the Pennsylvania Hospital* to publicize the worthy purpose of the institution. One thousand and five hundred copies were ordered printed by Franklin and Hall,[8] and they were distributed by the Board of Managers advantageously. In this account, Franklin mentioned "the pious Books that have been left in the Hospital, recommended to the Perusal of the Patients."[9] However, although there was established later a medical library for the hospital staff and students, it appears that there was no organized library for the patients. Not until 1810 did Dr. Benjamin Rush recommend a supervised reading program for mentally disturbed patients.[10]

In 1757 Franklin left for England, and therefore resigned from the Board of Managers. He kept their needs in mind, however, and visited hospitals when he toured England and Scotland. He collected from these hospitals some accounts of their rules and regulations, and sent them back to his friend, Hugh Roberts.

Possibly you may find a useful hint or two in some of them. I believe we shall be able to make a small collection here; but I cannot promise it will be very considerable.[11]

The hospital started a museum in 1757 with a skeleton donated by Deborah Morris. The museum was kept in a locked room except when visitors were admitted for a fee; it became the basis of medical lectures later on. In November, 1762, Dr. John Fothergill, London Quaker physician, donated seven cases of casts and anatomical drawings, valued at £350.[12] About the same time, Franklin returned to Philadelphia, and notified Dr. Fothergill that the drawings and casts had arrived safely, except the breaking of some of the glasses, which the Managers repaired.[13] Dr. Fothergill was a close associate of Franklin in London, having attended Franklin in his first illness there, and was also a fellow member of the Royal Society.

It was Dr. John Fothergill, also, who is credited with starting the organized medical library, through his donation of a book entitled *An Experimental History of the Materia Medica* by William Lewis, F.R.S., published in London. It was presented by William Logan, "lately returned from London," to a meeting of the Board of Managers on July 27, 1762.[14] The following May, the medical staff proposed that student fees be applied "to the founding of a Medical Library in the said Hospital, which we judge will tend greatly to the Advantage of the Pupils & the Honour of the Institution." The proposal was signed by Dr. Thomas Bond and Dr. Phineas Bond (both long-time members of the Library Company), Dr. Cadwallader Evans, and Dr. Thomas Cadwalader, who served as director of the Library Company for twenty-four years, and founded the public library in Trenton, New Jersey. This was a library-minded staff. The Board of Managers accepted the proposal with the stipulation that they were to approve books for purchase and to regulate loans. The Managers also agreed to provide suitable accommodations for the books, which were at first kept in the "Board Room," located in the east wing of the hospital.[15] In April, 1767, the "suitable accommodations" were expanded by adding another bookcase.[16]

Franklin was back in America for a two-year period beginning November, 1762. This was the period of the organization of the medical library. Franklin was no longer an official of the hospital, and since he was busy with post-office and Pennsylvania Assembly affairs, it is not certain that he had any part in shaping the policies and regulations. However, he was kept informed, since the doctors and members of the Board were old friends. After he returned to England, Dr. Cadwallader Evans reported the progress of the medical library, and Franklin answered on May 5, 1767:

I am pleased with your scheme of a Medical Library at the Hospital; and I fancy I can procure you some donations among my medical friends here, if you will send me a catalogue of what books you already have. Enclosed I send you the only book of the kind in my possession here, having just received it as a present from the author. It is not yet published to be sold, and will not be for some time, till the second part is ready to accompany it.[17]

Six months later, Dr. Evans returned a letter thanking Franklin for the "Pamphlet" and the interest he had taken in the scheme, and sending him the catalogue which he had requested.[18] In 1770 Franklin passed on another gift from Dr. John Fothergill, a "Treatise on the Materia Medica in two volumes quarto, Entitled Lectures on the Materia Medica, Containing the Natural History of Drugs their Values and Doses &c., published from the Manuscript of the late Dr. Charles Alston," edited by John Hope, both professors at the University of Edinburgh.[19]

In 1774 the Managers of the Pennsylvania Hospital

---

[6] Labaree, 1959—: **5**: p. 328.
[7] Morton, 1895: pp. 42, 405-409.
[8] Labaree, 1959—: **4**: p. 111.
[9] *Ibid.* **5**: p. 325.
[10] Rush, 1951: **2**: p. 1064.
[11] Van Doren, 1945: p. 127.
[12] Morton, 1895: pp. 356-359.
[13] American Philosophical Society, Franklin MSS, **45**: 25 (Dec. 8, 1762).
[14] Malin, 1830 (Manuscript), Historical Society of Pennsylvania, No. 989: p. 1 (not numbered).
[15] Packard, 1938: p. 64.
[16] Morton, 1895: p. 348.
[17] Smyth, 1905-1907: **5**: p. 24.
[18] American Philosophical Society, Franklin MSS, **2**: 104 (Nov. 20, 1767).
[19] Packard, 1938: p. 66.

asked William Strahan, who had served the Library Company, to be their book agent in London. The Managers set up a standing order:

When any new Books or Essays on any branch of Medicine appear we shall be glad to have Copies of such of them sent as are of small Cost and an acc't of such as are more costly than if we judge them necessary we may send for them.

Strahan accepted the agency, and not only filled the order compiled by the medical staff, but also donated books worth £100. After his death in 1785, the Managers were forced to seek another agent. This time they sent the order to Peter Wynne, specifying the ship to transport the books freight-free by agreement with the owners, and emphasizing

as they are for our Library and will be handled often, request that you will attend particularly to the binding that it may be both Neat and strong: . . .

Their next agent in 1790 was Dr. John Coakley Lettsom, a very close friend of Dr. John Fothergill (who had died in 1780), and also a friend of Franklin. Dr. Lettsom not only agreed to select and purchase the books, but also donated other books to the medical library.[20] Franklin's death in 1790 may have strengthened Dr. Lettsom's natural desire to patronize the Pennsylvania Hospital.

The medical library of the hospital was quite small compared to other Philadelphia libraries. It was not even as large as the private medical library of Dr. William Logan, a Bristol physician, whose books were shipped to Philadelphia, used by Dr. George Logan, and eventually deposited in the Loganian Library and in the Library Company.[21] When the first catalogue of the hospital library was printed in 1790, there were only 528 volumes. The Managers felt that they could not spare even one. They restricted the loans to the Managers, physicians, and past or present students attending the hospital, and required a promissory note and a deposit of the value of the book. In 1788, after discovering that a number of books were missing, they advertised in Hall and Sellers' *Pennsylvania Gazette* to request the return of the books, and strengthened their stand that the "Apothecary is ordered on no pretence to lend a book out of the Medical Library to a Manager, Physician, or to any other person, without taking a note or sufficient deposit." They printed and distributed the loan regulations agreed upon December 28, 1789, and finally printed 600 copies of their first catalogue in May, 1790. These were sold to students, but copies were given to Dr. Lettsom and to the Managers and the staff physicians.[22]

According to the regulations printed in the catalogue, the library was open only two mornings a week, from nine till eleven o'clock. There were about six reference books which could not be taken out, and therefore, their use was restricted severely by the limited hours. No person could borrow more than two books at a time.[23]

The 1790 catalogue failed to list many obvious donations as such. Among the books listed as donated by Dr. Lettsom were William May's *Essay on Pulmonary Consumptions* and three of his own works — *History of the Origin of Medicine* (London, 1778), *The Works of John Fothergill* (London, 1784), and *Memoirs of John Fothergill* (4th ed., London, 1786).[24] The library also had *Transactions* from the American Philosophical Society, the American Academy of Arts and Sciences (Boston), and the Royal Society of Edinburgh. Many of the Pennsylvania doctors went to Edinburgh for their medical education.

Franklin did not live to see this first printed catalogue, but he had remembered the Pennsylvania Hospital in his will. He had accumulated a lot of small outstanding debts in his business as stationer, printer, and postmaster, dating as far back as 1757 and not collected because he was in Europe for so many years.

These, as they are stated in my great folio Ledger E, I bequeath to the *contributors to the Pennsylvania Hospital,* hoping that those debtors, and the descendants of such as are deceased, who now, as I find, make some difficulty of satisfying such antiquated demands as just debts, may, however, be induced to pay or give them as charity to that excellent institution. I am sensible that much must inevitably be lost, but I hope something considerable may be recovered.[25]

Unfortunately, this bequest did not work out as Franklin had hoped. The Pennsylvania Hospital Contributors declined the legacy of old debts, because the debts were too small, too old, and too difficult to collect.[26]

One of the staff physicians of the Pennsylvania Hospital was Dr. Benjamin Rush, who had studied at Edinburgh and had dedicated his doctoral dissertation primarily to Benjamin Franklin,[27] for Franklin's aid and introductions while an agent in England. Dr. Rush, like Franklin, disapproved of the classical languages, Latin and Greek,[28] and his feelings on the subject undoubtedly affected the book selection policy of the Pennsylvania Hospital library. Rush and Franklin had also corresponded upon the possibility of transmitting colds through books,[29] and Franklin had included "Old Libraries, and damp old Books" in his "Preparatory Notes and Hints for Writing a Paper Concerning What Is Called Catching Cold."[30]

---

[20] Morton, 1895: pp. 347, 350.
[21] Tolles, 1953: p. 16.
[22] Morton, 1895: pp. 350-352.
[23] Pennsylvania Hospital, 1790-1794: pp. 3-5.
[24] *Ibid.,* pp. 39, 45, 49.
[25] Van Doren, 1945: pp. 692-693.
[26] Morton, 1895: pp. 68-69.
[27] Rush, 1948: p. 43 n. 12.
[28] Rush, 1951: 1: pp. 531-532. Rush, 1905: p. 27.
[29] Rush, 1951: 1: pp. 79-80. Van Doren, 1945: p. 294.
[30] Smyth, 1905-1907: 6: p. 66.

MEDICAL SOCIETY OF NEW FAIRFIELD, CONNECTICUT

In 1780 James Potter, President of the Medical Society of New Fairfield, Connecticut, wrote both to Franklin and to the Royal Medical Society of France and asked that a regular correspondence be established between the two societies. "The case is committed to the care of Dr. Franklin. The request, if granted, will have a salutary effect upon the medical profession in the United States, and will assist the Society in its efforts to be recognized by the Legislators."[31] Franklin had accepted membership in the Royal Medical Society in 1777.

The Medical Society of New Fairfield claimed to be the "First Medical Society in the Thirteen United States of America." However, it was not the first American medical society, for one established in Philadelphia in 1765 eventually became a part of the American Philosophical Society.

VI. GOVERNMENTAL LIBRARIES

NEW YORK CORPORATION LIBRARY

The New York Corporation Library was established in 1730 with the arrival of a huge bequest of 1642 volumes from the Reverend Dr. John Millington, English clergyman. To these, the city of New York added a collection of 238 volumes given by the Reverend John Sharpe in 1715 to establish a "Publick Library." Sharpe had drawn up specific suggestions for regulations for his proposed public library, but the books were held in trust by individuals while awaiting legislative support. The Sharpe collection was under the care of Governor Burnet in the spring of 1724,[1] and may have been a part of the Governor's conversation with young Benjamin Franklin, a lad of eighteen, traveling back to Philadelphia with a great load of books.

The then Governor of N York, Burnet, Son of Bishop Burnet hearing from the Captain that a young Man, one of his Passengers, had a great many Books, desired he would bring me to see him. I waited upon him accordingly, and should have taken Collins with me but that he was not sober. The Governor treated me with great Civility, show'd me his Library, which was a very large one, and we had a good deal of Conversation about Books and Authors.[2]

The Sharpe collection was small enough to be ignored by the New York officials. The Millington collection stirred them into action, and a room was prepared on the second floor of the City Hall to accommodate the New York Corporation Library. Alexander Lamb served as "Keeper of the Library" from 1734 to 1742, but after the end of his term of service, the dust began to collect upon the books.[3] Evidently the city of New York was unwilling to spend any money on the upkeep or care of the Corporation Library. On April 19, 1745, the city received a petition from James Parker, which began:

Whereas the Corporation is possessed of a Valuable Library which May be of very Great Use And Service to the Inhabitants of the Province; but More Especially to those of the City if a Library keeper was Appointed Under proper Regulations, the want of which at present Not only deprives Many persons of the Use of the Said Books, But Subjects the Books to be hurt Or Destroyed by the Dust and paper Worm Wherefore James Parker Printer for this Government Humbly proposes to Take the Care And Charge of the Said Library As Library keeper during the pleasure of the Corporation.[4]

James Parker at that time was a printing partner of Benjamin Franklin, publishing the *New York Gazette (Revived in the Weekly Post-Boy)* and public printer for New York.[5] He had worked for Franklin in Philadelphia, and had signed a partnership agreement on February 20, 1741/2, in which Franklin was to furnish a press and types, transport them to New York, pay one-third of the business expense and receive one-third of the profits. In the partnership agreement, Parker was not to engage in "any other Business but Printing, ... occasional Buying and Selling excepted."[6] This probably means that Franklin knew about and approved Parker's activities in the New York Corporation Library.

James Parker entered this venture with the New York Corporation Library for profit, charging a fee for the rental of the books, and assuming the cost of their care and repair. Whether or not any of the profits, if indeed there were any, went to Franklin under the terms of the partnership agreement is not known. Parker proposed:

1. to print a catalogue,
2. to charge six pence a week for loaning the books, with the borrowers assuming financial liability of double the value of the book,
3. to limit the loans to three books at a time for a period between a week and a month,
4. to permit the Common Council of New York free use with the same liability as other borrowers,
5. to attend the library once a week for two hours,
6. to receive the "Proffitts," keep the books in repair, and replace lost copies "at his Own Expence without any Charge to the Corporation."

The city officials were glad to be relieved of the burden of the city's library, and they approved the

---

[31] Hays, 1908: 2: p. 247; 4: p. 305.
[1] Keep, 1909: pp. 53-59.
[2] *Autobiography*, 1964: p. 85.

[3] Keep, 1909: pp. 64-73.
[4] New York (City), 1905: 5: p. 142.
[5] Van Doren, 1938: p. 120.
[6] Labaree, 1959—: 2: pp. 341-345.

petition.[7] It was August before James Parker took the first step of advertising for missing books. And it was not until the following June (1746) that he at last offered to the public free copies of his catalogue "to any Lovers of Reading, that will send and desire the same." The conditions of the loan had been changed to *"Four Pence Half-penny* per Week," limited to one book or one set each time. The library was opened on Tuesday afternoons at 4 o'clock.

In January, 1746/7, James Parker advertised in his paper the following offer:

As several Persons have signified their Desire of hiring Books from the Library belonging to the Corporation of this City; but the Time of Attendance being short, and the cold Weather rendering it uncomfortable, they neglect it; this is to give Notice, that on any Person's signifying a Day before-hand what Book they would have, they may at any Time have such Book of the Printer hereof, they giving the usual Security for the same. Catalogues to be had for sending for.

Fire broke out at the City Hall on January 14, 1746/7, but the minutes of the Common Council do not mention any damage to the Corporation Library.[8] Even so, public interest lagged, for the collection was not current and there was no provision for ordering new materials. James Parker turned away from the Corporation Library back to more profitable enterprises. News of the failure had reached Philadelphia by July, and James Logan tried to console Franklin with a note that he was "sorry thy Friend Parker could have no help to range their Library into some tolerable order."[9]

In 1754 the Corporation Library, having "for some years past been shut up, & the Books contained in it become of little or no advantage to the Public," was taken over by the New York Society Library, a subscription library, which promised to add new and fresh material to the collection. About 2,000 volumes of the Corporation Library were transferred to the custody of the New York Society Library; some of these were boxed and stored to make room for new books of contemporary interest. James Parker, glad enough to let somebody else take over the care and trouble of keeping the books, became a subscriber of the New York Society Library.[10]

PENNSYLVANIA ASSEMBLY LIBRARY

Much of Franklin's public life was spent in the service of the Pennsylvania Assembly. Beginning in 1736, he was appointed clerk; in 1751 he was elected a member; in 1757 he was sent to England as an agent of the Assembly to protest the exemption of the Proprietary estates from taxation. For the next eighteen years, except for two, he remained in England, serving Pennsylvania and several other colonies as agent. Early in the long career of service, he became public printer for Pennsylvania, "Printing the Votes, Laws, Paper Money, and other occasional Jobbs for the Public, that on the whole were very profitable."[11] He printed the two-volume edition of *The Charters and Laws of Pennsylvania* in 1742, a copy of which the Assembly donated to the Library Company.[12]

The Pennsylvania Assembly met in the State House, which is now preserved as a national historical shrine known as Independence Hall. This building was started in 1732 and took about twenty years to complete. By September, 1735, the Assembly room was in use, even though not finished. While the main building was being constructed, office wings on each side were also under construction to furnish a safe place for keeping public papers. In 1739, while serving as clerk to the Assembly, Franklin petitioned for permission to deposit the books of the Library Company in a room on the upper floor of the west wing.[13] The Library Company's books remained there until 1773, and this was the first library used by the Assembly.

The Pennsylvania Assembly started its own library on February 5, 1745/6 when it

Ordered, That the Clerk send to England for the best Edition of the Statutes at large, for the Use of the House, and also for some large Maps (one of *North America*) to be hung up in the Assembly Room.[14]

The "Clerk" designated was Benjamin Franklin. It was several months before he sent the order to William Strahan, asking that he

send me two setts of Popple's Mapps of N. America one bound the other in Sheets, they are for our Assembly; they also want the Statutes at large, but as I hear they are risen to an extravagant Price, I would have you send me word what they will cost before you send them.... P.S. I forgot to mention, that there must be some other large Map of the whole World, or of Asia, or Africa, or Europe, of equal Size with Popple's to match it; they being to be hung, one on each side the Door in the Assembly Room; if none can be had of equal Size, send some Prospects of principal Cities, or the like, to be pasted on the Sides, to make up the Bigness.[15]

After eighteen months had elapsed, and the maps had still not arrived, Franklin repeated the order:

I must desire you to send per first Opportunity the Maps formerly wrote for, viz. Popple's large One of North America pasted on Rollers; Ditto bound in a Book: and 8 or 10 other Maps of equal Size if to be had; they are

---

[7] New York (City), 1905: **5**: pp. 142-143.
[8] Keep, 1909: pp. 74-76. New York (City), 1905: **5**: pp. 190-191.
[9] Labaree, 1959—: **3**: p. 147. Labaree footnotes "Parker" as "Not identified," but the name and date tie so closely into the affairs of the New York Corporation Library, that it could hardly be any other than James Parker.
[10] Keep, 1909: pp. 76-80, 155.
[11] *Autobiography*, 1964: p. 171.
[12] Library Company of Philadelphia, 1807: p. 344.
[13] U. S. National Park Service, 1956: pp. 2-3.
[14] Pennsylvania, 1931-1935: **4**: p. 3080.
[15] Labaree, 1959—: **3**: p. 77.

FIG. 8. State House at Philadelphia about 1750. Courtesy of the Historical Society of Pennsylvania.

for the long Gallery and the Assembly Room in the Statehouse. If none so large are to be got, let Prospects of Cities, Buildings, &c. be pasted round them, to make them as large.[16]

Finally, two years after the date of the original order, the maps were received in April, 1748.[17]

In February, 1752, the Assembly ordered a room built adjoining the southeast corner of the building to be used for committee work and to house its library; it was completed the following year. According to a contemporary description, it was

a very elegant apartment. It is ornamented with a stucco ceiling, and chimney places. Round the room are glass cases, in which the books are deposited. These books consist of all the laws of England made in these later years, and besides these history and poetry. The Assembly only have recourse to this library. There is likewise deposited a most beautiful bust in wax of Thomas Penn Esqr, one of the Proprietors of the Province, which was sent as a present to the Assembly by the Lady Juliana Penn.[18]

With a special room now available, new books were ordered. On August 21, 1752, £170 was paid to Isaac Norris, Speaker, "towards purchasing Books, and Window-glass."[19] Franklin was appointed with the Speaker to procure books and maps on January 16, 1753:

The Speaker and *Benjamin Franklin* are requested to procure such Books and Maps as they may think suitable and necessary for the Use of this House; and it is
Ordered, That the Trustees of the Loan-Office do supply them with such Sums of Money as they may require for that Purpose; which shall be allowed by the Committee of Accounts, in their next Settlement with the said Trustees.[20]

These books came to the grand total of £850, approved by the House on September 11, 1753.[21]

During this period, Pennsylvania politics were rocked by controversies between Governor Morris and the Assembly over the right to tax the proprietary estates. The Assembly found Benjamin Franklin one of its most forceful speakers in this matter and in two replies to the Governor dated August 19 and September 29, 1755, the Assembly presented arguments extracted from the 23-volume work of Charles Viner, *A General Abridgment of Law and Equity, Alpha-*

---

[16] *Ibid.* 3: p. 214.
[17] *Ibid.* 3: p. 77 n. 3, p. 321.
[18] Jordan, 1899: p. 418.

[19] Pennsylvania, 1931-1935: 4: p. 3526.
[20] *Ibid.* 4: p. 3543.
[21] *Ibid.* 4: p. 3607.

betically Digested under Proper Titles, with Notes . . . to the Whole.

We find in *Viner's* Abridgment, an allowed Book, Title *Descent of Lands,* . . . arguments that a King (and therefore also proprietors) may own private lands (therefore subject to tax) as well as political lands by virtue of his title. Governor Morris fired back a hasty reply, and the impatient Assembly retorted:

If the Governor had given himself the Trouble of looking into *Viner* under the Title we mentioned, . . .[22]

Thus Franklin and other members of the Assembly were making full use of their new and costly library. The first librarian was chosen on December 26, 1754.

A Petition from *Charles Norris,* of the City of *Philadelphia,* was presented to the House and read, setting forth, that the Petitioner is informed that some of the Members of this House have lately represented the Necessity of having a Person to take Care of the Library belonging to the Assembly; the Petitioner therefore begs Leave to offer himself for that Service.
And the House taking the same into Consideration, *Resolved,* That *Charles Norris* be Keeper of the Assembly Library, and that he observe such Directions therein as shall be hereafter given him by this House.[23]

Even after Morris was replaced as governor, the Assembly still could not be pacified, and eventually, in 1757, sent Franklin to England as its agent. Once there, Franklin took care of the Assembly's library requests as well as the Assembly's petitions to the proprietors. He sent back pamphlets for the Speaker, purchased *Votes* of the House of Commons,[24] and filled a special request from Samuel Rhoads for separate printing of statutes relating to canals.[25] For the members of the Assembly, he sent fifty copies each of two publications he had financed — "Enquirys" (Charles Thomson's *Enquiry into the Causes of the Alienation of the Delaware and Shawonese Indians from the British Interest)* and "Reviews" *(Historical Review of the Constitution and Government of Pennsylvania).* In addition, 225 copies of the *Enquirys* and 450 more copies of the *Reviews* were sent for distribution in Pennsylvania and other colonies.[26] Both of these pamphlets were severely critical of proprietary government in Pennsylvania. Franklin also arranged for the purchase and shipment of a telescope ordered by the Assembly for the purpose of viewing the transit of Venus in 1769.[27]

The "Assembly Library" was also known as the "State Library" and the "Pennsylvania Library." As its usefulness became more evident, it received more attention from the legislators. The keeper, Charles Norris, had died in 1766. In 1767 the Clerk, Charles Moore, was ordered to make a catalogue of the books and have "Assembly of Pennsylvania" stamped in gilt letters on their covers. In 1773 a committee was appointed to draft regulations for use of the library and to advertise for any missing books.[28] Its books were used by the Second Continental Congress, which convened on May 10, 1775, in the Assembly room of the Pennsylvania State House. Franklin was a delegate to this Second Continental Congress, having arrived just a few days before from England. There he witnessed the use of the Assembly library room to cloak the modesty of George Washington, who darted into the library room when his name was proposed by John Adams for the commission of General and Commander-in-Chief of the Army. After being elected unanimously, Washington returned to the Assembly room and accepted the commission. During the war, the Pennsylvania Assembly met on the second floor of the State House so that the Continental Congress might use the first floor. Both legislative bodies found frequent need of consulting the British statutes in the library room. There were also times when the legislators were pushed out of the State House entirely by British troops quartered there during their occupation of Philadelphia, and by the hospitalization of wounded American soldiers.[29]

After Franklin returned from France in 1785, he again had occasion to utilize the Pennsylvania Assembly Library in fulfilling his official duties as President of the Supreme Executive Council of Pennsylvania for three years, and as a member of the Federal Constitutional Convention in 1787.

GENERAL ASSEMBLY OF RHODE ISLAND

In 1779 Franklin sent to the General Assembly of Rhode Island a six-volume edition of Berenget's *History of Geneva.* On October 5, the gift was acknowledged by Governor William Greene, husband of Catharine Ray Greene, who had been a correspondent of Franklin's for many years.

The General Assembly of this State received a letter from Mr Williams in your behalf of March 10th with a Package of books containing the History of Geneva by M. Berenget in Six Volums, as a Present to and for their use and benefit, for which they have requested me to return you their Sincere Thanks, and to inform you that they shall ever acknowledge The favour with gratitude as it greatly tends to discover your good Intentions to Promote the Publick welfare.[30]

Just what occasioned this gift is not known. Franklin's sister, Jane Mecom, had taken refuge at the Gov-

---

[22] *Ibid.* **5**: pp. 3988, 4026.
[23] *Ibid.* **5**: p. 3801.
[24] Eddy, 1931: pp. 104, 114. Smyth, 1905-1907: **3**: p. 434.
[25] Biddle, 1895: p. 69.
[26] Smyth, 1905-1907: **3**: p. 478. Sparks, 1836-1840: **7**: p. 209. Van Doren, 1938: pp. 284-286.
[27] American Philosophical Society, Franklin MSS, **2**: 179 (Thomas Bond to Franklin, June 7, 1769).

[28] Lamberton, 1918: pp. 216-219.
[29] U. S. National Park Service, 1956: pp. 13-19.
[30] Roelker, 1949: pp. 100-101.

ernor's estate at Warwick at times of danger during the Revolutionary War. Perhaps this was Franklin's way of repaying the favor. Coincidentally, 1779 was the year in which Franklin sent his grandson, Benjamin Franklin Bache, to Geneva for his education as "a Republican and a Protestant." There may have been some connection between his selection of Geneva and the *History of Geneva* sent to Rhode Island. In a letter to the boy's father, Richard Bache (June 2, 1779), Franklin remarked that he would like to see *"the old thirteen United States* of Switzerland."[31]

UNITED STATES CONGRESS

The Second Continental Congress convened on May 10, 1775, a few days after Benjamin Franklin arrived home from England. His days as colonial agent were over, and as a delegate, he was swept immediately into the activities of Congress. When the Proceedings of Congress were published, Franklin sent a copy to His Most Serene Highness, Don Gabriel of Bourbon (Spain), suggesting that it "may be a subject of some Curiosity at your Court."[32] Another copy went to Charles W. F. Dumas at the Hague, later United States secret agent, for translation into French. On December 9, 1775, Franklin acknowledged the receipt and approval of these translations, and thanked Dumas greatly for his gift of Vattel's *Law of Nations (Droits des Gens; ou, Principes de la Loi Naturelle Appliqués à la Conduite et aux Affaires des Nations et des Souverains* (1758).

It came to us in good season, when the circumstances of a rising state make it necessary frequently to consult the law of nations. Accordingly, that copy which I kept ... has been continually in the hands of the members of our Congress, now sitting, who are much pleased with your notes and preface, and have entertained a high and just esteem for their author. Your manuscript, *"Idée sur le Gouvernement et la Royauté"* is also well relished, and may, in time, have its effect. I thank you, likewise, for the other smaller pieces, which accompanied Vattel. *"Le court Exposé de ce qui est passé entre la Cour Britanique et les Colonies,"* &c. being a very concise and clear statement of facts, will be reprinted here for the use of our new friends in Canada.[33]

While in France from 1776 to 1785, Franklin sent Congress anything he thought might be useful to them in directing the war. Among these was a translation of the Amsterdam Resolutions on the proposed increase of the army, sent at the suggestion of Dumas, the translator.[34] He also sent maps of various kinds;[35] books for Robert Morris, the Superintendent of Finance;[36] a letter-copying machine for the Secretary of Congress, Charles Thomson;[37] books, political publications and papers for Robert Livingston, first Secretary for Foreign Affairs;[38] and for Benjamin Lincoln, Secretary of War, all the information he could get on "the state of the pay, rations, and subsistence of the officers and men in the service of France, Spain, and the Emperor of Germany."[39]

In a partial list covering Franklin's personal expense account with Congress, the following payments were made for books and periodicals:

1777: Feb. 11	Affairs d'Angleterre	36 livres
May 1	Books of Cavalry for Congress	315 livres
May 8	The Accoutrement of Troupes	69 livres
Oct. 14	Subscription for Affairs d'Angleterre	24 livres
1778: May 21	Blank Books & Maps	16 livres 10s.
June 9	Books and political Pamphlets	75 livres
June 15	Subscription for Courier de l'Europe	48 livres
July 4	5 Volumes of Atlas maritime (for pub. Use)	120 livres[40]

Once peace was declared, and Franklin could think of other things, he proposed the publication of a French translation of the *Constitutions of the United States of America,* printed by the U.S. Congress in 1781. It would be an octavo volume containing the state constitutions, the Articles of Confederation, the treaty with France, and "no foreign matter." The translating was done by the Duke de La Rochefoucauld; permission was granted by the French Foreign Minister, Vergennes, who communicated with the "Keeper of the Seals" so that the work could go forth without delay. The printer, Pierres, was allowed

to commence an impression of this work, on condition of his sending the sheets, as fast as they shall be printed, to M. de Neville, the director-general of the press, in order that he may intrust them to a censor for examination. The rules relative to the press make this last formality indispensable.[41]

Franklin's next step was to choose the proper binding:

I desire to have 50 of the 8vos bound in Calf and letter'd, and 50 half bound, that is, between Pasteboards with a Sheepskin Back, and Letter'd, but not cut. I desire also 6 of the 4tos copies bound in Morocco.[42]

On July 24, 1783, Franklin was able to present to Count de Vergennes one copy for the Count and one copy for King Louis XVI.[43] He did the same for all

---

[31] Van Doren, 1945: pp. 468, 471.
[32] Smyth, 1905-1907: 6: p. 437.
[33] *Ibid.* 6: pp. 432-433.
[34] Hays, 1908: 1: p. 522.
[35] *Ibid.* 2: p. 151 (Capitaine to Franklin, Oct. 8, 1779).
[36] Smyth, 1905-1907: 8: p. 404.
[37] Sparks, 1836-1840: 9: pp. 47, 77.
[38] *Ibid.* 9: pp. 163, 179, 444. Smyth, 1905-1907: 8: pp. 405-406.
[39] Sparks, 1836-1840: 9: p. 413.
[40] Bigelow, 1887-1889: 6: pp. 228-231, 236.
[41] Sparks, 1836-1840: 9: pp. 503, 508.
[42] Smyth, 1905-1907: 9: pp. 47-48.
[43] *Ibid.* 9: p. 73.

the other countries represented at the French court — one copy for the Foreign Minister and another for his sovereign. Franklin also sent a copy to Thomas Mifflin, then President of the Congress, with the following explanation:

> The extravagant Misrepresentations of our Political State in foreign Countries, made it appear necessary to give them better Information, which I thought could not be more effectually and authentically done, than by publishing a Translation into French, now the most general Language in Europe, of the Book of Constitutions, which had been printed by Order of Congress. This I accordingly got well done, and presented two Copies, handsomely bound, to every foreign Minister here, one for himself, the other more elegant for his Sovereign. It has been well taken, and has afforded Matter of Surprise to many, who had conceived mean Ideas of the State of Civilization in America, and could not have expected so much political Knowledge and Sagacity had existed in our Wildernesses. And from all Parts I have the satisfaction to hear, that our Constitutions in general are much admired. I am persuaded, that this Step will not only tend to promote the Emigration to our Country of substantial People from all Parts of Europe, by the numerous Copies I shall disperse, but will facilitate our future Treaties with foreign Courts, who could not before know what kind of Government and People they had to treat with. As, in doing this, I have endeavoured to further the apparent Views of Congress in the first Publication, I hope it may be approved, and the Expence allowed. I send herewith one of the Copies.[44]

Another copy had gone to Robert Livingston with a letter pointing out:

> It is particularly a Matter of Wonder, that, in the Midst of a cruel War raging in the Bowels of our Country, our Sages should have the Firmness of Mind to sit down calmly and form such compleat Plans of Government. They add considerably to the Reputation of the United States.[45]

Franklin referred to this edition of the *Constitutions* in his essay, "Information to Those Who Would Remove to America," and urged that it be read by those "who desire to understand the state of government in America."[46]

In representing the U.S. Congress to France, Franklin was called upon by the public as well as by the court. He struck commemorative medals of American independence, and the Royal Military School of Paris requested one of these for its library.[47] He was asked to criticize a history of the American Revolution written by Hilliard d'Auberteuil,[48] and was sent six copies of that work to be forwarded to America. He was asked to recommend the Swiss printing house of Le Banneret d'Ostervald to the leading libraries in America,[49] and to advise Michel Macklot of Carlsruhe, who wished to establish a library and a printing house at Philadelphia for one of his sons. Macklot also sent a military work by Baron O'Cahill, which he thought would be useful to America.[50] Franklin was asked to transmit a work on botany donated by Charles Louis L'Héritier de Brutelle to the U.S. Congress,[51] and numerous copies of *Du Gouvernement des Mœurs* by Pollier, an "old Gentleman in Switzerland," who "desired to know of me how he could convey a Number of the printed Copies, to be distributed gratis among the Members of Congress.... There are good Things in the Work, but his Chapter on the Liberty of the Press appears to me to contain more Rhetorick than Reason."[52]

After Franklin returned to America, he helped form the new constitution for the United States and felt that this, too, would be a worthy representative of the U.S. Congress abroad. He sent copies to his friends and correspondents, including M. Le Veillard. Duc de La Rochefoucauld, and Gaetano Filangieri. He kept abreast of European publications on government, and ordered eight copies of Filangieri's *Science of Legislation*.[53] In 1788 he wrote to Dupont de Nemours, expressing the hope that the latter's work, *Ouvrage sur les Principes et le Bien des Républiques en général,* would be ready to be put into the hands of the first Congress of the United States under the new constitution; "such a work from your hand I am confident, though it may not be entirely followed, will afford useful hints, and produce advantages of importance." Franklin also pointed out the necessity for a French–English commercial dictionary explaining the names of the different articles of manufacture in the two languages; otherwise, French manufacturers would have difficulty in understanding orders from America.[54]

Although the Library of Congress was not established until 1800 by Act of Congress, some of these materials that Franklin provided to members of Congress must have survived and found their way into the collection. On January 24, 1783, the Continental Congress had considered a library committee report which recommended the purchase of a long list of books, including Franklin's works. The proposal was rejected because of lack of funds.[55] The same fate awaited Thomas Jefferson's proposal in 1803 to purchase part of Franklin's private library at a public sale. A small part of Franklin's library was acquired by Congress in 1815, in the library of Thomas Jefferson, who had purchased some of Franklin's books from N. G. Dufief in Philadelphia.[56]

---

[44]*Ibid.* 9: pp. 131-132.
[45]*Ibid.* 9: p. 71.
[46]Sparks, 1836-1840: 2: p. 473.
[47]Hays, 1908: 4: p. 100.
[48]Sparks, 1836-1840: 9: p. 444.
[49]Hays, 1908: 3: p. 16.
[50]*Ibid.* 3: p. 81.
[51]*Ibid.* 3: p. 258.
[52]Smyth, 1905-1907: 9: p. 326.
[53]*Ibid.* 9: pp. 618-619, 637.
[54]Sparks, 1836-1840: 10: pp. 351-352.
[55]Mood, 1948: pp. 12, 23.
[56]Eddy, 1924: pp. 215-216.

A great many of Franklin's letters and papers have since come into the possession of the Library of Congress, particularly the Stevens collection; these are calendared in Worthington C. Ford's *List of the Benjamin Franklin Papers in the Library of Congress* (Washington, D. C., Government Printing Office, 1905).

VII. RELIGIOUS AND CHARITABLE ORGANIZATIONS

FRANKLIN, MASSACHUSETTS

The town of Franklin, Massachusetts, was incorporated in 1778, after being set off from the town of Wrentham. Because word had just been received that Franklin had signed a treaty of amity and commerce with King Louis XVI and the hopes of the colonists were revived, the new town was named in Franklin's honor.[1] Several years later, officials of the town wrote to Franklin, suggesting that he consider donating a bell for their meeting house. Franklin replied through his grand-nephew, Jonathan Williams, that he hoped that the good people of Franklin would "Prefer Sense to Sound," and would accept instead a donation of a parish library. As soon as his sister, Jane Mecom of Boston, heard the news, she came forth with a suggestion for the prospective library:

I cant doubt but such a Library will consist of some Authers on Divine Subjects I therefor hope you will not think it too Presuming in me to Propose won, Viz Discourses on Personal Religion in two Volumes by Samuel Stnnett D D Printed in London by R Hett in 1769 I borrowed them and Read them with a grat deal of Pleasure and I think you yourself would if you could find time tho there may be many things in them not altogether Agreable to your Sentiments, which I sopose may be the case with Every Volume you Read on any Subject.[2]

Franklin included her suggestion when he wrote to Richard Price in London and asked him to choose the books.

Passy, March 18, 1785.
Dear Friend: My nephew, Mr. Williams, will have the honour of delivering you this line. It is to request from a list of a few good books to the value of about twenty-five pounds, such as are most proper to inculcate principles of sound religion and just government. A new town in the State of Massachusetts having done me the honour of naming itself after me, and proposing to build a steeple to their meeting-house if I would give them a bell, I have advised the sparing themselves the expense of a steeple for the present, and that they would accept of books instead of a bell, sense being preferable to sound. These are therefore intended as the commencement of a little parochial library for the use of a society of intelligent, respectable farmers such as our country people generally consist of. Besides your own works, I would only mention, on the recommendation of my sister, Stennett's *Discourses on Personal Religion*, which may be one book of the number, if you know and approve it.
With the highest esteem and respect, I am ever, my dear friend, yours most affectionately. . . .[3]

Richard Price had been a correspondent of Franklin's for many years, and was well known both as a theologian and political philosopher who had befriended the American colonies in his writings. Franklin was old and tired and ready to "go home and go to bed" at this time, just a few months before he left France forever. He knew he could trust Dr. Price's judgment in selecting books for a parochial library, but it seems strange that he restricted the books to religion and government and made no provision for science.

Dr. Price responded immediately to the challenge:

Mr. Williams has given me much pleasure by calling upon me, and bringing me a letter from you. I have, according to your desire, furnished him with a list of such books on religion and government, as I think some of the best, and added a present to the parish that is to bear your name, of such of my own publications as I think may not be unsuitable. Should this be the commencement of parochial libraries in the States, it will do great good.[4]

Dr. Price could hardly have been ignorant of the parochial libraries established by Dr. Thomas Bray and his Associates at the beginning of the century (see below), but many of those had been ravaged by the Revolutionary War.

Jane Mecom received a catalogue of the books and the comforting news that "Those you recommended of Dr. Stennet are among them."[5] The books were consigned to Jonathan Williams, but were slow in coming and had not been received by the end of the year. On January 27, Franklin instructed Williams: "Pray write and enquire about them."[6] It was June, 1786, before the letter of thanks went out from the town of Franklin. The Reverend Nathanael Emmons, minister of the First Congregational Church, and Hezekiah Fisher acted as the committee to express the town's gratitude in a very flowery letter:

We beg leave to present to your Excellency, our most grateful Acknowledgments, for the very handsome Parish Library, which you have been pleased to bestow upon the Minister and the Parishioners of this Town, as a particular mark of your approbation and regard. This choice and valuable Collection of Books, . . . not only flatters our Understanding and Taste, but displays the brightest feature in your great and amiable Character. We only regret, that modesty should deny us the celebrated Productions of the greatest Philosopher and Politician in America. . . . May all the seeds of Science, which you have sown in this, and various other parts of the world, grow up into a living

---

[1] Blake, 1879: p. 43.
[2] Van Doren, 1950a: p. 232.
[3] Van Doren, 1945: pp. 637-638.
[4] Sparks, 1836-1840: 10: p. 182.
[5] Van Doren, 1950a: pp. 243, 246.
[6] American Philosophical Society, Franklin MSS, **38**: 165 (Jonathan Williams, Jr., to Franklin, Dec. 26, 1785). Bigelow, 1887-1889: **9**: p. 286.

THE DIGNITY OF MAN.

A

DISCOURSE

Addreſſed to the Congregation in

FRANKLIN,

Upon the Occaſion of their receiving from

Dr. FRANKLIN,

The Mark of his Reſpect, in a rich

DONATION OF BOOKS,

Appropriated to the Uſe of a

PARISH-LIBRARY.

By *NATHANAEL EMMONS*,
PASTOR OF THE CHURCH IN FRANKLIN.

PROVIDENCE:
PRINTED BY BENNETT WHEELER, IN WESTMINSTER-STREET.

FIG. 9. Title page of sermon commemorating Franklin's gift of a parish library to Franklin, Massachusetts. Courtesy of the Library of Congress.

Laurel, to adorn your illustrious Head in the Temple of Fame. . . .[7]

There were sixty-seven titles in this library, five of which were given by Dr. Price. They were heavy in theology, including a little philosophy and logic, works of Locke, Montesquieu, Priestley, Newton, Laws of Massachusetts, American Constitutions, eight volumes of the *Spectator,* one volume of poetry, and the life of Cromwell.[8]

On March 1, 1787, the Reverend Nathanael Emmons called his flock together and addressed them on the wonders of this library. His sermon, entitled *The Dignity of Man,* was printed with the following dedication:

TO
HIS EXCELLENCY
BENJAMIN FRANKLIN, ESQ.
PRESIDENT
OF THE STATE OF
PENNSYLVANIA;
THE ORNAMENT OF GENIUS,
THE PATRON OF SCIENCE,
AND THE BOAST OF MAN;
THIS DISCOURSE IS INSCRIBED,
*With the greatest Deference, Humility and Gratitude,
by his most obliged, and most obedient Servant,*
THE AUTHOR.

The text of the sermon was taken from David's charge to Solomon, "Shew thyself a man." Mr. Emmons urged his congregation to "Read for Use and not for Amusement," and concluded:

Your generous Benefactor hath set you an example, as well as given you the means of intellectual improvements. That Great Man, in the morning of life, was surrounded with uncommon difficulties and embarrassments, but by the mere dint of genius and of application. he surmounted every obstacle thrown in his way, and by his rapid and astonishing progress in knowledge, he hath risen, step by step, to the first offices and honours of his Country, hath appeared with dignity in the Courts of Britain and of France, and now fills more than half the globe with his Fame. Keep this illustrious example in your eye, and shew yourselves men.[9]

Evidently thirty years before, this congregation had assembled a parish library, and this was but an addition, which Parson Emmons interpreted as a fulfillment of the Scriptures: "Whosoever hath, to him shall be given, and he shall have more in abundance."[10]

There was some dissension about the use of the library. Ebenezer Guilde and others wrote to Franklin in September, 1786, to find out whether he really meant that the enjoyment of this gift should be limited to the members of one church:

We chearfully joined in that Tribute of Thanks which was publickly voted in consequence of your signal Favour to this Town, of which Meeting, to our Surprize, some Queries arose by certain Individuals of the Town. Whether all the Inhabitants were to receive a Privilege by the Books, or not, & urged the Propriety of a Part. being excluded therefrom. — Some Reasons (as they were called) were offered to show the propriety of the Exclusion. — We wishing that nothing might take place in anywise different from the original Intention of the Donor, were willing to rest the whole upon your Pleasure. Upon which a Clause

---
[7] Smyth, 1905-1907: 10: pp. 482-483.
[8] See Appendix for list. Blake, 1879: pp. 70-71.
[9] Emmons, 1787: pp. 38, 48.
[10] *Ibid.,* p. 34.

of your Excellency's Letter was construed by them for their Purpose, by which they would Understand, that none were to be benefitted by your Excellency's Donation, except those who did statedly attend in the Ministration of the Minister setled in the Town, by which Construction a considerable Part of the Inhabitants must quit all Pretentions to any Right in the Privilege.[11]

This must have been a matter of controversy over several years, for the use of the library was first limited to members of the parish, and the books were kept in the house of the minister. In November, 1788, the books were opened to the town. In June, 1789, the town directed Mr. Emmons to lend out the books "according to the directions in the letter accompanying said library"; and again in 1790, the books were opened "to the inhabitants of the town at large until the town shall order otherwise." The letter has long since disappeared. Despite all these efforts to permit circulation among the townspeople in general, this "choice and valuable Collection of Books" was not much used, and it was stored away in an old bookcase in a barn until it was resurrected in 1840 and returned to the people of Franklin.[12]

A town centennial was held in 1878, and a native of the place, the Reverend Albert M. Richardson, returned from Lawrence, Kansas, to address the townspeople:

Dr. Franklin builded better than he knew, when, in reply to the suggestion of a friend, that a bell for the church might be an acceptable present, he replied that "If the good people of Franklin were the sort of folk he took them to be, *they were more fond of sense than sound,*" and sent them *books* instead of a *bell*. That library was kept, in my boyhood, in my father's house, and to its perusal I was indebted for a taste for reading and a thirst for knowledge. But, sir, while books are better than bells, they also make more noise in the world.[13]

The collection of books which Franklin gave rests today in the Ray Memorial Library of Franklin, Massachusetts.

THE ASSOCIATES OF THE LATE DR. BRAY

The foundation of libraries in colonial America owes much to the English clergyman and philanthropist, Thomas Bray (1656-1730), founder of the Society for Promoting Christian Knowledge, the Society for the Propagation of the Gospel in Foreign Lands, and an enthusiastic organizer of libraries for the clergy and the public. When Dr. Bray was threatened with serious illness in 1723, he created a committee to help him administer a £900 legacy left by D'Allone of Holland. The committee became known as "The Associates of Dr. Thomas Bray for Founding Clerical Libraries and Supporting Negro Schools." Through the two religious societies and the Associates, Dr. Bray established at least thirty-nine parish libraries along the Atlantic Coast of the American colonies, to which were distributed about 34,000 books.[14] Some of these libraries were for the use of ministers only, some were open to the parishioners as reference and circulating libraries, and some were designated as traveling libraries.[15]

After the death of Dr. Bray, the Associates continued to establish clerical libraries in both England and the colonies, but the work of founding Negro schools in the colonies met with many disappointments and lagged far behind the goal of the society. In 1757 its secretary, John Waring, wrote to Franklin, asking his advice on organizing Negro schools in America, with instruction in both reading and religion.

Our fund at present is but Small, however I hope by the blessing of God we shall be able to furnish those worthy Clergymen who engage with zeal in this truly Christian Design with religious Books and tracts to enable them more effectualy to carry it on and perhaps also with some useful Books towards forming a parochial Library for the Use of themselves and Successors.[16]

This letter arrived in Philadelphia after Franklin had left for England, and Franklin's wife, Deborah, probably opened it and showed it to William Sturgeon, the assistant minister of Christ Church, employed also by the Society for the Propagation of the Gospel as catechist to the Negroes of Philadelphia. Sturgeon suggested that the education of Negro children would make his task much easier, as "I am forced chiefly to instruct them by the Ear."[17]

Eventually, Franklin's correspondence caught up with him in England, where he met John Waring. Franklin pointed out that there was a "Prejudice that Reading and Knowledge in a Slave are both useless and dangerous," and that public sentiment was definitely against the education of Negro and white children in the same classrooms. However, he felt that a separate school for Negro children might help overcome such prejudices, and he recommended the Reverend William Sturgeon as manager of such a school. He also advised starting the school by hiring a mistress first to teach about thirty boys and girls to read and write and to teach the girls to knit, sew, and mark. When the school became larger, then the classes could be divided and a separate master hired to instruct the boys. He felt that the owners of slaves might be willing to pay for their education, provided that some of the useful arts were included as well as reading and religious instruction.[18]

The first Philadelphia school was opened on Novem-

---

[11] American Philosophical Society, Franklin MSS, 34: 140 (Ebenezer Guilde, Joseph Millan, William Gillmer, Nathan Man, and Ebenezer Gude, Jr., to Franklin, Sept. 8, 1786).
[12] Blake, 1879: pp. 71-72.
[13] *Ibid.,* p. 217.
[14] Shera, 1949: pp. 26-28. *Dictionary of American Biography,* 1943: **2**: pp. 610-611.
[15] Thompson, 1952: pp. 20-21.
[16] Labaree, 1959—: **7**: pp. 100-101.
[17] *Ibid.,* **7**: pp. 252-253.
[18] Labaree, 1959—: **7**: pp. 356, 377-378. Shelling, 1939: pp. 285-286.

ber 20, 1758, with a woman teacher for thirty children, who were brought to the church every Wednesday and Friday for their catechism lessons. Deborah Franklin wrote to her husband that she had visited the catechism class and resolved to send Othello, her Negro slave, there for instruction;[19] her testimony was printed in the English newspapers, without previous clearance from either Franklin or his wife.

Franklin was elected chairman of the Bray Associates on March 6, 1760, and set about the business of distributing books in the colonies, according to the plan of the organization. The favors of the society were channeled into areas of Franklin's knowledge and interests. "One Set of D^r. Berriman's Sermons and Erasmi Ecclesiastes" went to the library at Philadelphia;[20] this brought the number of books sent to Philadelphia by 1762 up to 327. Woodbridge, New Jersey, home of James Parker, printing partner of Franklin, received a "Box of Books . . . for a Lending Library for the general Use of the Inhabitants of that Town." James Parker wrote on May 10, 1761,

that they all joined with him in gratefully acknowledging the Favour, and desired their Thanks might be given to the Associates for the Books, and also to a Person desiring to be unknown for the Present of a Guinea by the Hands of Dr. Franklin, to purchase a Press for the Reception of those and such other Books as may providentially be sent them.[21]

Other Negro schools were set up in New York City, Williamsburg, Virginia, and Newport, Rhode Island, through Franklin's personal correspondence with men that he knew in these areas. Among these correspondents was William Hunter, of Williamsburg, joint deputy postmaster-general with Franklin; news came on September 17, 1761, that Mr. Hunter had died, but that the school would be carried on. Franklin was also influential in soliciting donations for the Associates of the Late Dr. Bray and collected £3 3s. from Dr. William Heberden and £1 1s. from Philip Ludwell, who had contributed previously through Franklin to the Philadelphia Academy and the Pennsylvania Hospital. A sample yearly report (March 5, 1761 — March 4, 1762) listed the following expenditures:

	£ s. d.
Salaries to Negroe Schools	57-10- 0
Books for Negroe Schools	7- 1- 6
Books for Libraries	4- 2- 4
Rent, Stationery, Boxes, Porterage, etc.	10-12- 6.[22]

During his two-year stay in the colonies between 1762 and 1764, Franklin visited the Negro schools while on a post-office inspection tour, reported back to the Associates,[23] and gave special attention to the Philadelphia school when William Sturgeon's health failed.[24] The Abstract of the activities of the Bray Associates shows that in 1765 they sent 1,032 books and pamphlets to America for the instruction of Negroes; these were in addition to materials sent to parochial libraries.[25]

Franklin also suggested the purchase of land in the province of Pennsylvania "where Titles are generally clear," to be used for rental income.[26] In 1767 the Bray Associates appointed Benjamin Franklin, the Reverend Jacob Duché (rector of Christ Church), Francis Hopkinson, David Hall, and Edward Duffield as attorneys for any lands purchased in Pennsylvania.

The Negro schools were closed during the Revolutionary War and were reopened again about 1786.[27] By this time, Franklin was home again in Philadelphia and received power of attorney, along with Francis Hopkinson, to carry out whatever they thought best on behalf of the Associates of the Late Dr. Bray.[28] Francis Hopkinson carried the burden of management in these last years of Franklin's life; after Franklin's death in 1790, Hopkinson asked the Bray Associates for some one to replace Franklin "in the management of the Negroes School & charge of the Societies Lot of Ground in the City."[29]

Franklin's work on behalf of Negroes in America was not limited to their education, but extended to their freedom. As President of the Pennsylvania Society for Promoting the Abolition of Slavery and the Relief of Free Blacks, reactivated in 1787, Franklin tried in vain to force Congress to outlaw slavery forever. The Society, he explained in a letter to Washington, planned that their own committee on education would "superintend the school instruction of the children and youth of the free blacks."[30]

GERMAN CHARITY SCHOOLS

In the middle of the eighteenth century, German immigrants began pouring into the province of Pennsylvania at the rate of seven thousand each year.[31] Franklin became alarmed when he realized that large German settlements were being established within the borders of the English colonies, with little or no effort on the part of the Germans to assimilate with their English fellow colonists. "Why should the Palatine Boors be suffered to swarm into our Settlements, and

---

[19] Pennington, 1934: pp. 7-8.
[20] Shelling, 1939: pp. 286-287.
[21] Associates of Doctor Thomas Bray for Founding Clerical Libraries and Supporting Negro Schools, 1762: pp. 19, 25.
[22] Ibid., pp. 26, 34, 36.
[23] Shelling, 1939: pp. 286-288.
[24] Pennington, 1934: p. 9.
[25] Shelling, 1939: p. 287.
[26] Smyth, 1905-1907: 4: pp. 463-464.
[27] Pennington, 1934: pp. 10, 15-18.
[28] American Philosophical Society, Franklin MSS, 34: 45 (Thomas Lyttelton to Franklin, April 4, 1786).
[29] Pennington, 1934: p. 20.
[30] Bigelow, 1887-1889: 10: pp. 145-146.
[31] Bell, 1955: p. 381.

by herding together establish their Language and Manners to the Exclusion of ours?"[32] With the Boston publication of his "Observations Concerning the Increase of Mankind" in 1755, these words became very embarrassing to him and cast a ghostly chill over his relations with the Germans in trying to establish the German Charity Schools in Pennsylvania.

In May, 1753, Franklin wrote to Peter Collinson, explaining his concern:

Few of their children in the Country learn English; they import many Books from Germany; and of the six printing houses in the Province, two are entirely German, two half German half English, and but two entirely English; They have one German News-paper, and one half German. Advertisements intended to be general are now printed in Dutch and English; the Signs in our Streets have inscriptions in both languages, and in some places only German: They begin of late to make all their Bonds and other legal Writings in their own Language, which (though I think it ought not to be) are allowed good in our Courts, where the German Business so encreases that there is continual need of Interpreters; and I suppose in a few years they will be also necessary in the Assembly, to tell one half of our Legislators what the other half say; . . .[33]

Peter Collinson had quite a few suggestions for Franklin — to establish more English schools among the Germans, to prohibit deeds and bonds in the German language, to suppress printing houses printing only German, allowing bilingual publication and printing, and to prohibit importation of German books.[34]

The Society for the Relief and Instruction of Poor Germans was formed in England with the Reverend Samuel Chandler as secretary. Though not a member, Peter Collinson wrote to Franklin for information on March 7, 1754. Money was collected, and American trustees general were appointed, including Governor James Hamilton, Chief Justice William Allen, Richard Peters, William Smith, Conrad Weiser, and Benjamin Franklin. Franklin had been recommended by William Smith, who was then in England and was shortly to come to Philadelphia to head the Academy of Philadelphia. The American trustees met in August, 1754, after the Albany Congress was over. They decided to establish schools in Reading, York, Easton, Lancaster, New Hanover, and Skippack, appointing local trustees from both German and English factions to build schools and teachers' dwellings. The Reverend Michael Schlatter had been appointed Superintendent of the German schools by the English society.[35] A German professor of divinity was even established at the Philadelphia Academy to help train the German clergy.[36]

The German charity schools were unpopular with many of the German immigrants. Christopher Sauer, publisher of the *Pennsylvania Berichte*, saw the movement as an imperialistic scheme to Anglicize the Germans. To combat this distrust, the Reverend Henry Muhlenberg asked the trustees to establish a rival German newspaper; Franklin offered to sell a press and German type for £25 less than value. The offer was accepted, and the *Philadelphische Zeitung* appeared on July 12, 1755, under the imprint of Anthony Armbrüster and Benjamin Franklin.

To gain support for the cause, William Smith wrote *A brief history of the rise and progress of the charitable scheme . . . for the relief and instruction of poor Germans* (Philadelphia, Franklin and Hall, 1755), with a German translation printed by Armbrüster and Franklin. This pamphlet stressed the value of religious instruction in the charity schools, and the advantages of understanding English in the courts and market places.[37]

Instructions had been received from England from the Society in a letter dated January 28, 1755:

That the whole of what you aim at is, not to proselyte the Germans to any particular Denomination, but (leaving all of them to the entire Liberty of their own Judgments in speculative and disputed Points) to spread the knowledge of the avowed uncontroverted Principles of Religion and Morality among them, to render them acquainted with the English Language and Constitution, to form them into good Subjects to his Majesty King George whose protection they enjoy, and make them Friends to the Interests of that Nation which hath received them into her Bosom, blessed them with Liberty and given them a Share in her invaluable Privileges.

Five hundred copies of Henry Scougal's *Life of God in the Soul of Man* (in German) were distributed by the American trustees in 1756. It had been printed in German the year before by Christopher Sauer, but this particular edition contained a preface by William Smith explaining the Society's work.[38]

In 1756 Franklin became disenchanted with the political antics of William Smith, and confided his feelings to George Whitefield, the English evangelist, who had just sent a donation for the German schools:

I thank you cordially for your generous Benefaction to the German Schools. They go on pretty well, and will do better, when Mr. Smith, who has at present the principal Care of them, shall learn to mind Party-Writing and Party Politicks less and his proper Business more; which I hope time will bring about.[39]

Political pamphlets written by William Smith and the unfortunate timing of the Boston printing of Franklin's "Observations Concerning the Increase of Mankind" with that regretable reference to the "Palatine Boors" lost the cooperation of the Germans for the support of the charity schools. Indian raids on the frontier were also disruptive. The Reverend Mr. Schlatter resigned

---

[32] Labaree, 1959—: 4: p. 234.
[33] *Ibid.* 4: p. 484.
[34] Labaree, 1959—: 5: p. 21.
[35] Bell, 1955: pp. 383-384.
[36] Labaree, 1959—: 5: pp. 209-212.

[37] Bell, 1955: pp. 384-385.
[38] Labaree, 1959—: 6: pp. 533-535.
[39] *Ibid.* 6: p. 469.

as superintendent in 1757; the *Philadelphische Zeitung,* which had never exceeded four hundred copies in circulation, ceased publication the same year. Franklin sailed away to England in 1757, where he took no part in the Society's activities and was not even invited to the meetings. The attendance at the schools dwindled, and finally, in 1769, the remaining funds of the Society (£88 12s. 4d.) were turned over to the College of Philadelphia to be used for its charitable school.[40]

CONCLUSION

Benjamin Franklin was born into a world and time that was fully conscious of its poverty in books and libraries. As a printer, he developed a love of books strong enough to accumulate one of the largest private libraries of colonial times. He founded the Library Company of Philadelphia (the first subscription library in America), which stimulated the formation of other libraries, not only in Pennsylvania, but also in other colonies. He served as a trustee of the Loganian Library, which eventually joined with the Library Company. He founded the Philadelphia Academy (University of Pennsylvania); contributed to the libraries of Harvard and Yale; gave liberally to pioneer colleges in Pennsylvania; and urged American colleges to seek support from the people they served. He founded the American Philosophical Society and built up its library through an exchange program. He helped found the Pennsylvania Hospital, home of the first medical library in America. He ordered materials for the Pennsylvania Assembly library, and collected useful information from Europe for the United States Congress. He contributed a parish library to the town of Franklin, Massachusetts, which became the nucleus for the town's public library. He helped establish charity schools among the German immigrants in Pennsylvania and among the Negroes in all the colonies. His most significant contributions to eighteenth-century libraries were his promotion of public enterprises of an educational nature, and his emphasis upon modern languages (especially English) and upon useful knowledge (science, agriculture, commerce, geography, etc.).

[40] Bell, 1955: pp. 386-387.

APPENDIX

A. THE LONG ARM

FRANKLIN'S INVENTION FOR REACHING BOOKS ON HIGH SHELVES

(Printed in Sparks (ed.), *The Works of Benjamin Franklin* 6: pp. 562-564)

January, 1786.

Old men find it inconvenient to mount a ladder or steps for that purpose, their heads being sometimes subject to giddinesses, and their activity, with the steadiness of their joints, being abated by age; besides the trouble of removing the steps every time a book is wanted from a different part of their library.

For a remedy, I have lately made the following simple machine, which I call the *Long Arm*.

A B, the *Arm*, is a stick of pine, an inch square and 8 feet long. *C, D,* the *Thumb* and *Finger*, are two pieces of ash lath, an inch and half wide, and a quarter of an inch thick. These are fixed by wood screws on opposite sides of the end *A* of the arm *A B*; the finger *D* being longer and standing out an inch and half farther than the thumb *C*. The outside of the ends of these laths are pared off sloping and thin, that they may more easily enter between books that stand together on a shelf. Two small holes are bored through them at *i, k*. *E F,* the sinew, is a cord of the size of a small goosequill, with a loop at one end. When applied to the machine it passes through the two laths, and is stopped by a knot in its other end behind the longest at *k*. The hole at *i* is nearer the end of the arm than that at *k*, about an inch. A number of knots are also on the cord, distant three or four inches from each other.

To use this instrument; put one hand into the loop, and draw the sinew straight down the side of the arm; then enter the end of the finger between the book you would take down and that which is next to it. The laths being flexible, you may easily by a slight pressure sideways open them wider if the book is thick, or close them if it is thin by pulling the string, so as to enter the shorter lath or thumb between your book and that which is next to its other side, then push till the back of your book comes to touch the string. Then draw the string or sinew tight, which will cause the thumb and finger to pinch the book strongly, so that you may draw it out. As it leaves the other books, turn the instrument a *quarter* round, so that the book may lie flat and rest on its side upon the under lath or finger. The knots on the sinew will help you to keep it tight and close to the

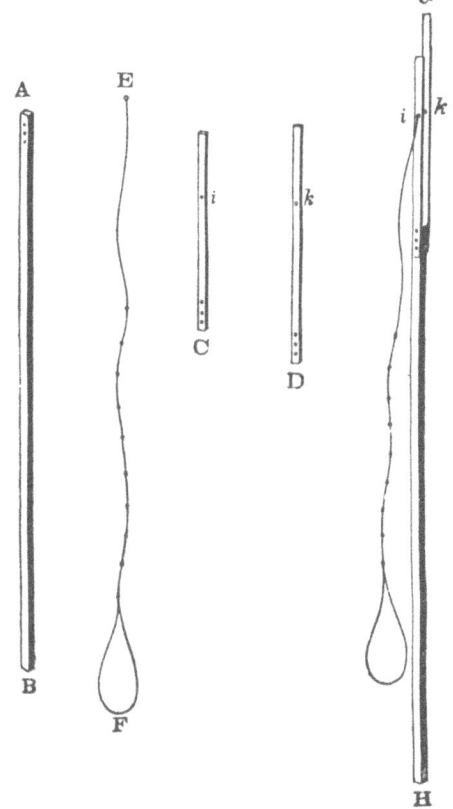

Fig. 10. The long arm. From Jared Sparks (ed.), *The Works of Benjamin Franklin* 6: p. 563.

side of the arm as you take it down hand over hand, till the book comes to you; which would drop from between the thumb and finger if the sinew was let loose.

All new tools require some practice before we can become expert in the use of them. This requires very little.

Made in the proportions above given, it serves well for books in duodecimo or octavo. Quartos and folios are too heavy for it; but those are usually placed on the lower shelves within reach of hand.

The book taken down, may, when done with, be put up again into its place by the same machine.

B. FRANKLIN'S "SHORT ACCOUNT OF THE LIBRARY"

Written to fill up a blank page of *A Catalogue of Books Belonging to the Library Company of Philadelphia* (Philadelphia, B. Franklin, 1741). [July 13, 1741]

A short Account of the LIBRARY.

THE Library-Company was form'd in 1731, by Constitutions or Articles entred into by 50 Persons, each obliging himself to pay 40 s. for purchasing the first Parcel of Books, and 10 s. *per annum* to defray Charges and encrease the Library.

Ten Directors or Managers of the Library, and a Treasurer, are chosen yearly by Vote, at a General Meeting of the Company.

The Number of Members are now encreased to upwards of 70. Persons enclining to be admitted, apply to any one of the Directors, who nominates them at the next monthly Meeting of Directors; and being allowed, and paying to the Treasurer the Value of a Share at the Time, and signing the Articles, they become Members.

Any Member may borrow a Book for 2, 3, or 4 Weeks, leaving his Note for double Value, and paying a small Penalty if 'tis not return'd at the Time agreed; which Penalties are applied to defraying Charges, or purchasing more Books.

Every Member has an absolute Property in his Share; may devise it in his Will, or dispose of it when he pleases to any Person the Directors approve. And Shares so sold have always hitherto yielded as much as they had cost. As Shares encrease yearly in Value 10 s. so much being yearly added by each Subscriber to the Stock of Books, a Share which at first was worth but 40 s. is now valued at 6 *l.* 10 s. But for this small Sum, which, laid out in Books, would go but a little Way, every Member has the Use of a Library now worth upwards of 500 *L.* whereby *Knowledge* is in this City render'd more cheap and easy to be come at, to the great Pleasure and Advantage of the studious Part of the Inhabitants.

Those who are not Subscribers may notwithstanding borrow Books, leaving in the Hands of the Librarian, as a Pledge, a Sum of Money proportion'd to the Value of the Book borrow'd, and paying a small Acknowledgment for the Reading, which is apply'd to the Use of the Library.

The Library is open and Attendance given every Saturday Afternoon from 4 a Clock 'til 8.

Besides the Books in this Catalogue given to the Library, the Company have been favour'd with several generous Donations; as, a curious Air-Pump, with its Apparatus, a large double Microscope, and other valuable Instruments, from the Hon. JOHN PENN, Esq; A handsome Lot of Ground whereon to build a House for the Library, from the Hon. THOMAS PENN, Esq; Proprietaries of the Province; and the Sum of 34 *L Sterl.* (to be laid out in Books) from Dr. *Sydserfe*, late of *Antigua*.

At present the Books are deposited in the West Wing of the State-House, by Favour of the General Assembly.

It is now Ten Years since the Company was first establish'd; and we have the Pleasure of observing, That tho' 'tis compos'd of so many Persons of different Sects, Parties and Ways of Thinking, yet no Differences relating to the Affairs of the Library, have arisen among us; but every Thing has been conducted with great Harmony, and to general Satisfaction. Which happy Circumstance will, we hope, always continue.

Note, A Copy of the Articles or Constitutions is left in the Library, for the Perusal of all that desire to be more fully inform'd.

FIG. 11. "A Short Account of the Library," from the 1741 *Catalogue* of the Library Company of Philadelphia. Reproduced with permission.

C. CATALOGUE OF THE FRANKLIN, MASSACHUSETTS, LIBRARY — 1786

(From Mortimer Blake, *History of the Town of Franklin, Mass.* (1879), pp. 70-71)

Clark's Works, 4 vols., folio
Hoadley's Works, 3 vols., folio
Barrows' Works, 2 vols., folio
Ridgeley's Works, 2 vols., folio
Locke's Works, 4 vols., octavo
Sydney's Works, 1 vol., octavo
Montesquieu's Spirit of Laws, 2 vols.
Blackstone's Commentaries, 4 vols.
Watson's Tracts, 6 vols.
Newton on the Prophesies, 3 vols.
Law on Religion, 1 vol.
Priestley's Institutes, 2 vols.
Priestley's Corruptions, 2 vols.
Price and Priestley, 1 vol.
Lyndsey's Apology and Sequel, 2 vols.
Abernethy's Sermons, 2 vols.
Duchal's Sermons, 3 vols.
Price's Morals, 1 vol.
Price on Providence, 1 vol.
Price on Liberty, 1 vol.
Price on the Christian Scheme, 1 vol.
Price's Sermons, 1 vol.
Needham's Free State, 1 vol.
West and Littleton on the Resurrection, 1 vol.
Stennet's Sermons, 2 vols.
Addison's Evidences, 1 vol.
Gordon's Tacitus, 5 vols.
Backus' History, 1 vol.
Lardner on the Logus, 1 vol., 8 vo.
Watts' Orthodoxy and Charity, 1 vol.
Brainerd's Life, 1 vol.
Bellamy's True Religion, 1 vol.
Doddridge's Life, 1 vol.
Bellamy's Permission of Sin, 1 vol.
Fordyce's Sermons, 1 vol.
Hemminway against Hopkins, 1 vol.
Hopkins on Holiness, 1 vol.
Life of Cromwell, 1 vol.
Fulfilling the Scriptures, 1 vol.
Watts on the Passions, 1 vol.
Watts' Logic, 1 vol.
Edwards on Religion, 1 vol.
Dickinson on the Five Points, 1 vol.
Christian History, 2 vols.
Prideaux's Connections, 4 vols.
Cooper on Predestination, 1 vol.
Cambridge Platform, 1 vol.
Stoddard's Safety of Appearing, 1 vol.
Burkett on Personal Reformation, 1 v.
Barnard's Sermons, 1 vol.
Shepard's Sound Believer, 1 vol.
History of the Rebellion, 1 vol.
Janeway's Life, 1 vol.
Hopkin's [sic.] System, 2 vols.
American Preacher, 4 vols.
Emmons' Sermons, 1 vol.
Thomas' Laws of Massachusetts, 1 vol.
American Constitutions, 1 vol.
Young's Night Thoughts, 1 vol.
Pilgrim's Progress, 1 vol.
Ames' Oration, 1 vol.
Spectators, 8 vols.
Life of Baron Trenk, 1 vol.
Cheap Repository, 2 vols.
Moral Repository, 1 vol.
Fitch's Poem, 1 vol.
Erskine's Sermons, 1 vol.

BIBLIOGRAPHY

A. GUIDES TO MANUSCRIPT COLLECTIONS

FORD, WORTHINGTON CHAUNCEY. 1905. *List of the Benjamin Franklin Papers in the Library of Congress* (Washington, D. C., Government Printing Office); includes papers in other collections besides the main collection by Henry Stevens.

HAYS, I. MINIS. 1908. *Calendar of the Papers of Benjamin Franklin in the Library of the American Philosophical Society* (5 v., Philadelphia, American Philosophical Society). Vol. IV Appendix lists "Papers of Benjamin Franklin in the Library of the University of Pennsylvania" (pp. 399-510); Vol. V is Index. This work is included as Vol. II-VI of *Franklin Bi-Centennial Celebration, Philadelphia, 1906*, published by the American Philosophical Society in 1908.

HISTORICAL SOCIETY OF PENNSYLVANIA. 1949. *Guide to the Manuscript Collections of the Historical Society of Pennsylvania* (2nd ed., Philadelphia).

B. PRINTED WORKS OF FRANKLIN

The Autobiography of Benjamin Franklin. 1964. Edited by Leonard W. Labaree and others (New Haven, Yale University Press).

BIGELOW, JOHN (ed.). 1887-1889. *The Complete Works of Benjamin Franklin* (10 v., New York, G. P. Putnam's Sons).

———. 1888. *The Life of Benjamin Franklin, Written by Himself; Now First Edited from Original Manuscripts and from His Printed Correspondence and Other Writings* (3 v., 2nd ed. rev., Philadelphia, J. B. Lippincott).

COHEN, I. BERNARD (ed.). 1941. *Benjamin Franklin's Experiments; a New Edition of Franklin's "Experiments and Observations on Electricity"* (Cambridge, Mass., Harvard University Press).

———. 1954. *Some Account of the Pennsylvania Hospital; Printed in Facsimile* (Baltimore, Johns Hopkins Press).

LABAREE, LEONARD W. (ed.). 1959—. *The Papers of Benjamin Franklin* (8 v. to date, New Haven, Yale University Press).

ROELKER, WILLIAM GREENE (ed.). 1949. *Benjamin Franklin and Catharine Ray Greene; Their Correspondence, 1755-1790*, Memoirs, American Philosophical Society **26** (Philadelphia).

SMYTH, ALBERT HENRY (ed.). 1905-1907. *The Writings of Benjamin Franklin* (10 v., New York, Macmillan).

SPARKS, JARED (ed.). 1836-1840. *The Works of Benjamin Franklin* (10 v., Boston, Tappan, Whittemore, and Mason).

VAN DOREN, CARL (ed.). 1945. *Benjamin Franklin's Autobiographical Writings* (New York, Viking Press).

———. 1947. *Letters and Papers of Benjamin Franklin and Richard Jackson, 1753-1785*, Memoirs, American Philosophical Society **24** (Philadelphia).

———. 1950a. *The Letters of Benjamin Franklin & Jane Mecom*, Memoirs, American Philosophical Society **27** (Philadelphia).

C. GENERAL BIBLIOGRAPHY

ABBOT, GEORGE MAURICE. 1913. *A Short History of the Library Company of Philadelphia; Compiled from the Minutes, together with some personal reminiscences* (Philadelphia, Library Company of Philadelphia).

ADAMS, PERCY G. 1947. "Crèvecœur and Franklin." *Pennsylvania History* **14**: pp. 273-279.

American Philosophical Society. 1824. *Catalogue of the Library of the American Philosophical Society, Held at Philadelphia, for Promoting Useful Knowledge* (Philadelphia, Joseph R. A. Skerrett).

———. 1838. *List of the Members of the American Philosophical Society, Held at Philadelphia, for Promoting Useful Knowledge. From Its Establishment, 2d January, 1769, to the 20th of April, 1838* (Philadelphia, Joseph William Kite).

———. 1885. "Early Proceedings of the American Philosophical Society for the Promotion of Useful Knowledge Compiled by one of the Secretaries, from the Manuscript Minutes of Its Meetings from 1744 to 1838." *Proceedings* **22**, 3: pp. 1-875.

———. 1902. *Fundamental Laws and Regulations (Adopted 1769), Charter (Granted 1780), Laws and Rules of Administration and Order (As Amended March 7, 1902)* (Philadelphia, American Philosophical Society).

Associates of Doctor Thomas Bray for Founding Clerical Libraries and Supporting Negro Schools. 1762. *An Account of the Designs of the Associates of the late Dr Bray: with an Abstract of Their Proceedings* (London).

BELL, WHITFIELD J., JR. 1955. "Benjamin Franklin and the German Charity Schools." *Proceedings, American Philosophical Society* **99**, 6: pp. 381-387.

BIDDLE, HENRY D. 1895. "Colonial Mayors of Philadelphia. Samuel Rhoads, 1774." *Pennsylvania Magazine of History and Biography* **19**: pp. 64-71.

BLAKE, MORTIMER. 1879. *A History of the Town of Franklin, Mass.; from Its Settlement to the completion of Its First Century, 2d March, 1878, . . .* (Franklin, Mass., Published by the Town).

"Books Taken from Dr. Franklin's Library by Major André." 1884. *Pennsylvania Magazine of History and Biography* **8**: p. 430.

BRIDENBAUGH, CARL, AND JESSICA BRIDENBAUGH. 1962. *Rebels and Gentlemen; Philadelphia in the Age of Franklin* (New York, Hesperides Book, Oxford University Press).

CHEYNEY, EDWARD POTTS. 1940. *History of the University of Pennsylvania, 1740-1940* (Philadelphia, University of Pennsylvania Press).

CLOYD, DAVID EXCELMONS. 1902. *Benjamin Franklin and Education; His Ideal of Life and His System of Education for That Ideal* (Boston, D. C. Heath).

COLEMAN, HELEN TURNBULL WAITE. 1956. *Banners in the Wilderness; Early Years of Washington and Jefferson College* (Pittsburgh, University of Pittsburgh).

Columbia Encyclopedia. 1950. (2nd ed., Morning Heights, N.Y., Columbia University Press).

CONKLIN, EDWIN G. 1963. "A Brief History of the American Philosophical Society." *Year Book 1962, American Philosophical Society* (Philadelphia), pp. 36-62.

"Correspondence between William Strahan and David Hall, 1763-1777." 1886-1888. *Pennsylvania Magazine of History and Biography* **10**: pp. 86-99, 217-232, 322-333, 461-473; **11**: pp. 98-111, 223-234, 346-357, 482-490; **12**: pp. 116-122, 240-251.

CUTLER, WILLIAM PARKER, AND JULIA PERKINS CUTLER. 1888. *Life, Journals and Correspondence of Rev. Manasseh Cutler, LL.D.* (2 v., Cincinnati, Robert Clarke & Co.).

Dictionary of American Biography. 1943. American Council of Learned Societies (21 v., New York, Charles Scribner's Sons).

DUBBS, JOSEPH HENRY. 1903. *History of Franklin and Marshall College* (Lancaster, Pa., Franklin and Marshall College Alumni Association).

DULLES, CHARLES WINSLOW. 1903. "Sketch of the Life of Dr. Thomas Cadwalader." *Pennsylvania Magazine of History and Biography* **27**: pp. 262-278.

DU PONCEAU, PETER STEPHEN. 1914. *An Historical Account of the Origin and Formation of the American Philosophical Society . . .* (Philadelphia, American Philosophical Society).

EDDY, GEORGE SIMPSON. 1924. "Dr. Benjamin Franklin's Library." *Proceedings, American Antiquarian Society* **34** (New Series): pp. 206-226.

―――――. 1928. *Account Books Kept by Benjamin Franklin, Ledger 1728–1739, Journal 1730–1737* (New York, Columbia University Press).
―――――. 1929. *Account Books Kept by Benjamin Franklin, Ledger "D", 1739–1747* (New York, Columbia University Press).
―――――. 1931. "Account Book of Benjamin Franklin kept by him during his First Mission to England as Provincial Agent, 1757–1762." *Pennsylvania Magazine of History and Biography* **55**: pp. 97-133.
EMMONS, NATHANAEL. 1787. *The Dignity of Man. A Discourse Addressed to the Congregation in Franklin, Upon the Occasion of their receiving from Dr. Franklin, The Mark of his Respect, in a rich Donation of Books, Appropriated to the Use of a Parish-Library* (Providence, R. I., Bennett Wheeler).
Federal Writers' Project of the Works Progress Administration for the State of New Jersey. 1939. *New Jersey, a Guide to Its Present and Past* ("American Guide Series"; New York, Viking Press).
FORD, PAUL LEICESTER. 1889. *Franklin Bibliography. A List of Books Written by, or Relating to Benjamin Franklin* (Brooklyn, N. Y.).
―――――. 1899. *The Many-Sided Franklin* (New York, Century Co.).
FOWLER, WILLIAM CHAUNCEY. 1866. *History of Durham, Connecticut, from the First Grant of Land in 1662 to 1866* (Hartford, Conn., Published by the Town, Press of Wiley, Waterman & Eaton).
GALLISON, JEFFERSON CUSHING. 1904. *Franklin and Wrentham* ... (Franklin, Mass., Sentinel Press).
GRAY, AUSTIN K. 1937. *Benjamin Franklin's Library* (New York, Macmillan).
GRIMM, DOROTHY F. 1956. "Franklin's Scientific Institution." *Pennsylvania History* **23**: pp. 437-462.
JORDAN, JOHN W. 1899. "A Description of the State-House, Philadelphia, in 1774." *Pennsylvania Magazine of History and Biography* **23**: pp. 417-419.
Juliana Library Company, Lancaster, Pennsylvania. 1766. *The Charter, Laws, Catalogue of Books, List of Philosophical Instruments, &c. of the Juliana Library-Company, in Lancaster ... With A Short Account of its Institution, Friends and Benefactors* (Philadelphia, D. Hall & W. Sellers).
KALM, PETER. 1937. *The America of 1750; Peter Kalm's Travels in North America; . . .*, edited by Adolph B. Benson (2 v., New York, Wilson-Erickson).
KEEP, AUSTIN BAXTER. 1909. *The Library in Colonial New York* (New York, De Vinne Press).
LAMBERTON, E. V. 1918. "Colonial Libraries of Pennsylvania." *Pennsylvania Magazine of History and Biography* **42**: pp. 193-234.
LANE, WILLIAM C. 1907. "Harvard College and Franklin." *Publications of the Colonial Society of Massachusetts* **10**: pp. 229-239.
Library Company of Philadelphia. 1731-1768. (Manuscript) "A Book of Minutes containing an Account of the Proceedings of the Directors of the Library Company of Philadelphia—Beginning November 8th 1731, taken by the Secretary to the Company. Vol. 1st. Collected, copied & continued by Fra. Hopkinson, 1759."
―――――. 1741 (1956). *A Catalogue of Books Belonging to the Library Company of Philadelphia; A Facsimile of the Edition of 1741 Printed by BENJAMIN FRANKLIN, With an Introduction by Edwin Wolf 2nd* (Philadelphia, Printed for the Library Company of Philadelphia to mark the 250th Anniversary of the Birth of Franklin, 1956).
―――――. 1764. *The Charter, Laws, and Catalogue of Books, of the Library Company of Philadelphia* (Philadelphia, Franklin & Hall).

―――――. 1770. *The Charter, Laws, and Catalogue of Books, of the Library Company of Philadelphia. With a Short Account of the Library prefixed* (Philadelphia, Joseph Crukshank).
―――――. 1807. *A Catalogue of the Books, Belonging to the Library Company of Philadelphia; To Which Is Prefixed, A Short Account Of The Institution, With The Charter, Laws, and Regulations* (Philadelphia, Bartram & Reynolds).
Library Company of Philadelphia, Loganian Library. 1795. *Catalogue of the Books Belonging to the Loganian Library: To Which Is Prefixed a Short Account of the Institution with the Law for Annexing the Said Library to That Belonging to "The Library Company of Philadelphia," and the Rules Regulating the Manner of Conducting the Same* (Philadelphia, Zachariah Poulson, Jr.).
"Library of the College of William and Mary." 1910. *William and Mary Quarterly* **19**, 1 (July): pp. 48-51.
LINGELBACH, WILLIAM E. 1946. "The Library of the American Philosophical Society." *William and Mary Quarterly* **3** (third series): pp. 48-69.
MALIN, WILLIAM G. 1830. (Manuscript) "Sketch of the History of the Medical Library of the Pennsylvania Hospital with a Brief Notice of the Medical Museum Formerly Belonging to That Institution. Jan. 30, 1830." Historical Society of Pennsylvania, No. 989.
MOFFAT, JAMES D. 1919. "Washington and Jefferson College." *A Cyclopedia of Education*, edited by Paul Monroe (5 v., New York, Macmillan) **5**: p. 749.
MONTGOMERY, THOMAS HARRISON. 1900. *A History of the University of Pennsylvania from Its Foundation to A.D. 1770, Including Biographical Sketches of the Trustees, Faculty, the First Alumni and Others* (Philadelphia, George W. Jacobs).
MOOD, FULMER. 1948. "The Continental Congress and the Plan for a Library of Congress in 1782–1783; an Episode in American Cultural History." *Pennsylvania Magazine of History and Biography* **72**: pp. 3-24.
MORRIS, RICHARD B. (ed.). 1953. *Encyclopedia of American History* (New York, Harper & Bros.).
MORTON, THOMAS G. 1895. *The History of the Pennsylvania Hospital, 1751–1895* (Philadelphia, Times Printing House).
New Jersey. 1894-1895. *Archives of the State of New Jersey, First Series; Documents Relating to the Colonial History of the State of New Jersey*, edited by William Nelson (Paterson, N. J., Press Printing & Publishing Co.), 11 and 12.
New York (City). 1905. *Minutes of the Common Council of the City of New York, 1675–1776* (8 v., New York, Dodd, Mead & Co.).
NOLAN, J. BENNETT. 1938. *Benjamin Franklin in Scotland and Ireland, 1759 and 1771* (Philadelphia, University of Pennsylvania Press).
OSWALD, JOHN CLYDE. 1917. *Benjamin Franklin, Printer* (Garden City, N.Y., Doubleday, Page & Co.).
―――――. 1937. *Printing in the Americas* (New York, Gregg Publishing Co.).
PACKARD, FRANCIS R. 1938. *Some Account of the Pennsylvania Hospital from its first Rise to the Beginning of the Year 1938* (Philadelphia, Engle Press).
PENNINGTON, EDGAR LEGARE. 1934. "The Work of the Bray Associates in Pennsylvania." *Pennsylvania Magazine of History and Biography* **58**: pp. 1-25.
Pennsylvania. 1853. *Colonial Records Published by the State. Vol. XVI, Containing the Proceedings of the Supreme Executive Council from February 7th, 1789, to December 20th, 1790, Both Days Inclusive* (Harrisburg, Theo. Fenn).
―――――. 1931-1935. *Pennsylvania Archives, Eighth Series; Votes and Proceedings of the House of Representatives of the Province of Pennsylvania*, to Sept. 26, 1776 (8 v., Harrisburg).
Pennsylvania Gazette. 1729-1789, *passim*. (On microfilm).

Pennsylvania Hospital, Philadelphia. 1790-1794. *A Catalogue of the Books Belonging to the Medical Library in The Pennsylvania Hospital; to which are prefixed, The Rules To be observed in the use of them* (Philadelphia, Zachariah Poulson, Jr.).

———. 1806. *A Catalogue of the Medical Library, Belonging to the Pennsylvania Hospital* . . . (Philadelphia, Archibald Bartram).

Pennsylvania, University of. Library. 1951. *Benjamin Franklin, Winston Churchill; an Exhibition Celebrating the Bicentennial of the University of Pennsylvania Library* . . . *May 8-June 15, 1951* (Philadelphia, Wm. F. Fells).

PETERSON, CHARLES E. 1953. "Library Hall: Home of the Library Company of Philadelphia 1790-1880." *Historic Philadelphia from the Founding until the Early Nineteenth Century* . . ., *Transactions, American Philosophical Society* **43**, 1: pp. 129-147.

PHILLIPS, JAMES W. 1947. "The Sources of the Original Dickinson College Library." *Pennsylvania History* **14**, 2: pp. 108-117.

POTTER, ALFRED CLAGHORN, AND CHARLES KNOWLES BOLTON. 1897. *The Librarians of Harvard College, 1667-1877* ("Harvard University Library, Bibliographical Contributions," No. 52; Cambridge, Mass.).

POTTER, ALFRED CLAGHORN, AND EDGAR H. WELLS. 1911. *Descriptive and Historical Notes on the Library of Harvard University* ("Harvard University Library, Bibliographical Contributions," No. 60; 2nd ed., Cambridge, Mass.).

QUINCY, JOSIAH. 1840. *The History of Harvard University* (2 v., Cambridge, Mass., John Owen).

Redwood Library and Athenaeum, Newport, R. I. 1860. *A Catalogue of the Redwood Library and Athenaeum in Newport, R.I.* . . . *To Which Is Prefixed a Short Account of the Institution; with the Charter, Laws, and Regulations* (Boston, John Wilson & Son).

RUSH, BENJAMIN. 1905. "Excerpts from the Papers of Dr. Benjamin Rush." *Pennsylvania Magazine of History and Biography* **29**: pp. 15-30.

———. 1948. *The Autobiography of Benjamin Rush, His "Travels Through Life" together with his Commonplace Book for 1789-1813*, edited by George W. Corner, Memoirs, American Philosophical Society **25** (Philadelphia).

———. 1951. *Letters of Benjamin Rush*, edited by L. H. Butterfield, Memoirs, American Philosophical Society **30** (2 v., Philadelphia).

SCUDDER, HORACE E. 1876. "Public Libraries a Hundred Years Ago." *Public Libraries in the United States of America, Their History, Condition, and Management*, Special Report, Part I, U.S. Bureau of Education (Washington, D.C., Government Printing Office), pp. 1-37.

SHELLING, RICHARD I. 1939. "Benjamin Franklin and the Dr. Bray Associates." *Pennsylvania Magazine of History and Biography* **63**: pp. 282-293.

SHERA, JESSE H. 1949. *Foundations of the Public Library: The Origins of the Public Library Movement in New England, 1629-1855* (Chicago, University of Chicago Press).

SHORES, LOUIS. 1935. *Origins of the American College Library, 1638-1800* (New York, Barnes & Noble).

SMITH, WILLIAM (of Philadelphia). 1792. *Eulogium on Benjamin Franklin, L.L.D., President of the American Philosophical Society . . . Delivered March 1, 1791, in . . . the City of Philadelphia* . . . (Philadelphia, Benjamin Franklin Bache).

SMITH, WILLIAM (of New York). 1830. *The History of the Late Province of New-York, from Its Discovery, to the Appointment of Governor Colden, in 1762* (2 v., New York, New-York Historical Society).

"Some Letters of Franklin's Correspondents." 1903. *Pennsylvania Magazine of History and Biography* **27**: pp. 151-175.

STILES, EZRA. 1901. *The Literary Diary of Ezra Stiles, D.D., LL.D., President of Yale College*, edited by Franklin Bowditch Dexter (3 v., New York, Charles Scribner's Sons).

THOMPSON, C. SEYMOUR. 1934. "The Gift of Louis XVI." *The University of Pennsylvania Library Chronicle* **2**: pp. 37-48, 60-67.

———. 1952. *Evolution of the American Public Library, 1653-1876* (Washington, D.C., Scarecrow Press).

THORPE, FRANCIS NEWTON. 1893. *Benjamin Franklin and the University of Pennsylvania*, U.S. Bureau of Education, Circular of Information, 1892, No. 2 (Washington, D.C., Government Printing Office).

TOLLES, FREDERICK B. 1953. *George Logan of Philadelphia* (New York, Oxford University Press).

———. 1957. *James Logan and the Culture of Provincial America* (Boston, Little, Brown and Co.).

TURNER, WILLIAM L. 1953. "The Charity School, the Academy, and the College." *Historic Philadelphia from the Founding until the Early Nineteenth Century* . . ., *Transactions, American Philosophical Society* **43**, 1: pp. 179-186.

U.S. National Park Service. 1956. *Independence National Historical Park, Philadelphia, Pa.*, by Edward M. Riley ("National Park Service Historical Handbook Series," No. 17; rev. ed., Washington, D.C., Government Printing Office).

VAN DOREN, CARL. 1938. *Benjamin Franklin* (New York, Viking Press).

———. 1950b. *Jane Mecom, the Favorite Sister of Benjamin Franklin: Her Life here first fully narrated from their entire surviving Correspondence* (New York, Viking Press).

VAN RENSSELAER, MRS. JOHN KING. 1898. *The Goede Vrouw of Mana-ha-ta At Home and in Society, 1609-1760* (New York, Charles Scribner's Sons).

WERTENBAKER, THOMAS JEFFERSON. 1946. *Princeton, 1746-1896* (Princeton, N.J., Princeton University Press).

WOLF, EDWIN, 2ND. 1956a. "B. Franklin, Bookman." *American Library Association Bulletin* **50**: pp. 13-16.

———. 1956b. "Franklin and His Friends Choose Their Books." *Pennsylvania Magazine of History and Biography* **80**: pp. 11-36.

———. 1962. "The Reconstruction of Benjamin Franklin's Library: An Unorthodox Jigsaw Puzzle." *The Papers of the Bibliographical Society of America* **56**: pp. 1-16.

WOODWARD, CARL RAYMOND. 1941. *Ploughs and Politicks: Charles Read of New Jersey and His Notes on Agriculture, 1715-1774* (New Brunswick, N.J., Rutgers University Press).

INDEX

Aberdeen University, 52
Academia Naturae Curiosorum, 52
Académie des Inscriptions et Belles Lettres, Paris, 57
Académie Royale des Sciences, Paris, 54; history of, 55
Academy of Philadelphia, 27, 30-36, 37, 70-72. *See also* College of Philadelphia; University of Pennsylvania
Academy of Sciences, Belles Lettres, and Arts, Lyons, 54
Adams, George, 12, 31
Adams, John, 64
Addison, Joseph (author), 8
Affaires de l'Angleterre, 65
Air pump, 11-12, 40
Albany Congress, 25, 71
Alexander, James, 25, 47
Alexander, William, 25
Allen, Andrew, 16
Allen, William, 28, 31, 48, 71
Allison, Francis, 11, 33
Almanacs, 5, 56
Alston, Charles (author), 59
American Academy of Arts and Sciences, Boston, 51, 56-57, 60
American Philosophical Miscellany, 51
American Philosophical Society, 16, 18, 20, 22-23, 25, 35, 40, 47-57, 60, 72; buildings, 18, 51; charter, 50; donations from individuals, 54-56; early years, 47-51; exchange program, 51-54; librarians, 50-51, 56; museum, 50-51
American Revolution, 16, 23, 28, 35, 38-39, 41, 43, 53-54, 64-67, 70
American Society held at Philadelphia for Promoting Useful Knowledge, *see* American Philosophical Society
Amicable Company, Philadelphia, 22
André, Major John, 54
Antigua, 13, 24
Armbrüster, Anthony (printer), 71
Articles of Confederation, 65
Les Arts et les Métiers, 19, 57
Associates of the Late Dr. Bray, 69-70
Association Library, Philadelphia, 22
Atlases, 8, 54, 65
Auberteuil, Hilliard d', 66

Bache, Benjamin Franklin (grandson of BF), 18, 65
Bache, Richard (son-in-law of BF), 56, 65
Bache, Sarah (Sally) Franklin (daughter of BF), 18
Bache collection of Franklin papers, 56
Bailly, Jean-Sylvain (author), 41
Balloon experiments, 53, 57
Banks, Sir Joseph, 55
Barton, Rev. Thomas, 49
Bartram, John, 13-14, 22, 26, 47
Baskerville edition of Virgil, 37

Batavian Philosophical Society, 53
Beatty, Rev. Charles, 23, 42-43
Beaumont, Eli de, 55
Bell, Robert (bookseller), 44
Bentham, Jeremy (author), 46
Bérenger (Berenget), Jean-Pierre (author), 64
Bergmann, Torbern, 46, 55
Berkeley, Bishop George, 21, 24, 36, 39
Berlin, Royal Society, 52-53
Berne Society, 52
Berriman, William (author), 70
Biddle, Owen, 49
Bingham, William, 18
Bird, John, 38
Black, Joseph, 40
Blackwall, Anthony (author), 33
Blair, John (author), 33
Bodley, Sir Thomas, 27
Bologna, Academy of Sciences, Letters, and Arts, 52-54
Bond, Dr. Phineas, 47, 59
Bond, Dr. Thomas, 47-49, 57-59
Bonnycastle, John (author), 46
Book Company of Durham, Conn., 21
Books and the transmission of colds, 60
Bossu (Bosser), Jean-Bernard (author), 54
Boston, 25, 38, 42; BF visits, 13, 21, 36-37
Boston, American Academy of Arts and Sciences, *see* American Academy of Arts and Sciences, Boston
Bowdoin, James, 12, 38-39, 51, 56-57
Bower, Archibald (author), 23, 39
Bradford, David, 46
Bradford, William (printer), 22
Bray, Dr. Thomas (and Associates), 67, 69-70
Breintnall, Joseph, 6-7, 9-11, 13
Brillon collection of Franklin papers, 56
British Museum, 52
Brockden, Charles, 7
Brown University, *see* Rhode Island College
Budd, Robert M. (Back Number), 46-47
Buffon, Georges-Louis Le Clerc, Comte de, 27, 35, 52, 54
Burgoyne, General, 20
Burlington, New Jersey, Library Company, 21, 23-24
Burnet, Gov. William, 61
Byles, Mather, 37

Cabanis, Pierre J. G., 55
Cadwalader, Dr. Thomas, 7, 23, 48, 59
Calder, Dr. John, 20
Cambridge University, 9, 49, 52
Campomanès, Conde de, 54
Canonsburg, Pennsylvania, 47
Cape Henlopen, 49
Capitaine (French map maker), 65 (fn. 35)

Carlisle College, *see* Dickinson College
Carmichael, William, 54
Carpenters' Hall, Philadelphia, 16-17, 50-51
Cave, Edward (London publisher), 12
Cercle des Philadelphes, Cap François, Haiti, 53
Chamberlin's portrait of Franklin, 38
Chandler, Rev. Samuel, 71
Charity School of Philadelphia, *see* Academy of Philadelphia
Charles II, 11
Charles, Jacques A. C., 55
Charleston Library Society, 24
Chastellux, Marquis de, 35, 41, 55
Chatham, Lord (William Pitt, the Elder), 38
Chattin, James (printer), 22
Chaulnes, Duc de, 55
Chauncey, Elihu, 21
Chauncey, Rev. Nathaniel, 21
Chester, Pennsylvania, library, 23
Chew, Benjamin, 33
Childs, Francis (printer), 47, 56
China, Jesuits' description, 54; papermaking, 55
Clap, Thomas (President of Yale), 39-40
Clarke, John (author), 10, 33
Clarkson, Lt. Col. Mathew, 43-44
Classical languages, *see* Greek language and literature; Latin language and literature
Clerical libraries, 69-70. *See also* Religion, books on
Clinton, George, 43
Clymer, George, 16
Colden, Cadwallader, 32, 47, 51
Coleman, William, 6-7, 9-12, 31, 34
College of Glasgow, 42
College of New Jersey (Princeton), 23, 42-44
College of Philadelphia, 32-35, 41, 72. *See also* Academy of Philadelphia; University of Pennsylvania
College of William and Mary, 35, 41
Collins, Henry, 24
Collins, John, 19, 61
Collinson, Peter, 8, 11-15, 19, 22, 28, 31, 33-34, 36, 40, 71
Columbia College, 43
Condorcet, Marquis de, 55
Connecticut Academy of Arts and Sciences, New Haven, 57
Connecticut Gazette, 39
Constitutional Convention, 16, 45-46
Constitutions of the United States of America, 65-66, 68, 75
Continental Congress, 16, 25, 64-66. *See also* U. S. Congress
Cooke, Captain, 55
Cooper, Samuel, 38-39, 56
Cornwallis, Gen., 20

Courier de l'Europe, 65
Court de Gebelin, Antoine, 54, 56–57
Coxe, John, 23, 47
Crèvecœur, J. Hector St. John, 45, 55
Cromwell, Oliver (biography), 68, 75
Cutler, Rev. Manasseh, 16–17, 35, 57

Dalibard, Thomas François, 36
Darby, Pennsylvania, library, 22
Dartmouth College, 42–43
Dashkov, Princess Catherine, 53–55
Declaration of Independence, 16, 50
Decquemare, Abbé, 54
Defay, 54
Dennis, 54
Dickinson, John, 16, 44
Dickinson College, 44–45
The Dignity of Man, reproduction of title page, 68
Dilly, Charles and Edward (London booksellers), 53
Dod, Thaddeus, 46
Duane, James, 43
Dublin Society, 52
Dublin University, 52
Dubourg, Barbeu, 38, 55
Duché, Rev. Jacob, 34, 48, 70
Duffield, Edward, 70
Dufief (Philadelphia bookseller), 19, 56, 66
Dumas, Charles W. F., 20, 39, 42, 65
Dunlap, William (printer), 34
Dunn, Samuel, 54
Du Perron, Anquetil (author), 40
Dupont de Nemours, Samuel, 66
Du Port Royal, 8, 19
Durham, Conn., *see* Book Company of Durham, Conn.

Eckhardt, F. A., 55
Edinburgh Philosophical Society, 52, 54
Edinburgh, Royal Society, *see* Royal Society of Edinburgh
Edinburgh University, *see* University of Edinburgh
Edwards, George (naturalist), 14
Edwards, Morgan, 41
Eliot, Jared, 13, 27, 39
Ellicott, John, 38
Ellis, Henry (author), 27
Emmons, Rev. Nathanael, 67–69, 75
Encyclopedias and dictionaries, 16, 33, 41, 44, 46, 55
English language and literature, 10, 32–34, 36, 45, 71–72
English school, Academy of Philadelphia, 32–33, 36
Erasmus, Desiderius (author), 70
Erskine, John, 44
European learned societies, 52–54, 57
Evans, Dr. Cadwallader, 48, 59
Ewing, John, 34–35, 52

Fénelon, François (author), 33
Ferguson, Adam, 40
Ferguson, James, 46, 52
Feutry, Aimé A. J., 55
Filangieri, Gaetano, 66
Finley, Samuel, 42
Fisher, Edward (engraver), 38

Fisher, Hezekiah, 67
Fleury, M., 20
Florence Academy (of sciences), 52
Flores, Don Joseph Miguel de, 54
Folard, Jean-Charles de (author), 27
Forster, John Reinhold, 54
Fothergill, Dr. John, 12, 20, 27, 44, 52, 54, 59–60
Fox collection of Franklin papers, 56
Francis, Tench, 31
Franking privileges, 47–48
Franklin (and Marshall) College, 45–46
Franklin, Benjamin
 author, 19, 55–56; *An Account of the New-Invented Pennsylvanian Fire-places*, 11, 19; *Autobiography*, 5–8, 12, 21, 24, 26, 39, 48 57; Cornerstone inscription for Library Co. of Philadelphia, 17–18; Cornerstone inscription for Pennsylvania Hospital, 58; *A Dissertation on Liberty and Necessity, Pleasure and Pain*, 6; *Dr. Franklin's account of the inoculation for the small pox, in England and America . . .*, 19; *Experiments and Observations on Electricity* (1751), 36, 39; French edition (1752), 36; 1754 edition, 39; *Supplemental Experiments and Observations* (1753), 36; *New experiments and observations on electricity* (1760), 19; *Experiments and Observations on Electricity . . . To which are added, Letters and Papers on Philosophical Subjects* (1769), 19, 38; *The general magazine, and historical chronicle, for the British plantations in America*, 19; "Idea of the English School," 32–33, 36; "Information to Those Who Would Remove to America," 66; "The long arm," 57, 73; *Maritime Observations*, 57; *A Modest Enquiry into the Nature and Necessity of a Paper Currency*, 26; "Observations Concerning the Increase of Mankind," 71; "Observations on my Reading History in Library, May 9, 1731," 6; *Observations Relative to the Intentions of the Original Founders of the Academy in Philadelphia*, 36; *Œuvres de M. Franklin*, 38; *Political, miscellaneous and philosophical pieces*, 19; "Preparatory Notes and Hints for Writing a Paper Concerning What Is Called Catching Cold," 60; "A Proposal for Promoting Useful Knowledge among the British Plantations in America," 47; *Proposals Relating to the Education of Youth in Pensilvania*, 26, 30–32; "A short Account of the Library," 10; facsimile reproduction, 74; *Silence Dogood papers*, 36; *Some Account of the Pennsylvania Hospital*, 59
 donations, 19–20, 34, 36–41, 44–47, 51, 55–57, 59, 64–65, 67–69, 72
 electrical and scientific experiments, 11–13, 22, 27, 36–37, 40, 47–48
 eulogies of Franklin, 41, 46, 48
 government service, 13, 15–16, 25, 27, 30, 36–37, 41, 45–48, 58–60, 62–67, 70
 ladder-chair, illustration, 56
 library, 19, 51, 56, 66, 72
 papers, 56, 67
 portraits, 25, 40, 47, 51
 printer, 6–7, 10–11, 21–27, 30, 33–34, 39, 42, 47, 56, 59–62, 71–72; *see also Pennsylvania Gazette*
 will, 18, 39, 55, 57, 60
Franklin, Deborah (wife of BF), 15, 23, 69–70
Franklin, James (brother of BF), 21, 25
Franklin, John (brother of BF), 25, 37, 42
Franklin, Peter (brother of BF), 25
Franklin, Sarah (Sally, daughter of BF), *see* Bache, Sarah Franklin
Franklin, William (son of BF), 18, 24, 27, 42–43, 48
Franklin, William Temple (grandson of BF), 50
Franklin, Massachusetts, 67–69, 72, 75
French language and literature, 16, 26, 32, 35, 41–42, 44, 53, 55–57, 65–66
Frenicle de Bessy, Bernard (author), 27
Frossard, Benjamin-Sigismond (author), 20

Gabriel of Bourbon, Don, 65
Galloway, Joseph, 41, 48
Gastelier, René G., 55
Gates, Gen. Horatio, 28
Gauger, Nicolas (author), 11
Gazette of the United States, 46–47
Geneva, history of, 64
Gentleman's Magazine, 12
Gerbier, Humbert (Thibert), 55
German Charity Schools, 45, 70–72
German language and literature, 22, 45, 53, 70–72
Germantown Library Company, 22
Gillmer, William, 69 (fn. 11)
Glasgow, *see* College of Glasgow; University of Glasgow
Godfrey, Thomas, 6–8, 26, 47
Göttingen, Königliche Gesellschaft der Wissenschaften, 52–54
Government and law, books on, 44, 62–68, 75
Government libraries, 61–67
Grace, Robert, 6–9, 11, 13
Gray, Stephen, 27
Greek language and literature, 26, 28, 31, 36, 38, 50, 60
Greene, Catharine Ray, 56, 64
Greene, Gov. William, 40, 64–65
Greenwood, Isaac, 12
Grivel, Guillaume, 55
Gude, Ebenezer, Jr., 69 (fn. 11)
Guilde, Ebenezer, 68–69

Hahn, Johann D. (Utrecht), 52
Hall, David, 22–24, 30, 33–34, 44, 48, 59–60, 70
Hamilton, Andrew, 25
Hamilton, Gov. James, 12, 22, 48–49, 71
Hancock, Thomas, 37
Harvard, 12, 21, 36–41, 72
Hatborough, Pa., Union Library Co., 23

Hauksbee, Francis, 27
Heberden, Dr. William, 70
Hebrew language and literature, 26, 40, 50
Hemmer, Abbé Jacob, 53
Henry, David (London publisher), 15
Herschell, William, 54
Hett, R. (London publisher), 67
Hewson, William, 54
Hibernian Magazine, 52
Historical Review of the Constitution and Government of Pennsylvania, 64
Hogarth, William, engravings, 15
Home, Archibald, 47
Hoogeveen, Henricus (author), 38
Hope, John (editor), 59
Hopkins, Stephen, 42
Hopkinson, Francis, 11, 15–16, 21, 31, 48, 50, 53, 70
Hopkinson, Thomas, 7–12, 47
House of Commons, 44, 64
Hubbard, Thomas, 37
Hume, David, 40
Hunter, William, 37, 70

Independence Hall, *see* Pennsylvania State House
Indians, American, 10, 42, 57, 64, 71
Ingenhousz, Jan, 54–55
Inglis, Captain, 49
Ireland, Royal Irish Academy, 53

Jackson, Richard, 55
Jackson and Dunn (Philadelphia booksellers), 44
Jefferson College, *see* Washington (and Jefferson) College
Jefferson, Thomas, 16, 66
Jeffries, John, 57
Jenkins, Samuel, 11
Jesuits' "Account of China," 54
Johnson, David, 46
Johnson, Dr. Samuel (Stratford, Conn.), 32–33
Johnson's dictionary, 33
Jones, John, Jr., 7
Jones, Robert Strettell, 52
Jones's Alley (Pewter-Platter Alley), Philadelphia, 6, 8
Journals of the House of Commons, 44
Juliana Library Company, Lancaster, Pa., 22, 49
Junto, 5–7, 26, 30, 47–48

Kalm, Peter, 11, 20, 24, 54
Kames, Lord, 40
Keimer, Samuel, 19, 24
Keith, George (London bookseller), 22
Keith, Gov. William, 26
King, Charles B., 25
Kinnersley, Ebenezer, 12, 22, 34, 36, 48
Klingstedt, Timothy, Baron de (Russia), 52, 55
Knight, Gowin, 27

Lamb, Alexander, 61
Lamy, Bernard (author), 33
Lancaster, Pa., *see* Franklin and Marshall College; Juliana Library Company; German Charity Schools

La Rochefoucauld, Duc de, 55, 65–66
Latin language and literature, 26, 28, 31–33, 36, 40, 50, 60
Latin School, Academy of Philadelphia, 31–33, 36
Lavoisier, Antoine Laurent, 54
Le Banneret d'Ostervald (Swiss printing firm), 66
Le Roy, Jean Baptiste, 54
Le Roy, Julien David, 54
Letterpress copier, 57
Lettsom, Dr. John Coakley, 44, 55, 60
Le Veillard, Louis, 55, 66
Lewis, William (author), 59
L'Héritier de Brutelle, Charles Louis, 54, 66
Library Company of Philadelphia, 5–25, 27, 30–31, 37, 47, 49–52, 59–60, 62, 72, 74; agents, 13–15; building and cornerstone inscription, 17–18; catalogues, 8–11, 13, 19, 23–24, 27, 74; charter and by-laws, 11; classification system, 8–9; donations, 18–20; early years, 5–11; influence, 20–25; Junto, 5–7; librarians, 9–10, 13–17, 20, 24; museum, 13, 17; scientific activities, 11–13, 36; "A short Account of the Library," 74
Library of Congress, 20, 66–67
Lincoln, Benjamin, 65
Linné, Karl von (Uppsala), 52
Literary and Philosophical Society, Manchester, 54
Literary and Philosophical Society, Newport, R. I., 24
Literary Society, London, 54
Livingston, Philip, 25
Livingston, Robert R., 25, 43, 65–66
Livingston, William, 25
Locke, John, 6, 10, 19, 68, 75
Logan, Deborah, 54
Logan, Dr. George 28, 30, 60
Logan, James, 8–9, 11, 14, 22–23, 26–31, 62
Logan, James, II (son of James Logan), 20, 28–30
Logan, William (son of James Logan), 28, 59
Logan, Dr. William (Bristol physician), 60
Loganian Library, 20, 23, 26–31, 33, 60, 72
London, *see* Literary Society; Medical Society; Royal Society of London; Society for Promoting Arts, Manufactures, and Commerce; Society of Antiquaries
Long arm, 57, 73
Lottery financing, 33, 42
Louis XVI, 20, 35, 41–42, 54, 65, 67
Ludlam, William, 54
Ludwell, Col. Philip 34, 70
Lyons (author), 6
Lyons, France, Academy of Sciences, Belles Lettres, and Arts, 54

McKean, Thomas, 16
Mackenzie, William, 19
Macklot, Michel (Carlsruhe), 66
Madison, Bishop James, 41
Madrid, Royal Academy of History, 53–54
Magaw, Samuel, 22

Magellan, John Hyacinth de, 53, 55
Mahon, Lord (son of Lord Stanhope), 55
Man, Nathan, 69 (fn. 11)
Manchester, Literary and Philosophical Society, 54
Mandeville, Dr. Bernard (author), 6
Manning, James, 42, 51
Maps, 31, 36, 62–63, 65
Marchant, Henry, 25, 40
Marshall College, *see* Franklin (and Marshall) College
Martin, David (artist), 51
Martin, David (Trenton), 23, 47
Martin, Col. Josiah, 33
Maseres, Francis (mathematician), 38
Maskelyne, Nevil (Royal astronomer), 38, 52, 55
Mather, Cotton, 6
Mather, Increase, 37
Maugridge, William, 6
May, Dr. William (author), 60
Mazarin, Cardinal, library, 27
Mazzei, Philip, 53
Mecom, Jane Franklin (sister of BF), 38, 40, 46, 56, 64, 67
Medical library, Pennsylvania Hospital, 57–60, 72
Medical Society of London, 54
Medical Society of New Fairfield, Conn., 61
Medical Society of New Haven County, 51
Medical Society of Philadelphia, 48, 61
Mercersburg, Pa., Marshall College, 46
Mercury, transit of, 13, 38, 52
Meredith, Hugh (printer), 6–7
Mico, Joseph, 37
Mifflin, John, 10
Mifflin, Thomas, 16, 66
Milan, La Société Patriotique, 53–54
Millan, Joseph, 69 (fn. 11)
Miller, Philip (author), 8, 54
Millington, Rev. John, 61
Montesquieu, Charles de Secondat (author), 68, 75
Montgomery, John, 44–45
Moore, Mrs., 15
Moore, Charles, 64
Morellet, Abbé, 45
Morris, Deborah, 59
Morris, Robert, 16, 65
Morris, Gov. Robert Hunter, 47, 63–64
Morton, John, 16
Muhlenberg, Rev. Henry, 45, 71
Muhlenberg, Peter, 45
Mullen, Thomas, 11

Nairne, Edward, 38, 55
Negro schools, 69–70, 72
Neville, M. de (French director-general of the press), 65
New Fairfield, Conn., Medical Society of, 61
New Haven, Conn., *see* Connecticut Academy of Arts and Sciences; Medical Society of New Haven County
New York (City), 21, 35, 39, 42–43, 46–47, 61–62, 70
New York Corporation Library, 25, 61–62

New York Gazette (revived in the *Weekly Post-Boy*), 61
New York Society Library, 25, 62
Newenham, Sir Edward, 55
Newport, R. I., *see* Redwood Library
Newton, Sir Isaac, 6, 8, 68, 75
Nicholas, Anthony, 7
Norris, Charles (librarian for Pennsylvania Assembly), 64
Norris, Isaac, 44, 63
Northwest Company, 13, 27

O'Cahill, Baron (author), 66
Orléans, Société Royale de Physique, d'Histoire Naturelle, et des Arts, 54
Osborne, Thomas (London bookseller), 34
Owen, Owen, 7, 23
Oxford University, 40, 52

Padua, Royal Academy of Arts and Sciences, 54
Palatinate Academy of Sciences, 53
Palmer, Samuel (London printer), 10
Papermaking, Chinese, 55
Paris, *see* Académie des Inscriptions et Belles Lettres; Académie Royale des Sciences; Royal Medical Society; Royal Military School; Royal Observatory
Parker, James (printer), 25, 39, 61–62, 70
Parsons, William (librarian for Library Company of Philadelphia), 6–7, 9–10, 26, 47
Paschall, Isaac, 49
Paschall, Joseph, 49
Patterson, Robert (librarian of American Philosophical Society), 51
Peale, Charles Willson, 50–51
Pemberton, Dr. Henry, 6
Pemberton, Israel, Jr., 28
Penington, Isaac, 7
Penn, John, 10–12, 13 (fn. 74), 48, 50
Penn, Juliana, 22, 63
Penn, Richard, 11, 52
Penn, Thomas, 9–13, 22, 31, 34, 63
Penn, William, 11, 26
Pennsylvania Assembly, 10, 15–16, 19, 25, 27, 30, 33–34, 44–45, 48–51, 58, 62–64
Pennsylvania Assembly Library, 51, 62–64, 72
Pennsylvania Berichte, 71
Pennsylvania Chronicle, 48
Pennsylvania Gazette, 9–10, 12, 19, 21–23, 28, 30, 35–36, 39, 45, 48, 60
Pennsylvania Hospital, 51, 57–60, 70, 72; illustration, 58
Pennsylvania Society for the Abolition of Slavery, 20, 70
Pennsylvania State House (Independence Hall), 10–12, 16–17, 48–50, 62–63; illustration, 63
Pennsylvania Supreme Executive Council, 45–47, 50. *See also* Franklin, Benjamin, government service
Percival, Dr. Thomas, 55
Peters, Rev. Richard, 12, 15, 28, 30–31, 33–34, 48, 71
Pewter-Platter Alley (Jones's Alley, Philadelphia), 6, 8

Philadelphia Academy, *see* Academy of Philadelphia
Philadelphia College, *see* College of Philadelphia
Philadelphia libraries, 21–22
Philadelphia Library Company, *see* Library Company of Philadelphia
Philadelphia school for Negroes, 69–70
Philadelphische Zeitung, 9, 71–72
The Philosophical Dictionary, 46
Philosophical Transactions, see Royal Society of London
Phoenician language, 57
Picts, language of, 27
Pierres, Philippe-Denis (French printer), 65
Pitt, William, the Elder (Lord Chatham), 38
Plutarch (author), 8
Poetry, books on, 68, 75
Political pamphlets, 64–65, 71
Pollier (Swiss author), 66
Ponçins, Marquis de, 20
Popple (map maker), 62
Potter, James, 61
Potts, Stephen, 6
Poulson, Zachariah, Jr., 17, 19–20, 51
Pownall, Thomas, 39
Price, Richard, 20, 44, 55, 67–68, 75
Priestley, Joseph, 20, 34, 38–39, 55, 68, 75
Princeton (College of New Jersey), 23, 42–44
Pringle, Sir John, 27, 55
Printers and publishers, *see* Armbrüster, Baskerville, Bradford, Cave, Chattin, Childs, Dunlap, Edwards, Franklin, Hall, Hett, Le Banneret d'Ostervald, Meredith, Palmer, Parker, Pierres, Rivington, Sauer, Sellers, Timothy, Wheeler, Zenger
Providence, R. I., *see* Rhode Island College (Brown University)
Prussian Academy of Sciences, 53

Queens' College, Cambridge, classification system, 8–9

Ramsay, Andrew Michael (author), 33
Read, Charles, Jr. (1715–1774), 23–24
Read, Charles, Sr. (1686–1737), 23
Read, James, 23
Redick, David, 46
Redwood, Abraham, 24
Redwood Library, 24–25, 40
Reed, Joseph, 35
Reland, Adrien (author), 40
Religion, books on, 40, 67–72, 75
Religious toleration, 40, 45
Rhoads, Samuel, 16, 47, 64
Rhode Island College, 41–42, 51
Rhode Island Gazette, 21
Rhode Island General Assembly, 64–65
Richardson, Rev. Albert M., 69
Rittenhouse, David, 35, 49–50
Rivington, James (printer), 24
Roberts, Hugh, 11, 59
Robertson, William, 40
Robeson, Andrew, 25
Rochambeau, Jean Baptiste, Comte de, 35

Rolland d'Erceville, Barthélemi-Gabriel, 55
Ross, George, 16
Rotterdam, Bataafsch Genootschap der Proefondervindelijke Wijsbegeerte, 54
Royal Academy of Arts and Sciences, Padua, 54
Royal Academy of History, Madrid, 53–54
Royal Academy of Sciences, Paris, 19, 52–53
Royal College of Physicians, London, 52
Royal Medical Society, Paris, 54, 61
Royal Military School, Paris, 66
Royal Observatory, Paris, 56
Royal Society of Arts, London, *see* Society for Promoting Arts, Manufactures, and Commerce
Royal Society of Edinburgh, 54, 60
Royal Society of London (and *Philosophical Transactions*), 12, 16, 33, 36, 38, 40, 48, 51–55, 57, 59
Rozier, L'Abbé, 55
Rush, Dr. Benjamin, 16, 42, 44–45, 53, 55, 58–60
Russell, James, 40

St. Andrews University, 52
St. Petersburg, Imperial Academy of Sciences, 52–54
Saltonstall, Gov., portrait, 40
Samaritan coins, book given to Yale by Franklin, 41
Sauer, Christopher (printer), 71
Saville, Sir George, 52
Schlatter, Rev. Michael, 71–72
Science, books on, 8, 12–13, 19, 34, 36, 43–44, 47–57
Scott, John Morin, 25
Scott, Thomas, 46
Scougal, Henry (author), 71
Scull, Nicholas, 6–8
Sellers, William (printer), 60
Shakespeare, William, 33
Sharp, Granville, 44
Sharpe, Rev. John, 61
Shippen, Edward, 22, 49
Short, James, 38
Sinclair (or St. Clair), John, 24
Small, Dr. Alexander, 20, 55
Smeaton, John, 33, 40
Smith, Hannah Logan (Mrs. John), 28
Smith, James, 16
Smith, John (son-in-law of James Logan), 28
Smith, Captain John (author), 15, 27
Smith, William (of New York), 25
Smith, William (of Philadelphia), 33–34, 41, 48, 52, 71
La Société Patriotique, Milan, 53–54
Société Royale de Physique, d'Histoire Naturelle, et des Arts, Orléans, France, 54
Society for Promoting Arts, Manufactures, and Commerce, London, 52, 54
Society for Promoting Christian Knowledge, 69
Society for the Propagation of the Gospel in Foreign Lands, 69

Society for the Relief and Instruction of Poor Germans, 71
Society of Antiquaries, London, 54
Society of the Free and Easy (United Party for Virtue), 7
Socrates, 8
Soulavie, Jean L. G., Abbé, 35, 55
South Carolina Gazette, 9, 24
The Spectator, 8, 32, 68, 75
Spencer, Dr. A., 12
Stæhlin-Storksburg, Jacob von, 55
Stanhope, Lord, 55
Stennett, Samuel (author), 67, 75
Stenton (home of James Logan), 8, 26–27
Stifel (Stifelius), Michael (author), 27
Stiles, Ezra, 25, 39–41, 57
Stockholm, Royal Society, 52
Stockton, Annis Boudinot, 45
Strahan, William, 14–15, 22–24, 60
Sturgeon, Rev. William, 69–70
Subscription financing, 7, 30, 37, 39, 46, 51, 57–58, 62
Swaine, Captain Charles, 13, 27
Syng, Philip, Jr., 7, 11–12

Thomas, Gov. George, 11
Thomas, Mr. (tutor), 46
Thomson, Charles, 48, 64–65
Timothy (Timothée), Lewis (Louis), 9, 13, 24
Timothy, Peter, 24
Trumbull, Jonathan, 42
Turin, Royal Academy of Arts and Sciences, 52–54

Union Library Company, Hatborough, Pa., 23
Union Library Company, Philadelphia, 21–22, 48–49
United Party for Virtue (Society of the Free and Easy), 7
U. S. Congress, 65–67, 70, 72. *See also* Continental Congress; Library of Congress
U. S. Constitution, 66
University of Edinburgh, 40, 42, 44, 52, 60
University of Glasgow, 52
University of Pennsylvania, 30–36, 41, 45–46, 50–51, 72. *See also* Academy of Philadelphia; College of Philadelphia
University of the State of New York, 42–44
Uppsala, Royal Society, 52

Vattel, Emerich de (author), 20, 39, 65
Vaughan, Benjamin, 55
Vaughan, John (librarian of American Philosophical Society), 56
Vaughan, Samuel, 16, 30, 53
Venus, transit of, 13, 38, 48–49, 52, 64
Vergennes, Charles Gravier, Comte de, 35, 55, 65
Vernon, Samuel, 25
Vernon, Thomas, 25
Verona, Societá Italiana, 53
Viel de St. Maux, 55
Viner, Charles (author), 63–64
Virgil, Baskerville edition, 37
Von Stæhlin, *see* Stæhlin-Storksburg

Walsh, John, 55
Waring, John, 69
Washington (and Jefferson) College, 46–47
Washington, George, 42, 64, 70
Watson, William, 40
Wayne, Gen. Anthony, 20
Webb, George, 6
Weiser, Conrad, 71
Wells, Richard, 17–18
West, Benjamin, 13, 52
Wheeler, Bennett (printer), 68
Wheelock, Eleazar, 42
Wheelock, James, 42–43
Wheelock, John, 42–43
Whiston, John (London bookseller), 31
Whitefield, George, 30–31, 71
Whitehurst, John, 55
Willard, Joseph, 56
William and Mary, *see* College of William and Mary
Williams, Jonathan (grandnephew of BF), 57, 64, 67
Williamsburg, Va., Negro school, 70
Wilson, James, 16
Wilson, Prof. Patrick, 52
Winthrop, James, 39
Winthrop, John, 36–40
Witherspoon, John, 42–44
Woodward, Bezaleel (librarian of Dartmouth College), 42
Wren, Thomas, 43
Writing, Franklin's idea of good, 6
Wynne, Peter, 60

Yale College, 13, 21, 25, 39–42, 57, 72
Yale, Gov., portrait, 40

Zenger, Peter (printer), 25
Zoroaster, 40

www.ingramcontent.com/pod-product-compliance
Lightning Source LLC
LaVergne TN
LVHW081316060526
838201LV00006B/179